Commodore 64 Favorite Programs Explained

Donald C. Kreutner

Que Corporation
Indianapolis

Library of Congress Catalog No.: LC 83-63254

ISBN 0-88022-073-2

88 87 86 85 84 8 7 6 5 4 3 2

Interpretation of the printing code: the rightmost double-digit number is the year of the book's printing; the rightmost single-digit number, the number of the book's printing. For example, a printing code of 83-4 shows that the fourth printing of the book occurred in 1983.

Editor
Virginia D. Noble, M.L.S.

Editorial Director
David F. Noble, Ph.D.

Managing Editor
Paul L. Mangin

About the Author

Donald C. Kreutner received his B.A. in history from Valparaiso University in 1967 and his M.S. in education from Indiana University in 1974. In addition to taking course work in computer science, business, and accounting, he has done work toward an M.B.A. degree at Indiana University.

Over the past fifteen years, Mr. Kreutner has worked as a teacher, linguist, data processing manager, programmer/analyst, and director of data processing.

Because of his familiarity with many programming languages and a wide variety of computers and microcomputers, Mr. Kreutner is an expert programmer. His teaching and linguistic experiences have made him an exceptional communicator as well.

Dedication

To my wife Janet,
my sons Derek and Jay,
my parents Albert and Pauline,
and Robert and Sally Bard

Table of Contents

Introduction xi

Chapter 1 Math and Problem Solving Programs

ADDMACH1 1

Recalls numbers entered to the screen, changes entries, and alters totals

ADDSUB1 7

Gives addition and subtraction problems of easy or difficult levels and keeps a fine score

BSKTSTAT 10

Keeps cumulative statistics for a team

CALC1 20

Performs like a calculator--adding, subtracting, multiplying, dividing, and taking the powers and roots of numbers

CALENDAR 23

Produces a calendar for any year from 1800 through 2099

DIVMULT1 29

Gives multiplication and division problems and provides drills in multiplication and division tables

GRAPH1 32

Draws a horizontal bar graph for any set of figures

MORTGAGE 34

Gives the monthly payment and a loan amortization schedule for any principal to be repaid over any number of months at any interest rate

SAVE1 37

Allows you to analyze various savings, investments, and annuities, both yearly and monthly

SCORE1 43

Performs a variety of scorekeeping applications, from a bridge club's scores to a team's cumulative scores in several games

Chapter 2 Games and Miscellaneous Programs

BEEP1 49

Allows you to key any message on the screen and display it repetitively

BIRTHDAY 51

Provides a list of birthdays in a given month (or for all months) for all the people whose data has been provided, as well as an alphabetical listing of birthdays (by name)

DRAW1 55

Enables you to "draw" any picture or diagram on the screen, using blocks or asterisks

EDIT1 57

Creates multipurpose data files, used as input for other programs, to which you can add, delete, or alter records

EDIT2 61

Creates data files, like EDIT1, but manipulates data differently, providing a choice of "tools" to create and alter files

EDITMASK 65

Edits a number, adding commas and a decimal point

FIGURE1 67

Uses graphics to draw patterns on the screen

GAMBLE 70

Enables up to ten players to play a simulated dice game and keeps all players' cumulative scores

GUESS3 73

Allows you to guess a three-digit number, based on clues obtained from previous guesses

GUESS4 75

Allows you to guess a four-digit number, based on clues obtained from previous guesses

HANGMAN 77

Enables one or two players to guess the program's word, or one another's hidden words, until one player "hangs" or the word is guessed

LABEL1 82

Uses a file from the EDIT programs as input for printing mailing labels on a printer

LABELP 84

Prints any number of labels from keyed input instead of from a file

PRTRCMDS 86

Causes a printer to go into and out of certain modes of printing and also acts as a typewriter

RECIPE1 90

Allows you to recall from a file or the program's DATA statements the ingredients, quantities, and preparation steps for your favorite recipes, paint formulas, or other mixtures

SCREEN1 93

Displays repetitively up to five lines of data on the screen and then removes the data one character at a time, from right to left and from bottom to top

SORT1 95

Sorts any file created by the EDIT programs in a variety of ways, with up to ten different sort fields located anywhere within a record

TAG 100

Allows one player to try to catch another player, with each taking turns at being "it"

TICHUMAN 104

Enables two people to play tick-tack-toe, with the Commodore 64 keeping score

TICTACTO 110

Allows you to play tick-tack-toe with the computer, which uses built-in logic to figure out the best moves possible, and keeps cumulative scores

Chapter 3 Business and Educational Programs

CKBOOK 117

Balances a checkbook, comparing checks written to checks returned

EXPENSE 122

Produces an expense summary from details keyed, using one of the EDIT programs in Chapter 2

FLASHCARD 126

Allows you to drill on any set of facts from files you have created using the EDIT programs

GENLED1 130

Allows you to key transactions to be added to a year-to-date accumulation of income and expense records

GENLED2 135

Produces a summary of transactions for a given month, calculating year-to-date and monthly figures for all accounts

GRADES 144

Keeps track of cumulative scores for a class and the maximum scores possible on quizzes and tests

MEMO 148

Keeps a list of appointments or other memos by time and date

PHONEADD 151

Provides a directory of phone numbers, names, and addresses, by alphabetical lookup keys

PRICELIST 154

Gives an estimate sheet of prices and costs, with item numbers and descriptions, for any number of items to be sold to a customer

RULE78 160
Gives a loan payout (using the "rule of 78s" formula) for any number of months, giving the payoff balance each month

Chapter 4 Commodore BASIC Commands, Statements, and Functions 163
Provides an alphabetical list of Commodore BASIC commands, statements, and functions, with accompanying program illustrations

Appendix 187
Gives a summary of new and old Commodore peripherals and other computer products

Introduction

Commodore 64 Favorite Programs Explained is a unique book in several ways.

First, the book contains many interesting programs that are both practical and entertaining. Other books often contain program examples that are too undeveloped in the uses of BASIC or too short to be meaningful. *Commodore 64 Favorite Programs Explained* is designed to help users learn better the applications of Commodore 64 BASIC. The book is fun to use as well.

Second, *Commodore 64 Favorite Programs Explained* provides with each program clear and concise explanations of what actually takes place within the program. On reading (and rereading) these discussions, you can learn more about why the programs work the way they do.

The programs in this book can be run on the simplest Commodore 64 setup. With only the computer and perhaps a cassette recorder, practically every program can be run satisfactorily. But if you do have available a disk drive or a printer, many of the programs here can already make full use of these devices without any changes needed in the BASIC code.

Finally, this book is unique because it provides programs for one of the most powerful computers available for its price. If you already own a Commodore 64, with its many built-in capabilities, you have made a good investment. You do not need to worry about your computer becoming quickly outdated, even as newer and different machines become available. Commodore has committed its resources to continued support of the 64, regarding both future hardware peripherals and new software availability.

Despite the large amount of testing and proofreading that has been done in the preparation of this book, neither it nor the programs are necessarily perfect. Every program, however, has been thoroughly tested on the Commodore 64. As you read *Commodore 64 Favorite*

Programs Explained, you will acquire techniques in Commodore 64 BASIC that may be helpful in other ways. After reading the book, you will have available useful programs for both work and play.

To key in any program, simply follow the guidelines in your Commodore reference manuals. If you need to modify any of the lines (for instance, to put your own DATA statements in the programs), you may need to skip the line numbers for the "test" DATA statements in the programs. Just key in your own statements, instead. (Be certain to end your DATA statements with the data element "END," or whatever ends the DATA statements in the book, so that the program can identify the end of data.)

Chapters 1, 2, and 3 contain different kinds of programs, including math and problem-solving, games and miscellaneous, and business and educational applications. Dividing the programs into such groupings was not an easy task since many of the programs are quite versatile. For instance, some of the math programs are also educational, and some miscellaneous programs have uses in business, too.

Whenever a printer is allowed within a program, an OPEN statement is necessary for the device, such as "OPEN 128,2,0,CHR$(8)". This particular statement is needed for a system whose printer is attached to a VIC 1011A RS-232 interface cartridge and set at a baud rate of 1200 BPS (bits per second). If your printer has a different baud rate (or other options), you may need to alter these OPEN statements to suit the printer you are using. The CHR$(8) portion of the statement means 1200 baud, and the 128 file number causes a line feed after each line that is sent to the printer. Any file number lower than 128 causes no line feed to be generated automatically. For each program that uses a printer, you may choose either a Commodore 1525 printer or the RS-232 printer described.

In *Commodore 64 Favorite Programs Explained*, an illustration that is contained within a box, as shown below, represents a screen illustration:

Throughout the book these boxes show examples of pictures or displays on your TV or monitor that result from running the programs being described.

To run any program, key it in as printed and then save it to cassette or disk immediately (so that you do not have to retype the program again), as in the following:

SAVE

or

SAVE "(program name)",8

You can reload any program by typing

LOAD

or

LOAD "(program name)",8

Then you can run the program by simply stating

RUN

In addition to the methods described in the book for terminating the programs, any program can be ended without damage by holding down the RUN/STOP key or the RUN/STOP and RESTORE keys simultaneously.

Whenever a program asks you to key data by an INPUT statement, you must hit the RETURN key (sometimes called the ENTER key) after keying the desired input.

An acknowledgment should be made to Commodore for providing the fine photographs that appear in this book and for permitting the use of portions of their reference manuals in Chapter 4.

Thanks also are given to Donna S. Padgett for permission to use her programs, TICTACTO and TICHUMAN, and to Bob and Sally Bard for literally thousands of photocopies.

The Commodore 64 Computer

1

Math and Problem Solving Programs

ADDMACH1

```
100 REM *************************
110 REM *        ADDMACH1        *
120 REM *                        *
130 REM *     COPYRIGHT 1983     *
140 REM *   DONALD C. KREUTNER   *
150 REM *************************
160 PRINT CHR$(147):POKE 53280,14:POKE
    53281,6:PRINT CHR$(5)
170 INPUT "1525 PRTR(1), RS232(2),
    NONE(3)";PX$
175 IF PX$="3" THEN 214
180 IF PX$="1" THEN 195
185 IF PX$="2" THEN 195
190 GOTO 170
195 PT=VAL(PX$)
200 PT=PT+126
205 IF PT=127 THEN 212
210 OPEN PT,2,0,CHR$(8):PT=128:PX$="2":
    GOTO 214
212 OPEN PT,4
214 DIM E$(200)
216 C1=0
218 TTL=0
```

ADDMACH1 is a program that performs like an adding machine, only better. When you key numbers to be added or subtracted, they are stored in memory in the same order in which you enter them. They can be reviewed later at any time, along with the total that has accumulated to that point. Any entries made in error can be changed or eliminated. In this manner, the memory serves the same purpose as an adding machine tape. On an adding machine, however, you have to subtract out and add back incorrect entries. With ADDMACH1 you can get a new list of numbered entries as soon as you have made one or more corrections.

In addition, ADDMACH1 does not need a printer, since about 40 numbers can be easily displayed on the screen. When all the entries are recalled, they are displayed in two columns. For example, if 20 numbers have been entered, ten would be displayed on each side of the screen, with entries

```
219 YN$="N"
220 PRINT CHR$(147)
230 PRINT "******************"
240 PRINT "HELP              INSTRUCTIONS"
250 PRINT "#/ OR #X"
260 PRINT "#=                TO GET RESULT"
270 PRINT "END               END PROGRAM"
280 PRINT "S                 SUBTOTAL"
290 PRINT "T                 TOTAL (CLR MEMORY)"
300 PRINT "(TO ADD/          # AND +,-,A,S"
310 PRINT "SUBTRACT)         A FOR +, S FOR -"
320 PRINT "ON                TURN PRINTER ON"
330 PRINT "OFF               TURN PRINTER OFF"
340 PRINT
350 PRINT
360 PRINT
370 PRINT
380 INPUT A$
390 IF A$="HELP" THEN 220
400 IF A$="END" THEN 1930
410 IF A$="S" THEN 980
420 IF A$="T" THEN 1000
430 IF A$="ON" THEN 460
440 IF A$="OFF" THEN 500
450 GOTO 540
460 IF YN$="Y" THEN 490
470 YN$="Y"
475 IF PX$="3" THEN YN$="N"
490 GOTO 380
500 IF YN$="N" THEN 530
510 YN$="N"
530 GOTO 380
540 LA=LEN(A$)
550 IF LA>0 THEN 580
560 A$=E$(C1)
570 LA=LEN(A$)
580 O$=MID$(A$,LA,1)
590 IF YN$<>"Y" THEN 610
600 PRINT# PT,A$
610 IF O$="A" THEN 670
```

1-10 clearly labeled on the left half and 11-20 on the right. To correct item #13, you need only answer **Y** (for Yes) to the question "PRINT DETAILS?" Then you answer **13** to the prompt asking for the detail # and enter the addition or subtraction desired to replace the incorrect entry.

Lines 240-330 indicate the possible commands you may use. **HELP** will redisplay the instructions in these lines. The instructions come up on the screen automatically at the startup of the program.

Line 160 clears the screen by printing the character **CHR$(147)**, which has the same effect as entering the keystroke **SHIFT/CLR HOME** between quotation marks after a print statement. This second option will produce a listing with a heart between quotation marks on the screen. Using **CHR$(147)** makes the printout perhaps a bit more readable.

ADDMACH1 is the first of many programs in this book that can use a printer. Lines 160-210 allow you to choose a Commodore 1525 printer by keying **1**, an RS-232 printer by keying **2**, or no printer by keying **3** in line 80.

Line 200 gives the value of 127 or 128 to the file number for a 1525 printer or an RS-232 printer, respectively. Opening the file as number 128 causes a line feed to be generated automatically after each carriage return sent to the printer. PT is the variable that contains that file number. If your RS-232 printer does not require a line feed to be generated, change line 200 (and similar statements in other programs using a printer) to the following:

```
620 IF O$="/" THEN 740
630 IF O$="X" THEN 740
640 IF O$="=" THEN 780
650 IF O$="S" THEN 690
660 GOTO 700
670 O$="+"
680 GOTO 700
690 O$="-"
700 IF O$="+" THEN 890
710 IF O$="-" THEN 890
720 PRINT "ERROR - LAST CHAR MUST
    BE A,S,+,-"
730 GOTO 380
740 NUM$=MID$(A$,1,LA-1)
750 NA=VAL(NUM$)
760 OA$=O$
770 GOTO 380
780 NUM$=MID$(A$,1,LA-1)
790 NB=VAL(NUM$)
800 IF OA$="X" THEN 850
810 PRINT NA/NB
820 IF YN$<>"Y" THEN 840
830 PRINT# PT,NA/NB
840 GOTO 380
850 PRINT NA*NB
860 IF YN$<>"Y" THEN 380
870 PRINT# 1,NA*NB
880 GOTO 380
890 NUM$=MID$(A$,1,LA-1)
900 N1=VAL(NUM$)
910 IF O$="+" THEN 940
920 TTL=TTL-N1
930 GOTO 950
940 TTL=TTL+N1
950 C1=C1+1
960 E$(C1)=NUM$+O$
970 GOTO 380
980 PRINT "SUBTOTAL = ";TTL
990 GOTO 1010
1000 PRINT "TOTAL = ";TTL
```

```
200 PT=125+PT
```

The **CHR$(8)** causes the baud rate to be 1,200.

Whenever the cursor is located in the second position without a preceding prompt, you may make a new entry by keying a number with or without a decimal point and ending the number with a + or -, or an **A** or **S**. An **A** (for add) and an **S** (for subtract) can be used for quick entry of a + or - since the letters can be easily accessed without a shift on the Commodore typewriter-style keyboard. With this method, you can enter one entry after another until you want either a subtotal (enter an **S** alone) or a total (**T**). The difference between the two is that **T** will automatically clear the memory and total accumulations, whereas **S** will show the total to that point, allowing you to continue making entries after viewing the subtotal, as well as making any needed corrections.

The commands **ON** and **OFF** will turn a printer on or off to provide a printed copy of the entries you are making on the screen. You can turn the printer on or off whenever desired. As mentioned earlier, however, you can use ADDMACH1 without a printer and therefore save paper—either printer paper or adding machine tape.

One final feature is that you may obtain intermediate results which do not interfere with memory storage. These are accomplished by entering a number followed by a **/** (for division) or an **X** (for multiplication) and by pressing **RETURN**. Then by entering the number to be multiplied by or divided by, followed by an equal sign, and by

```
1010 IF YN$<>"Y" THEN 1060
1020 IF A$="S" THEN 1050
1030 PRINT# PT,"TOTAL = ";TTL
1040 GOTO 1060
1050 PRINT# PT,"SUBTOTAL = ";TTL
1060 INPUT "PRINT DETAILS";PYN$
1070 IF A$="S" THEN 1090
1080 IF A$="T" THEN 1110
1090 IF PYN$<>"Y" THEN 380
1100 GOTO 1120
1110 IF PYN$<>"Y" THEN 1900
1120 PRINT
1130 C2=0
1140 CA=C1/2
1150 IF CA=INT(CA) THEN 1170
1160 CA=INT(CA)+1
1170 FOR I=1 TO CA
1180 I$=STR$(I)
1190 LI=LEN(I$)
1200 IF LI<2 THEN 1230
1210 I2$=I$+". "
1220 GOTO 1240
1230 I2$=" "+I$+". "
1240 PRINT I2$;E$(I);
1245 S1=20-(LEN(I2$)+LEN(E$(I)))
1250 IF YN$<>"Y" THEN 1270
1260 PRINT# PT,I2$;E$(I);
1270 IX=I+CA
1280 IF IX>C1 THEN 1380
1290 IX$=STR$(IX)
1300 LX=LEN(IX$)
1310 IF LX<2 THEN 1340
1320 X2$=IX$+". "
1330 GOTO 1350
1340 X2$=" "+IX$+". "
1350 PRINT TAB(15);X2$;E$(IX);
1360 IF YN$<>"Y" THEN 1380
1370 PRINT# PT,SPC(S1);X2$;E$(IX);
1380 PRINT
1390 IF YN$<>"Y" THEN 1410
```

pressing **RETURN**, you will obtain the answer. For example, if you first key **12.34X** and a **RETURN**, then **25**= and a **RETURN**, you will get the answer 308.5. Then you can add or subtract 308.5 by entering **308.5**+ or **308.5-** and by pressing **RETURN**.

You can add or subtract the same number repetitively without re-entering it. Just enter one time the number to be added or subtracted and key **RETURN** for each calculation. For instance, by entering **25.37-** and keying **RETURN RETURN RETURN RETURN RETURN RETURN**, you are subtracting 25.37 six times. Lines 460-530 turn the printer on or off (if one is used) as you enter **ON** or **OFF**. When the printer has been turned on, a flag is set to "Y" (YN$ in line 470) or "N" (line 510). The program, then, is always aware of whether to print the desired details to the printer as well as display them on the screen.

Lines 610-720 evaluate the arithmetic operator keyed as the last character of an entry. If the character is not an **A**, **/**, **X**, =, **S**, +, or **-**, the operator is considered invalid, and an error message is displayed (line 720).

Lines 740-770 evaluate the number keyed before an **X** or a **/** so that the next number keyed before an equal sign can be evaluated in lines 780-880. In lines 810 and 830, the intermediate division result is listed on the screen and/or to the printer. Likewise, an intermediate multiplication product is printed in lines 850 and 870.

Lines 890-970 accumulate the number keyed into the total, either adding or subtracting, depending on the ending operator (+, **-**, **A**, or **S**). Furthermore, the entry is saved

```
1400 PRINT# PT
1410 NEXT I
1420 IF YN$<>"Y" THEN 1490
1430 PRINT# PT
1440 IF A$="S" THEN 1470
1450 PRINT# PT,"TOTAL = ";TTL
1460 GOTO 1480
1470 PRINT# PT,"SUBTOTAL = ";TTL
1480 PRINT# PT,"********************"
1490 PRINT
1500 IF A$="S" THEN 1530
1510 PRINT "TOTAL = ";TTL
1520 GOTO 1540
1530 PRINT "SUBTOTAL = ";TTL
1540 PRINT "********************"
1550 IF A$="T" THEN 1900
1560 INPUT "CHG DETAIL";CYN$
1570 IF CYN$<>"Y" THEN 380
1580 INPUT "DETAIL# ";DN
1590 IF DN>C1 THEN 1560
1600 INPUT "NEW VALUE";A$
1610 LA=LEN(A$)
1620 IF LA=0 THEN 1600
1630 O$=MID$(A$,LA,1)
1640 IF O$="A" THEN 1670
1650 IF O$="S" THEN 1690
1660 GOTO 1700
1670 O$="+"
1680 GOTO 1700
1690 O$="-"
1700 IF O$="+" THEN 1740
1710 IF O$="-" THEN 1740
1720 PRINT "ERROR - LAST CHAR MUST
     BE A,S,+,-"
1730 GOTO 1600
1740 NUM$=MID$(A$,1,LA-1)
1750 N1=VAL(NUM$)
1760 LE=LEN(E$(DN))
1770 OE$=MID$(E$(DN),LE,1)
1780 NE$=MID$(E$(DN),1,LE-1)
```

in the memory array E$ (line 960). Note that if an **S** or **A** was keyed, a **-** or + replaces the operator keyed in memory.

The subtotal or total is printed in lines 980-1550. The number of entries contained in memory (CTR1 in line 1140) is divided by two to determine how many rows of two columns should be displayed or printed.

As previously mentioned, each item is clearly numbered so that any entry can be easily located and changed. Lines 1560-1890 allow you to make changes or deletions to the displayed entries. To replace an entry with a correction, you need only to key the new entry after responding to the prompt that asks for the detail number in line 1580. The old entry is then either subtracted from the total (if the entry had been added to it) or added to the total (if the entry had been subtracted from it). The keyed replacement is stored in the same location of the memory array.

Lines 1900-1920 clear the TOTAL accumulator and set the pointer for the memory array back to zero.

```
1790 NE=VAL(NE$)
1800 IF OE$="+" THEN 1830
1810 TTL=TTL+NE
1820 GOTO 1840
1830 TTL=TTL-NE
1840 IF O$="+" THEN 1870
1850 TTL=TTL-N1
1860 GOTO 1880
1870 TTL=TTL+N1
1880 E$(DN)=NUM$+O$
1890 GOTO 1560
1900 C1=0
1910 TTL=0
1920 GOTO 380
1930 IF PX$="3" THEN 1950
1940 CLOSE PT
1950 END
```

```
SUBTOTAL = 987.79
 1. 24.00+      18. 54.00-
 2. 24.00+      19. 35.00+
 3. 24.00+      20. 35.00+
 4. 24.00+      21. 35.00+
 5. 24.00+      22. 35.00+
 6. 24.00+      23. 35.00+
 7. 24.00+      24. 35.00+
 8. 24.00+      25. 41.21-
 9. 34.00+      26. 65.00+
10. 34.00+      27. 65.00+
11. 34.00+      28. 65.00+
12. 34.00+      29. 65.00+
13. 34.00+      30. 23.00+
14. 34.00+      31. 23.00+
15. 34.00+      32. 23.00+
16. 34.00+      33. 23.00+
17. 34.00+      34. 23.00+

SUBTOTAL =  987.79
***************************
```

ADDSUB1

```
100 REM *************************
110 REM *          ADDSUB1          *
120 REM *                           *
130 REM *       COPYRIGHT 1983      *
140 REM *    DONALD C. KREUTNER     *
150 REM *************************
160 PRINT CHR$(147):POKE 53280,14:POKE
    53281,6:PRINT CHR$(5)
170 REM ADDSUB1
190 NEG$="N"
200 PRINT CHR$(147):REM CLR HOME
210 INPUT "WITH BORDER (Y/N)";YN$
220 INPUT "TOP # FROM 1 TO (2/999)";T1
230 IF T1<2 THEN 220
240 IF T1>999 THEN 220
250 INPUT "BOTTOM # 1 TO (2/999)";B1
260 IF B1<2 THEN 250
270 IF B1>999 THEN 250
280 ERRS=0
290 C1=0
300 INPUT "ADD, SUB, OR BOTH (A/S/B)";ASB$
310 IF ASB$="A" THEN 350
320 IF ASB$="S" THEN 350
330 IF ASB$="B" THEN 350
340 GOTO 300
350 PRINT CHR$(147):IF YN$="N" THEN 450
355 R=8
360 FOR C=12 TO 25
365 PT=1024+C+40*R:POKE PT,102
370 PT=55296+C+40*R:POKE PT,1
375 NEXT C
380 R=18
385 FOR C=13 TO 26
390 PT=1024+C+40*R:POKE PT,102
395 PT=55296+C+40*R:POKE PT,1
400 NEXT C
```

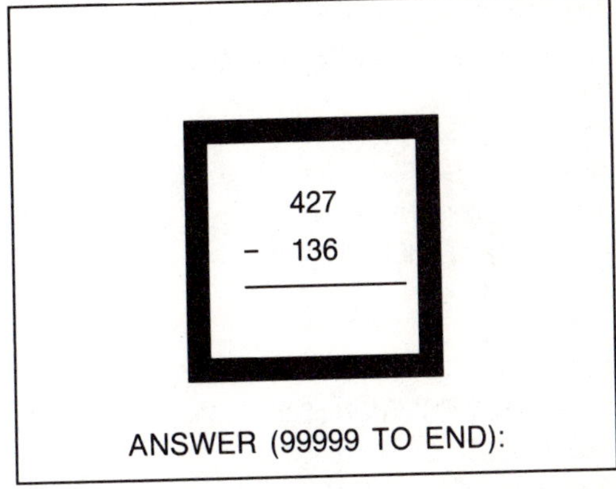

ADDSUB1 is a mathematical skills builder designed for improving performance in addition and subtraction.

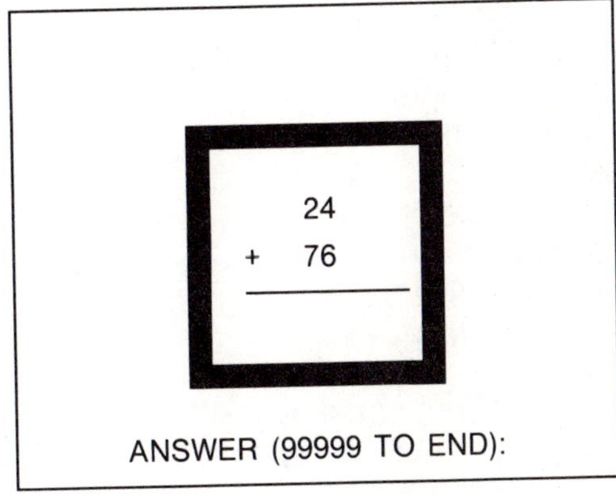

As is evident in the illustrations, the program will draw a border in the middle of the screen (if desired) in line 210. By answering any number from **2** to **999** in lines 220 and 250, the user can easily select the

```
405 C=12
410 FOR R=8 TO 18
415 PT=1024+C+40*R:POKE PT,102
420 PT=55296+C+40*R:POKE PT,1
425 PT=1024+26+40*R:POKE PT,102
430 PT=55296+26+40*R:POKE PT,1
435 NEXT R
450 N1=INT(T1*RND(1))+1
460 N2=INT(B1*RND(1))+1
470 IF NEG$<>"N" THEN 520
480 IF N1>N2 THEN 520
490 NX=N1
500 N1=N2
510 N2=NX
520 IF ASB$="S" THEN 580
530 IF ASB$="A" THEN 560
540 O1=INT(2*RND(1))+1
550 GOTO 590
560 O1=1
570 GOTO 590
580 O1=2
590 IF O1=1 THEN 600
600 N1$=STR$(N1)
610 N2$=STR$(N2)
620 IF O1=1 THEN 650
630 OP$="-"
640 GOTO 660
650 OP$="+"
660 L1=LEN(N1$)
670 L2=LEN(N2$)
680 J=21
690 FOR I=L1 TO 1 STEP -1
700 J=J-1
705 V=ASC(MID$(N1$,I,1))
710 PT=1024+J+40*12:POKE PT,V
720 PT=55296+J+40*12:POKE PT,1
730 NEXT I
740 J=21
750 FOR I=L2 TO 1 STEP -1
760 J=J-1
```

upper and lower ranges of the top and bottom numbers to be added or subtracted. The totals of the correct and incorrect answers are set to zero in lines 280 and 290. You can select addition only, subtraction only, or a mixture of both, selected randomly.

Two special characters are defined for this program: a checkered block and a horizontal line through the middle of the character grid.

Lines 355 to 435 draw the checkered squares by poking the value for the graphic square (102) into the appropriate memory address for the row and column desired. This process is computed by the formula in lines 365, 390, 415, and 425. Then the color value (1) is poked to the color memory map by the formula in lines 370, 395, 420, and 430. The square is used to draw the rectangular box in which each generated problem is displayed. The underline character is used to draw the dark bar beneath the problem, just as one would draw it on paper. The random selection process for the top and bottom numbers is given in lines 450 and 460. If you want a random number between 1 and 50, for example, use the statement

```
10 N1=INT(50*RND(1))+1
```

To avoid negative answers, the value N is given to NEG$ in line 190.

To display the problem in the middle of the screen, the two numbers are converted to character strings in N1$ and N2$. The lengths of these two alphanumeric (another word for string) items are determined in

```
770 V=ASC(MID$(N2$,I,1))
780 PT=1024+J+40*13:POKE PT,V
790 PT=55296+J+40*13:POKE PT,1
795 NEXT I
800 O2=ASC(OP$)
810 PT=1024+16+13*40:POKE PT,O2
815 PT=55296+16+13*40:POKE PT,1
820 FOR I=17 TO 20
830 PT=1024+I+14*40:POKE PT,67
835 PT=55296+I+14*40:POKE PT,1
840 NEXT I
845 INPUT "ANSWER (99999 TO END)";X
847 IF X=99999 THEN 1000
850 IF O1=2 THEN 880
860 IF X=N1+N2 THEN 960
870 GOTO 890
880 IF X=N1-N2 THEN 960
890 PRINT CHR$(147)
900 IF O1=2 THEN 930
910 PRINT "INCORRECT ";N1;" + ";N2;" = ";N1+N2
920 GOTO 940
930 PRINT "INCORRECT ";N1;" - ";N2;" = ";N1-N2
940 ERRS=ERRS+1
950 GOTO 980
960 C1=C1+1
970 GOTO 350
980 INPUT X$
990 GOTO 350
1000 PRINT CHR$(147):REM CLEAR SCREEN
1010 PRINT "************************"
1020 PRINT "*";TAB(23);"*"
1030 PRINT "*CORRECT=";C1;TAB(23);"*"
1040 PRINT "*";TAB(23);"*"
1050 PRINT "*ERRORS=";ERRS;TAB(23);"*"
1060 PRINT "*";TAB(23);"*"
1070 IF C1>0 THEN 1100
1080 IF ERRS>0 THEN 1100
1090 ERRS=1
1100 PRINT "*SCORE=";INT(C1/(C1+ERRS)*100);
     "%";TAB(23);"*"
```

lines 660 and 670. The characters of the top and bottom numbers are then moved in, one digit at a time, from the 20th position on the screen, right to left. This move is accomplished by two **FOR-NEXT** loops that have a negative step (that is, I decreases from the length of the string to 1). At the same time, each digit is moved to the 20th position of the screen, then the 19th, etc., in rows 12 and 13, using the **POKE** statements in lines 710, 720, 780, and 790.

Lines 680 to 840 are similar to lines 355-435 in that the locations for the digits of the numbers N1 and N2 are determined by the formulas of lines 710 and 780. Then the operator + or - and the underline of the problem are drawn by lines 810-835.

After the problem is displayed, you are prompted at the bottom for an answer. If the answer you give is correct, the program goes on to another problem. If your answer is incorrect, you are shown the correct answer. You must then press **RETURN** to continue.

To end the program, key **99999** as the answer to any problem. You are then shown a summary of your correct and incorrect responses.

```
1110 PRINT "*";TAB(23);"*"
1120 PRINT "************************"
1130 PRINT
1140 PRINT
1150 END
```

BSKTSTAT

```
10 REM **************************
30 REM *          BSKTSTAT           *
40 REM *                            *
50 REM *       COPYRIGHT 1983        *
60 REM *     DONALD C. KREUTNER      *
70 REM **************************
72 PRINT CHR$(147):POKE 53280,14:
   POKE 53281,6:PRINT CHR$(5)
75 PRINT CHR$(147):REM CLR SCREEN
80 INPUT "1525 PRTR(1), RS232(2),
   NONE(3)";PX$
85 IF PX$="3" THEN 130
90 IF PX$="1" THEN 105
95 IF PX$="2" THEN 105
100 GOTO 80
105 PT=VAL(PX$)
110 PT=126+PT
115 IF PT=127 THEN 125
120 OPEN PT,2,0,CHR$(8):PT=128:
    P$="2":GOTO 130
125 OPEN PT,4
130 ECTR=0
135 DIM D$(100)
140 DIM P$(100)
145 GOSUB 3500
150 B$="                    "
155 REM B$ IS TWENTY SPACES LONG
160 PRINT CHR$(147)
170 PRINT "ED   ENTER DETAILS"
180 PRINT "RD   READ DETAILS FILE"
190 PRINT "WD   WRITE DETAILS FILE"
200 PRINT "SD   SORT DETAILS"
210 PRINT "LD   LIST DETAILS"
220 PRINT "PD   PRINT DETAILS"
230 PRINT "C    CLEAR DETAILS"
240 PRINT "RP   READ PLAYER FILE"
```

BSKTSTAT is a multipurpose, basketball statistics accumulation program. As indicated by the menu in lines 170-260, this program will enter new details for a team's game statistics. Old details can be read from a file prior to entering new details in order to obtain cumulative totals. Details can then be sorted and listed as raw data, or the details and total statistics can be displayed on the screen or printed on the printer, or both. A player file can be read in from cassette or disk, or a new player file with names and numbers can be entered and written to tape or disk.

Based on the action requested in line 310, the allowable options above are taken by the program (lines 310-420).

Note that when the program starts, the subroutine in lines 3500-3530 is executed, blanking out the names of the player string array P$. This array will hold up to 100 names that can then be accessed by player number. The **GOSUB** statement is particularly useful for accomplishing a routine that will be done at more than one place within a program. Here **GOSUB** allows you to perform a routine of four lines simply by stating **GOSUB** 3500. Control is then returned to the next sequential line (150) after the **RETURN** statement is encountered in line 3530.

Lines 440-610 accomplish the reading into P$ of a player name file that had been previously written either to disk or tape,

```
250 PRINT "WP   WRITE PLAYER FILE"
260 PRINT "END  END PROGRAM"
270 PRINT "**********************"
280 PRINT
290 PRINT
300 PRINT
310 INPUT "ACTION";AC$
320 IF AC$="ED" THEN 880
330 IF AC$="RD" THEN 1660
340 IF AC$="WD" THEN 1850
350 IF AC$="SD" THEN 2000
360 IF AC$="LD" THEN 2170
370 IF AC$="PD" THEN 2290
380 IF AC$="END" THEN 3590
390 IF AC$="C" THEN 3470
400 IF AC$="RP" THEN 440
410 IF AC$="WP" THEN 630
420 GOTO 160
430 REM *******************
440 GOSUB 3500
450 INPUT "CASSETTE/DISK (C/D)";CD$
460 IF CD$<>"C" THEN 490
470 OPEN 2,1,0:REM OPEN TAPE FOR INPUT
480 GOTO 510
490 INPUT "FILENAME";FILE1$
500 OPEN 2,8,2,"0:"+FILE1$+",S,R"
510 INPUT#2,I$
515 PRINT I$
520 IF I$="END" THEN 590
525 IF ST>0 GOTO 590
530 PN$=MID$(I$,1,2)
540 LI=LEN(I$)
550 P1NAME$=MID$(I$,3,LI-2)
560 PN=VAL(PN$)
570 P$(PN)=P1NAME$
580 GOTO 510
590 CLOSE 2
600 PRINT "END OF PLAYER READ -
    HIT RETURN"
605 GET Z$:IF Z$="" THEN 605
```

using the **WP** (write player file) command of this program. Line 450 controls whether the file will be read from a cassette recorder or a disk drive. The answer you key will then cause one or the other type of file to be opened for input (lines 470 and 500). Both files are sequential in nature, and I$ is input from the file. The first two characters are the player number. From position 3 to the end of the string is the player's name. Note that the **VAL** function of line 560 obtains the numeric value of the player number string.

Lines 630-860 similarly write a player file to tape or disk. Be sure to note, however, that you will have to enter the player number and name for every player you wish to have in the file. Once you have the file stored on disk or cassette, you can later recall that "team" whenever you want to access the same information.

If you have already entered a team file, you should perform the read function first to have all the players' names and numbers in memory each time you run the program. If this is the first time you are entering data for a team, you should perform the write function first. Obviously, you can have several files with information about different teams so that whenever you want to enter data for a particular team, you can easily recall from a file that team's names and numbers.

Notice in line 710 the **STR$** function, which does the opposite of the **VAL** function discussed earlier. **STR$** causes the numeric value of PN to be changed into the string value PN$. This number can then be joined together into one string with the name (P1NAME$) and written ("printed") to the

```
610 GOTO 160
620 REM *******************
630 INPUT "CASSETTE/DISK (C/D)";CD$
640 IF CD$<>"C" THEN 670
650 OPEN 2,1,2:REM OPEN TAPE FOR OUTPUT
660 GOTO 690
670 INPUT "FILENAME";FILE1$
680 OPEN 2,8,2,"@0:"+FILE1$+",S,W"
690 INPUT "PLAYER ##";PN
700 IF PN=999 THEN 830
710 PN$=STR$(PN)
720 IF PN>99 THEN 690
730 IF PN<0 THEN 690
740 IF PN>9 THEN 755
750 PN$="0"+MID$(PN$,2,1):GOTO 760
755 PN$=MID$(PN$,2,2)
760 INPUT "PLAYER NAME
    (20 CHARS)";P1NAME$
765 REM PRINT "X";PN$;"X";PN;"X"
770 LPN=LEN(P1NAME$)
780 IF LPN>20 THEN 760
790 IF LPN=20 THEN 810
800 P1NAME$=P1NAME$+MID$(B$,1,20-LPN)
810 PQ$=PN$+P1NAME$
812 PRINT PQ$
814 PRINT# 2,PQ$
820 GOTO 690
830 PRINT# 2,"END"
840 CLOSE 2
850 PRINT "END OF PLAYER WRITE"
855 INPUT "RETURN TO CONTINUE";Z$
860 GOTO 160
870 REM ***********************
880 INPUT "PLAYER ##";PL
890 IF PL=999 THEN 160
900 IF PL>99 THEN 880
910 INPUT "MONTH";MO
920 IF MO<1 THEN 840
930 IF MO>12 THEN 840
940 INPUT "DAY";DY
```

file as a single string or group of characters (lines 810-814). As in the read routine discussed above, file #2 in lines 650, 680, 814, 830, and 840 is either a cassette or a disk file. The writing is terminated when **999** is entered for the player number (line 700).

Game details for players are entered in lines 880-1640. Again, the entry is terminated by entering player number **999** in line 880. Data to be entered includes game date, opponent (limited to an eight-character abbreviation), and the player's statistics (points, field goals, field goals attempted, free throws, free throws attempted, rebounds, assists, steals, minutes played, and personal fouls).

This data is then strung together in a set sequence so that the details can be easily sorted. Each field that was keyed is changed to a string of a specified length. For example, lines 1230-1305 make the points field three digits long, even if fewer than 10 points were scored. Then all of these string values are joined together into the next available detail array element (D$). In this manner, if you have already input a file of details (see the next paragraph), each detail you key will be added to the data already read in. Line 1620 keeps track of what position within the array is available for the next detail entry.

To input a file of details previously saved to tape or diskette, lines 1660-1830 are used. Another feature is that you don't have to clear the details already in memory just because you want to read in a new details file. You can merge two files together in memory (the D$ array), then write them out

```
950 IF DY<1 THEN 940
960 IF DY>31 THEN 940
970 INPUT "YEAR";YR
975 IF YR<80 THEN 970
976 IF YR>99 THEN 970
980 INPUT "OPPONENT";O$
990 LO=LEN(O$)
1000 IF LO>8 THEN 980
1010 INPUT "POINTS";P1PT
1020 INPUT "FG";G
1030 INPUT "FGA";GA
1040 INPUT "FT";F2FT
1050 INPUT "FTA";F3FTA
1060 INPUT "REBS";REB
1070 INPUT "ASSISTS";A
1080 INPUT "STEALS";S
1090 INPUT "MINUTES";MIN1
1100 INPUT "PF";PF
1110 INPUT "ACCEPT (Y/N)";YN$
1120 IF YN$<>"Y" THEN 880
1130 PL$=STR$(PL)
1140 IF PL>9 THEN 1155
1150 PL$="0"+MID$(PL$,2,1):GOTO 1160
1155 PL$=MID$(PL$,2,2)
1160 MO$=STR$(MO)
1170 IF MO>9 THEN 1185
1180 MO$="0"+MID$(MO$,2,1):GOTO 1190
1185 MO$=MID$(MO$,2,2)
1190 DY$=STR$(DY)
1200 IF DY>9 THEN 1215
1210 DY$="0"+MID$(DY$,2,1):GOTO 1220
1215 DY$=MID$(DY$,2,2)
1220 YR$=STR$(YR)
1225 YR$=MID$(YR$,2,2)
1230 REM POINTS FIELD IS 3 DIGITS
1240 PT$=STR$(P1PT)
1250 IF P1PT<10 THEN 1280
1260 IF P1PT<100 THEN 1300
1270 GOTO 1305
1280 PT$="00"+MID$(PT$,2,1)
```

to a single file. Likewise, you can read in one or more files and also add more keyed details before writing them out to a file.

Note that when the string "END" is read from the file, the input sequence is terminated (line 1780). You can, of course, clear all previous details in memory by responding **Y** in line 1660. This has the effect of resetting the counter ECTR to 0, instead of continuing from the value it had reached from a previous file read or from a keying of details.

Lines 1850-1980 save all the data details to either a diskette or a tape file. Notice that in line 1910 you have complete control over the file name you want for data files. This is true in all cases where you request to read or write a disk file. For a cassette file, you are simply asked to rewind the tape, hit play/record (or play), etc., as described in the Commodore manual for the operation of cassette recorders.

The sorting of player details is a "bubble sort," which goes through the array D$ and swaps the "position prior" to the "position after" if the data is greater than that of the following position. With this method the data elements "bubble" from one end of the array to the end where they belong. If any one element is detected out of order and is switched, the check through the array is done again until no swaps are made and the data is in the desired sequence. Note that only the first eight characters (which contain the player number and the date of the game) are compared. Line 2130 checks for a change having been made, and lines 2080-2100 accomplish the "swap."

```
1290 GOTO 1310
1300 PT$="0"+MID$(PT$,2,2):GOTO 1310
1305 PT$=MID$(PT$,2,3)
1310 G$=STR$(G)
1320 IF G>9 THEN 1335
1330 G$="0"+MID$(G$,2,1):GOTO 1340
1335 G$=MID$(G$,2,2)
1340 GA$=STR$(GA)
1350 IF GA>9 THEN 1365
1360 GA$="0"+MID$(GA$,2,1):GOTO 1370
1365 GA$=MID$(GA$,2,2)
1370 F2FT$=STR$(F2FT)
1380 IF F2FT>9 THEN 1395
1390 F2FT$="0"+MID$(F2FT$,2,1):GOTO 1400
1395 F2FT$=MID$(F2FT$,2,2)
1400 F3FTA$=STR$(F3FTA)
1410 IF F3FTA>9 THEN 1425
1420 F3FTA$="0"+MID$(F3FTA$,2,1):GOTO 1430
1425 F3FTA$=MID$(F3FTA$,2,2)
1430 REB$=STR$(REB)
1440 IF REB>9 THEN 1455
1450 REB$="0"+MID$(REB$,2,1):GOTO 1460
1455 REB$=MID$(REB$,2,2)
1460 A$=STR$(A)
1470 IF A>9 THEN 1485
1480 A$="0"+MID$(A$,2,1):GOTO 1490
1485 A$=MID$(A$,2,2)
1490 ST$=STR$(S)
1500 IF S>9 THEN 1515
1510 ST$="0"+MID$(ST$,2,1):GOTO 1520
1515 ST$=MID$(ST$,2,2)
1520 MIN$=STR$(MIN1)
1530 IF MIN1>9 THEN 1545
1540 MIN$="0"+MID$(MIN$,2,1):GOTO 1550
1545 MIN$=MID$(MIN$,2,2)
1550 PF$=STR$(PF)
1560 O2$="        "
1565 REM O2$ IS 8 SPACES LONG
1570 LO2=8-LO
1580 O3$=O$+MID$(O2$,1,LO2)
```

A simple data listing is the result of lines 2170-2270. The data is displayed either on the screen or on both the screen and a printer in the form in which the data is stored in the detail array. If a sort has been done, the data will be in player number/date sequence. Otherwise, the data will be in the order entered and/or read from a file or files.

Lines 2290-3030 print formatted details and totals, including averages for each player, if desired. You can make the display of data on the screen pause by answering **Y** to the input statement in line 2305. **GOSUB** 3540 in line 2340 prints a heading on the printer. **GOSUB** 3340 in line 2360 zeroes out the player totals at the beginning and after a player's last detail has been read.

LASTPL$ in line 2350 keeps track of the last player number of the previous record read from the array. When that number changes, the totals of the previous player are computed and printed. Lines 2370-2630 "unstring" the data into its elements so that totals can be added. The **MID$** function is used to break up the large detail string array. For example, rebounds are in the 28th position of the D$ field for a length of two positions (see line 2480). A player summary is printed by the subroutine 3040-3330.

```
1590 R1REC$=PL$+YR$+MO$+DY$+O3$+PT$+G$
1600 R2REC2$=GA$+F2FT$+F3FTA$+REB$+A$
1610 R3REC3$=ST$+MIN$+PF$
1620 ECTR=ECTR+1
1630 D$(ECTR)=R1REC1$+R2REC2$+R3REC3$
1640 GOTO 880
1650 REM ********************
1660 INPUT "CLEAR OLD DETAILS (Y/N)";CYN$
1670 IF CYN$<>"Y" THEN 1690
1680 ECTR=0
1690 INPUT "DISK/CASSETTE (D/C)";DC$
1700 IF DC$="C" THEN 1730
1710 IF DC$="D" THEN 1750
1720 GOTO 1690
1730 OPEN 2,1,0:REM OPEN TAPE FOR INPUT
1740 GOTO 1770
1750 INPUT "FILENAME";FILE1$
1760 OPEN 2,8,2,"0:"+FILE1$+",S,R"
1770 INPUT# 2,D1$
1775 IF ST>0 THEN 1820
1780 IF D1$="END" THEN 1820
1790 ECTR=ECTR+1
1800 D$(ECTR)=D1$
1810 GOTO 1770
1820 CLOSE 2
1825 INPUT "RETURN TO CONTINUE";Z$
1830 GOTO 160
1840 REM *********************
1850 INPUT "DISK/CASSETTE (D/C)";DC$
1860 IF DC$="C" THEN 1890
1870 IF DC$="D" THEN 1910
1880 GOTO 1850
1890 OPEN 2,1,1:REM OPEN TAPE FOR OUTPUT
1900 GOTO 1930
1910 INPUT "FILENAME";FILE1$
1920 OPEN 2,8,2,"@0:"+FILE1$+",S,W"
1930 FOR I=1 TO ECTR
1940 PRINT# 2,D$(I)
1950 NEXT I
1960 PRINT# 2,"END"
1970 CLOSE 2
1975 INPUT "RETURN TO CONTINUE";Z$
1980 GOTO 160
1990 REM **********************
2000 REM SORT BY ##/BY DATE
2010 SRTCTR=0
2020 CHGFLAG$="N"
2030 SRTCTR=SRTCTR+1
2040 PRINT CHR$(147)
2050 PRINT "SORT PASS #";SRTCTR
2060 FOR I=1 TO ECTR-1
2070 IF MID$(D$(I),1,8)<=MID$(D$(I+1),1,8)
     THEN 2120
2080 SAV$=D$(I)
2090 D$(I)=D$(I+1)
2100 D$(I+1)=SAV$
2110 CHGFLAG$="Y"
2120 NEXT I
2130 IF CHGFLAG$="Y" THEN 2020
2140 PRINT "SORT COMPLETED"
2150 GOTO 160
2160 REM ********************
2170 INPUT "PRINTER (Y/N)";PYN$
2175 IF PX$="3" THEN PYN$="N"
2200 FOR I=1 TO ECTR
2210 PRINT I;D$(I)
2220 IF PYN$<>"Y" THEN 2240
2230 PRINT# PT,I;D$(I)
2240 NEXT I
2260 INPUT "RETURN TO CONTINUE";Z$
2270 GOTO 160
2280 REM ***********************
2290 INPUT "PRINTER (Y/N)";PYN$
2300 IF PX$="3" THEN PYN$="N"
2305 INPUT "PAUSE (Y/N)";PAYN$
2310 INPUT "PRINT TOTALS (Y/N)";TTLYN$
2320 IF PYN$<>"Y" THEN 2350
2340 GOSUB 3540
2350 LASTPL$="XX"
2360 GOSUB 3340
```

```
2370 FOR I=1 TO ECTR
2380 PL$=MID$(D$(I),1,2)
2390 YR$=MID$(D$(I),3,2)
2400 MO$=MID$(D$(I),5,2)
2410 DY$=MID$(D$(I),7,2)
2420 O$=MID$(D$(I),9,8)
2430 PT$=MID$(D$(I),17,3)
2440 G$=MID$(D$(I),20,2)
2450 GA$=MID$(D$(I),22,2)
2460 F2FT$=MID$(D$(I),24,2)
2470 F3FTA$=MID$(D$(I),26,2)
2480 REB$=MID$(D$(I),28,2)
2490 A$=MID$(D$(I),30,2)
2500 ST$=MID$(D$(I),32,2)
2510 MIN$=MID$(D$(I),34,2)
2520 PF$=MID$(D$(I),36,2)
2530 PL=VAL(PL$)
2540 P1PT=VAL(PT$)
2550 G=VAL(G$)
2560 GA=VAL(GA$)
2570 F2FT=VAL(F2FT$)
2580 F3FTA=VAL(F3FTA$)
2590 REB=VAL(REB$)
2600 A=VAL(A$)
2610 S=VAL(ST$)
2620 MIN1=VAL(MIN$)
2630 PF=VAL(PF$)
2640 IF PL$=LASTPL$ THEN 2700
2650 IF LASTPL$="XX" THEN 2700
2660 IF TTLYN$<>"Y" THEN 2700
2670 REM *PLAYER SUMMARY*
2680 GOSUB 3040
2690 GOSUB 3340
2700 T6TTLPT=T6TTLPT+P1PT
2710 T7TTLFG=T7TTLFG+G
2720 T8TTLFGA=T8TTLFGA+GA
2730 T5TTLFT=T5TTLFT+F2FT
2740 T4TTLFTA=T4TTLFTA+F3FTA
2750 T3TTLREB=T3TTLREB+REB
2760 T1TTLA=T1TTLA+A
2770 T2TTLST=T2TTLST+S
2780 T9TTLMIN=T9TTLMIN+MIN1
2790 TG=TG+1
2800 LASTPL$=PL$
2810 TPF=TPF+PF
2820 IF PYN$<>"Y" THEN 2880
2830 PRINT# PT,PL$;" ";P$(PL);SPC
     MO$;"/";DY$;"/";YR$;
2840 PRINT# PT," ";O$;SPC(9-LEN(O$));PT$;
     SPC(5-LEN(PT$));REB$;
2850 PRINT# PT,SPC(4-LEN(REB$));A$;
     SPC(4-LEN(A$));ST$;SPC(4-LEN(ST$));MIN$;
2860 PRINT# PT,SPC(4-LEN(MIN$));
     PF$;SPC(1);G$;"/";GA$;
2870 PRINT# PT,SPC(3);F2FT$;"/";F3FTA$
2880 PRINT "#";PL$;SPC(1);P$(PL)
2890 PRINT "DATE ";MO$;"/";DY$;"/";YR$
2900 PRINT "OPP: ";O$
2910 PRINT "PTS: ";PT$;" REBS: ";REB$;" A: ";A$
2920 PRINT "ST: ";ST$;" MIN: ";MIN$;" PF: ";PF$
2930 PRINT "FG/FGA: ";G$;"/";GA$;" FT/FTA:
     ";F2FT$;"/";F3FTA$
2940 PRINT "************************"
2950 IF PAYN$<>"Y" THEN 2970
2960 GET Z$:IF Z$="" THEN 2960
2970 NEXT I
2980 IF TTLYN$<>"Y" THEN 3000
2990 GOSUB 3040
3000 GET Z$:IF Z$="" THEN 3000
3030 GOTO 160
3040 REM **********************
3042 GP=0:PPG=0:RPG=0:MPG=0
3044 F1FTP=0
3046 IF T8TTLFGA=0 THEN 3055
3050 GP=INT(T7TTLFG*100000/T8TTLFGA)
3055 IF TG=0 THEN 3085
3060 PPG=INT(T6TTLPT/TG*100)/100
3070 RPG=INT(T3TTLREB/TG*100)/100
3080 MPG=INT(T9TTLMIN/TG*100)/100
3085 IF T4TTLFTA=0 THEN 3110
```

```
3090 F1FTP=INT(T5TTLFT*100000/T4TTLFTA)
3100 F1FTP=F1FTP/1000
3110 GP=GP/1000
3120 PRINT "*PLAYER TOTALS* #GAMES; ";TG
3130 PRINT "PTS:";T6TTLPT;" REBS:";
    T3TTLREB;" A:";T1TTLA
3140 PRINT "ST:";T2TTLST;" MIN:";T9TTLMIN;
    " PF:";TPF
3150 PRINT "FG/FGA:";T7TTLFG;
    "/";T8TTLFGA;SPC(4);GP;"%"
3160 PRINT "FT/FTA:";T5TTLFT;"/";
    T4TTLFTA;SPC(4);F1FTP;"%"
3170 PRINT "PTS/GM:";PPG
3180 PRINT "MIN/GM:";MPG
3190 PRINT "REB/GM:";RPG
3200 PRINT "**************************"
3205 IF PYN$<>"Y" THEN 3330
3210 PRINT# PT
3220 PRINT# PT,"*PLAYER TOTALS*
    #GAMES:";TG
3230 PRINT# PT,"PTS:";T6TTLPT;
    " REB:";T3TTLREB;" A:";T1TTLA;
3240 PRINT# PT," ST:";T2TTLST;
    " MIN:";T9TTLMIN;" PF:";TPF
3250 PRINT# PT,"FG/FGA:";T7TTLFG;
    "/";T8TTLFGA;SPC(4);GP;"%"
3260 PRINT# PT,"FT/FTA:";T5TTLFT;
    "/";T4TTLFTA;SPC(4);F1FTP;"%"
3270 PRINT# PT,"PTS/GM:";PPG;SPC(4);
3280 PRINT# PT,"MIN/GM:";MPG;SPC(4);
3290 PRINT# PT,"REB/GM:";RPG
3300 PRINT# PT,"********************
    ******************************";
3310 PRINT# PT,"
    *****************************"
3330 RETURN
3340 T8TTLFGA=0
3350 T5TTLFT=0
3360 T4TTLFTA=0
3370 T3TTLREB=0
3380 T1TTLA=0
3390 T2TTLST=0
3400 T9TTLMIN=0
3410 TPF=0
3420 TG=0
3430 T6TTLPT=0
3440 T7TTLFG=0
3450 RETURN
3460 REM *********************
3470 ECTR=0
3480 PRINT "DETAILS CLEARED"
3490 GOTO 160
3500 FOR I=1 TO 100
3510 P$(I)=" "
3520 NEXT I
3530 RETURN
3540 PRINT# PT,"## NAME";SPC(19);"DATE";
    SPC(3);"OPP";SPC(6);"PTS";SPC(2);
3550 PRINT# PT,"REB A";SPC(3);"ST";
    SPC(2);"MIN PF FG/FGA";SPC(2);"FT/FTA"
3560 PRINT# PT
3580 RETURN
3590 IF PX$="3" THEN 3610
3600 CLOSE PT
3610 END
```

```
## NAME                   DATE     OPP      PTS  REB A   ST  MIN PF FG/FGA  FT/FTA

08 JAY K.                 03/12/83 RED      014  08  02  01  12  3  06/09   02/03
08 JAY K.                 03/20/83 BLUE     020  04  02  00  13  2  08/13   04/06

*PLAYER TOTALS* #GAMES: 2
PTS: 34   REB: 12   A: 4  ST: 1   MIN: 25   PF: 5
FG/FGA: 14 / 22     63.636 %            FT/FTA: 6 / 9         66.666 %
PTS/GM: 17          MIN/GM: 12.5        REB/GM: 6
********************************************************************************
12 DEREK                  03/12/83 RED      015  07  02  02  13  4  04/05   07/10
12 DEREK                  03/20/83 BLUE     018  06  01  01  10  1  09/10   00/01

*PLAYER TOTALS* #GAMES: 2
PTS: 33   REB: 13   A: 3  ST: 3   MIN: 23   PF: 5
FG/FGA: 13 / 15     86.666 %            FT/FTA: 7 / 11        63.636 %
PTS/GM: 16.5        MIN/GM: 11.5        REB/GM: 6.5
********************************************************************************
15 JAY H.                 03/12/83 RED      020  06  04  03  14  5  10/15   00/02
15 JAY H.                 03/20/83 BLUE     010  08  01  00  10  2  03/06   04/07

*PLAYER TOTALS* #GAMES: 2
PTS: 30   REB: 14   A: 5  ST: 3   MIN: 24   PF: 7
FG/FGA: 13 / 21     61.904 %            FT/FTA: 4 / 9         44.444 %
PTS/GM: 15          MIN/GM: 12          REB/GM: 7
********************************************************************************
19 VAUGHN                 03/12/83 RED      012  06  01  01  12  2  05/09   02/02

*PLAYER TOTALS* #GAMES: 1
PTS: 12   REB: 6    A: 1  ST: 1   MIN: 12   PF: 2
FG/FGA: 5 / 9       55.555 %            FT/FTA: 2 / 2         100 %
PTS/GM: 12          MIN/GM: 12          REB/GM: 6
********************************************************************************
24 RICK                   03/12/83 RED      016  09  03  02  13  2  06/12   04/07
24 RICK                   03/20/83 BLUE     006  06  00  01  10  5  03/03   00/01

*PLAYER TOTALS* #GAMES: 2
PTS: 22   REB: 15   A: 3  ST: 3   MIN: 23   PF: 7
FG/FGA:  9 / 15     60 %                FT/FTA: 4 / 8         50 %
PTS/GM: 11          MIN/GM: 11.5        REB/GM: 7.5
********************************************************************************
```

```
29 BOBBY                03/12/83 RED      008  10  04  03  08  3  04/07   00/00
29 BOBBY                03/20/83 BLUE     021  12  01  01  16  2  09/10   03/03

*PLAYER TOTALS* #GAMES: 2
PTS: 29   REB: 22   A: 5  ST: 4   MIN: 24   PF: 5
FG/FGA: 13 / 17     76.47 %           FT/FTA: 3 / 3         100 %
PTS/GM: 14.5        MIN/GM: 12        REB/GM: 11
****************************************************************************
33 TONY                 03/12/83 RED      010  04  01  00  09  3  04/05   02/02
33 TONY                 03/20/83 BLUE     009  01  03  04  12  2  04/05   01/01

*PLAYER TOTALS* #GAMES: 2
PTS: 19   REB: 5    A: 4  ST: 4   MIN: 21   PF: 5
FG/FGA: 8 / 10      80 %              FT/FTA: 3 / 3         100 %
PTS/GM: 9.5         MIN/GM: 10.5      REB/GM: 2.5
****************************************************************************
```

CALC1

```
100 REM **************************
110 REM *          CALC1          *
120 REM *                         *
130 REM *      COPYRIGHT 1983     *
140 REM *    DONALD C. KREUTNER   *
150 REM **************************
160 REM
170 REM
175 PRINT CHR$(147):POKE 53280,14:
    POKE 53281,6:PRINT CHR$(5)
180 TTL=0
190 PRINT CHR$(147):REM CLR SCREEN
200 INPUT A$
210 LA=LEN(A$)
220 IF LA=0 THEN 200
230 IF A$="END" THEN 1250
240 IF A$<>"C" THEN 280
250 TTL=0
260 PRINT CHR$(147)
270 GOTO 200
280 N1$=" "
290 N2$=" "
300 O1$=" "
310 O2$=" "
320 C1N1=0
330 C2N2=0
340 IF MID$(A$,1,1)>="0" THEN 360
350 GOTO 370
360 IF MID$(A$,1,1)<="9" THEN 390
370 FLOPER$="Y"
380 GOTO 400
390 FLOPER$="N"
400 FOR I=1 TO LA
410 A2$=MID$(A$,I,1)
420 IF A2$="X" THEN 700
430 IF A2$="/" THEN 700
```

CALC1 performs like a calculator—adding, subtracting, multiplying, dividing, and taking the powers and roots of various numbers. The total accumulator (TTL) is cleared to zero by line 180 at the program startup. Every calculation to be performed is entered in line 200. Whatever you key in is then evaluated by lines 220 to the program end. After every evaluation, control is returned to line 220 for the next operation.

Two numbers can be entered, which are separated by an operator and terminated by an equal sign, as in

243.5/12.2=

When a number starts the keyed expression, the previously accumulated total (TTL) is automatically cleared. This is determined in lines 340 to 390, where the first character entered is inspected to see whether it is numeric or an operator.

Lines 420-550 ensure that the operation is valid (either **X**, **/**, +, -, ^, **A**, **S**, a period, or a number).

Then, depending on whether the number being read one character at a time is the first or the second number, lines 560-690 move the numbers and/or decimal points into N1$ or N2$. The string entered is examined for the length of the string (LA in line 400). When that has been completed, N1 and N2 are given numeric values from the strings N1$ and N2$ (lines 770 and 800). Lines 810 and 820 clear the total if the first

```
440 IF A2$="^" THEN 700
450 IF A2$="+" THEN 700
460 IF A2$="-" THEN 700
470 IF A2$="A" THEN 700
480 IF A2$="S" THEN 700
490 IF A2$="=" THEN 700
500 IF A2$="." THEN 560
510 IF A2$>"9" THEN 540
520 IF A2$<"0" THEN 540
530 GOTO 560
540 PRINT "MUST BE # OR X,/,^,+,-,A,S,="
550 GOTO 200
560 IF O1$=" " THEN 640
570 IF FLOPER$="Y" THEN 640
580 C2N2=C2N2+1
590 IF C2N2>1 THEN 620
600 N2$=MID$(A2$,1,1)
610 GOTO 630
620 N2$=N2$+MID$(A2$,1,1)
630 GOTO 740
640 C1N1=C1N1+1
650 IF C1N1>1 THEN 680
660 N1$=MID$(A2$,1,1)
670 GOTO 690
680 N1$=N1$+MID$(A2$,1,1)
690 GOTO 740
700 IF O1$=" " THEN 730
710 O2$=A2$
720 GOTO 740
730 O1$=A2$
740 NEXT I
750 IF LEN(N1$)<1 THEN 780
760 IF N1$=" " THEN 780
770 N1=VAL(N1$)
780 IF LEN(N2$)<1 THEN 810
790 IF N2$=" " THEN 810
800 N2=VAL(N2$)
810 IF FLOPER$="Y" THEN 1030
820 TTL=0
830 IF O1$="A" THEN 910
```

character keyed is numeric. Lines 830-1020 then compute the total to be the result of N1 and N2, acted on by the first operator. Then, if the second operator is an equal sign, the result is printed (lines 1000 and 1010). However, if the first character is an operator, the previous total is added to, multiplied, etc., to obtain a new total. Once again, whenever an equal sign is encountered, the total is displayed on the screen.

Following are statements of particular interest.

Line 410 evaluates the characters entered one character at a time. **MID$**(A$,I,1) represents the segment of A$, starting at position number I for a length of one character. Note that I increases by one as the **FOR-NEXT** loop of lines 400-740 is executed.

Line 210 determines the length of A$ so that it can be evaluated character by character. The function **LEN**(A$) determines the length of A$. Finally, remember that **A** and **S** can be used alternately in place of the + and - keys.

```
89.5X16 =
1432
/2 =
716
14.52-6.2
-5
=
3.32
C
X10 =
0
```

```
840 IF O1$="+" THEN 910
850 IF O1$="S" THEN 930
860 IF O1$="-" THEN 930
870 IF O1$="X" THEN 950
880 IF O1$="/" THEN 970
890 IF O1$="^" THEN 990
900 GOTO 200
910 TTL=N1+N2
920 GOTO 1000
930 TTL=N1-N2
940 GOTO 1000
950 TTL=N1*N2
960 GOTO 1000
970 TTL=N1/N2
980 GOTO 1000
990 TTL=N1^N2
1000 IF O2$<>"=" THEN 200
1010 PRINT "*TOTAL* ";TTL
1020 GOTO 200
1030 IF O1$="=" THEN 1230
1040 IF O1$="+" THEN 1120
1050 IF O1$="A" THEN 1120
1060 IF O1$="-" THEN 1140
1070 IF O1$="S" THEN 1140
1080 IF O1$="X" THEN 1160
1090 IF O1$="/" THEN 1180
1100 IF O1$="^" THEN 1200
1110 GOTO 200
1120 TTL=TTL+N1
1130 GOTO 1210
1140 TTL=TTL-N1
1150 GOTO 1210
1160 TTL=TTL*N1
1170 GOTO 1210
1180 TTL=TTL/N1
1190 GOTO 1210
1200 TTL=TTL^N1
1210 IF O2$="=" THEN 1230
1220 GOTO 200
1230 PRINT "*TOTAL* ";TTL
1240 GOTO 200
1250 END
```

CALENDAR

```
100 REM ************************
120 REM *          CALENDAR            *
130 REM *                              *
140 REM *       COPYRIGHT 1983         *
150 REM *    DONALD C. KREUTNER        *
160 REM ************************
162 PRINT CHR$(147):POKE 53280,14:POKE
    53281,6:PRINT CHR$(5)
165 INPUT "1525 PRTR(1), RS232(2),
    NONE(3)";PX$
170 IF PX$="3" THEN 215
175 IF PX$="1" THEN 190
180 IF PX$="2" THEN 190
185 GOTO 165
190 PT=VAL(PX$)
195 PT=126+PT
200 IF PT=127 THEN 210
205 OPEN PT,2,0,CHR$(8):PT=128:PX$="2":
    GOTO 215
210 OPEN PT,4
215 REM 1980 IS BASE FOR LY/3(TUE)
217 REM 1981 IS BASE FOR LY+1/5(THU)
218 REM 1982 IS BASE FOR LY+2/6(FRI)
219 REM 1983 IS BASE FOR LY+3/7(SAT)
220 REM 01/01/80 FELL ON TUE, 3RD DAY
    OF WEEK
221 REM 1983 IS BASE FOR LY+3/7(SAT)
223 REM 01/01/80 FELL ON TUE, 3RD DAY
    OF WEEK
230 INPUT "DESIRED 4 DIGIT YR FOR
    CALENDAR";Y1
235 IF Y1=0 THEN 2180
240 IF Y1<1800 THEN 230
250 IF Y1>2099 THEN 230
270 IYRDIV1=INT(Y1/4)
280 L1=IYRDIV1*4
```

CALENDAR produces a calendar for any year from 1800 to 2099. With this program you can find anyone's birth date to the exact day of the week or print out any number of calendars for any year.

The logic behind the calculation is briefly explained in the remarks of lines 215-223. Each day of the week is given a number (Sundays are 1, Mondays are 2, and so on, through Saturdays, which are 7.) Each succeeding year has January 1st falling one day number greater than the day number of January 1st for the previous year. The only exceptions to this rule are the following:

1. Two days are added on the year following a leap year.
2. Not all century years are leap years even though they are divisible by four.

These "centesimal" years, which end with two zeros, are only leap years if they are evenly divisible by 400. Hence, 1800 and 1900 were not leap years, whereas the year 2000 will be.

As noted, this program computes calendars for only the years from 1800 to 2099. If you want to extend the upper and lower ranges beyond these limits, lines 390-480 set up the parameters for the 1800s, lines 490-570 for the 1900s, and lines 580-660 for the 21st century. To add other centuries, you need only add similar modules for the

```
290 BASE1=Y1-L1
300 REM BASE1=0 (LEAP YEAR)
310 REM BASE1=1 (LY + 1)
320 REM BASE1=2 (LY + 2)
330 REM BASE1=3 (LY + 3)
340 REM 1800 & 1900 WERE NOT LY'S
350 IF Y1<1900 THEN 390
360 IF Y1<2000 THEN 490
370 IF Y1<2100 THEN 580
380 REM ********************
390 BEGY=1801
400 EY=1899
410 IF Y1<>1800 THEN 450
420 R1=4
430 BASE1=1
440 GOTO 900
450 DAY1=4
460 LF=99
470 REM *LF=99 MEANS COMMON
    CENTURY YR*
480 GOTO 670
490 BEGY=1901
500 EY=1999
510 IF Y1<>1900 THEN 550
520 R1=2
530 BASE1=1
540 GOTO 1900
550 DAY1=2
560 LF=99
570 GOTO 670
580 BEGY=2001
590 EY=2099
600 IF Y1<>2000 THEN 640
610 R1=7
620 BASE1=0
630 GOTO 900
640 DAY1=7
650 LF=0
660 GOTO 670
670 FOR I=BEGY TO EY
```

beginning and ending years. Note that R1 being 4 in line 420 indicates that January 1st in 1800 fell on Wednesday. BASE1 in line 430 is 1, meaning that 1800 was not a leap year. And LF (leap year flag) is 99, which means that 1800 was a nonleap (or common) century year.

From this basic information, by counting from 1800, 1900, or 2000 to the desired calendar year, you can easily calculate exactly what day January 1st was in any year and whether or not that year was a leap year. The generation of a calendar for the year is then a simple matter.

Now let's discuss some specific program statements. As mentioned earlier, lines 230-660 set up the desired parameters for the first year of the century for the year a calendar was requested. You will note that you can end the program by keying **0** for the desired year in line 230. Obviously, this program, as any other, can also be terminated by holding down the **RUN/STOP** key.

Lines 670-890 contain a **FOR-NEXT** loop that computes the day of the week for January 1st of the year asked for. The loop starts (line 670) with BEGY—defined earlier as 1800, 1900, or 2000—and ends when the year being computed equals the requested year (line 880 when the counter I = Y1, the keyed year in line 230). DAY1 (the day of the week of the first day of the year) is added to, one by one, as each year is counted off, except when the previous year was a leap year. In that event, two is added to DAY1 (lines 770-780). Whenever DAY1 exceeds 7, the value is changed to DAY1 minus 7 (lines 840-850).

```
680 LF=LF+1
690 IF LF>90 THEN 810
700 IF LF<4 THEN 770
710 LF=0
720 REM LF=0 MEANS LY
730 REM LF=1 MEANS LY + 1
740 REM LF=2 MEANS LY + 2
750 REM LF=3 MEANS LY + 3
760 REM LF=99 MEANS COMMON CENTURY YR
770 IF LF<>1 THEN 810
780 DAY1=DAY1+2
790 GOTO 840
800 DAY1=5
810 DAY1=DAY1+1
820 IF LF<90 THEN 840
830 LF=1
840 IF DAY1<8 THEN 860
850 DAY1=DAY1-7
860 R1=DAY1
870 REM PRINT "LF=";LF;" DAY1=";DAY1
880 IF I=Y1 THEN 900
890 NEXT I
900 REM R1 IS REMAINDER (DAY FOR JAN 1ST)
920 R1=R1-1
930 IF R1>0 THEN 950
940 R1=7
950 REM PRINT "R1=";R1
960 INPUT "PRINTER(Y/N)";X$
970 IF PX$="3" THEN X$="N"
990 PRINT CHR$(147):REM CLR SCREEN
1000 FOR I=1 TO 12
1010 PRINT
1020 MO$=" "
1030 IF I=1 THEN 1150
1040 IF I=2 THEN 1170
1050 IF I=3 THEN 1190
1060 IF I=4 THEN 1210
1070 IF I=5 THEN 1230
1080 IF I=6 THEN 1250
1090 IF I=7 THEN 1270
```

Note that in line 870 the residue of a "debugging" statement still exists within the program. In this case the values of LF and DAY1 were displayed on the screen to determine what was going on within the program logic. **PRINT** statements (to the screen) can help show you values of some key variables you may be concerned about.

Once the day of the week of the first day of the year has been determined and whether or not the selected year is a leap year, the program is ready to generate a calendar. Lines 1000-2080 contain two loops, an I loop counting from 1 to 12 for the months, and a J loop counting from 1 to 31 for the days of each month. Lines 1030-1370 give the month abbreviations for the months being displayed. Lines 960-970 cause the calendar to be printed on a printer as well as be displayed on the screen. CALENDAR, like all other programs, can be used with or without a printer. Obviously, the program is more useful if you own a printer.

Lines 1540-1720 determine how many days each month has (from the famous "30 days hath September . . . ." rhyme). Likewise, the day of the week is increased by 1 (from 1 to 7,) and the number of the day of the month is printed in the proper day of the week column by tabbing (lines 1760-2010). Line 1760 uses the **ON-GOTO** statement, which causes a branch to the desired line when R1 = 1, 2, 3, 4, 5, 6, or 7. When the calendar has been completed, the printer file is closed (if it was used), and control returns to line 230 from line 2100.

```
1100 IF I=8 THEN 1290
1110 IF I=9 THEN 1310
1120 IF I=10 THEN 1330
1130 IF I=11 THEN 1350
1140 IF I=12 THEN 1370
1150 MO$="JAN"
1160 GOTO 1380
1170 MO$="FEB"
1180 GOTO 1380
1190 MO$="MAR"
1200 GOTO 1380
1210 MO$="APR"
1220 GOTO 1380
1230 MO$="MAY"
1240 GOTO 1380
1250 MO$="JUN"
1260 GOTO 1380
1270 MO$="JUL"
1280 GOTO 1380
1290 MO$="AUG"
1300 GOTO 1380
1310 MO$="SEP"
1320 GOTO 1380
1330 MO$="OCT"
1340 GOTO 1380
1350 MO$="NOV"
1360 GOTO 1380
1370 MO$="DEC"
1380 PRINT " ";MO$;" / ";Y1
1390 PRINT "---------------------------"
1400 PRINT " SU   MO   TU   WE";
1410 PRINT "TH   FR   SA"
1420 IF X$<>"Y" THEN 1520
1430 IF I<>7 THEN 1470
1440 FOR K=1 TO 10
1450 PRINT# PT
1460 NEXT K
1470 PRINT# PT
1480 PRINT# PT," ";MO$;" / ";Y1
1490 PRINT# PT,"---------------------------"
```

```
JAN / 1984
---------------------------
SU  MO  TU  WE  TH  FR  SA
1   2   3   4   5   6   7
8   9   10  11  12  13  14
15  16  17  18  19  20  21
22  23  24  25  26  27  28
29  30  31

FEB / 1984
---------------------------
SU  MO  TU  WE  TH  FR  SA
            1   2   3   4
5   6   7   8   9   10  11
12  13  14  15  16  17  18
19  20  21  22  23  24  25
26  27  28  29

MAR / 1984
---------------------------
SU  MO  TU  WE  TH  FR  SA
                1   2   3
4   5   6   7   8   9   10
11  12  13  14  15  16  17
18  19  20  21  22  23  24
25  26  27  28  29  30  31

APR / 1984
---------------------------
SU  MO  TU  WE  TH  FR  SA
1   2   3   4   5   6   7
8   9   10  11  12  13  14
15  16  17  18  19  20  21
22  23  24  25  26  27  28
29  30

MAY / 1984
---------------------------
SU  MO  TU  WE  TH  FR  SA
        1   2   3   4   5
6   7   8   9   10  11  12
13  14  15  16  17  18  19
20  21  22  23  24  25  26
27  28  29  30  31

JUN / 1984
---------------------------
SU  MO  TU  WE  TH  FR  SA
                    1   2
3   4   5   6   7   8   9
10  11  12  13  14  15  16
17  18  19  20  21  22  23
24  25  26  27  28  29  30
```

```
1500 PRINT# PT," SU     MO     TU     WE";
1510 PRINT# PT,"TH     FR     SA"
1520 FOR J=1 TO 31
1530 IF J<28 THEN 1730
1540 IF I=1 THEN 1700
1550 IF I=3 THEN 1700
1560 IF I=5 THEN 1700
1570 IF I=7 THEN 1700
1580 IF I=8 THEN 1700
1590 IF I=10 THEN 1700
1600 IF I=12 THEN 1700
1610 IF I=9 THEN 1720
1620 IF I=4 THEN 1720
1630 IF I=6 THEN 1720
1640 IF I=11 THEN 1720
1650 IF BASE1=0 THEN 1680
1660 IF J>28 THEN 2040
1670 GOTO 1730
1680 IF J>29 THEN 2040
1690 GOTO 1730
1700 IF J>31 THEN 2040
1710 GOTO 1730
1720 IF J>30 THEN 2040
1730 R1=R1+1
1740 IF R1<8 THEN 1760
1750 R1=1
1760 ON R1 GOTO 1770,1810,1850,1890,1930,
     1970,2010
1770 PRINT J;
1780 IF X$<>"Y" THEN 1800
1790 PRINT# PT,J;:GOSUB 2110
1800 GOTO 2040
1810 PRINT TAB(4);J;
1820 IF X$<>"Y" THEN 1840
1824 IF J<>1 THEN 1830
1825 PRINT# PT,SPC(4);
1830 PRINT# PT,J;:GOSUB 2110
1840 GOTO 2040
1850 PRINT TAB(8);J;
1860 IF X$<>"Y" THEN 1880
```

JUL / 1984

SU	MO	TU	WE	TH	FR	SA
1	2	3	4	5	6	7
8	9	10	11	12	13	14
15	16	17	18	19	20	21
22	23	24	25	26	27	28
29	30	31				

AUG / 1984

SU	MO	TU	WE	TH	FR	SA
			1	2	3	4
5	6	7	8	9	10	11
12	13	14	15	16	17	18
19	20	21	22	23	24	25
26	27	28	29	30	31	

SEP / 1984

SU	MO	TU	WE	TH	FR	SA
						1
2	3	4	5	6	7	8
9	10	11	12	13	14	15
16	17	18	19	20	21	22
23	24	25	26	27	28	29
30						

OCT / 1984

SU	MO	TU	WE	TH	FR	SA
	1	2	3	4	5	6
7	8	9	10	11	12	13
14	15	16	17	18	19	20
21	22	23	24	25	26	27
28	29	30	31			

NOV / 1984

SU	MO	TU	WE	TH	FR	SA
				1	2	3
4	5	6	7	8	9	10
11	12	13	14	15	16	17
18	19	20	21	22	23	24
25	26	27	28	29	30	

```
1864 IF J<>1 THEN 1870
1865 PRINT# PT,SPC(8);
1870 PRINT# PT,J;:GOSUB 2110
1880 GOTO 2040
1890 PRINT TAB(12);J;
1892 IF X$<>"Y" THEN 1920
1894 IF J<>1 THEN 1910
1895 PRINT# PT,SPC(12);
1910 PRINT# PT,J;:GOSUB 2110
1920 GOTO 2040
1930 PRINT TAB(16);J;
1940 IF X$<>"Y" THEN 1960
1944 IF J<>1 THEN 1950
1945 PRINT# PT,SPC(16);
1950 PRINT# PT,J;:GOSUB 2110
1960 GOTO 2040
1970 PRINT TAB(20);J;
1980 IF X$<>"Y" THEN 2000
1984 IF J<>1 THEN 1990
1985 PRINT# PT,SPC(20);
1990 PRINT# PT,J;:GOSUB 2110
2000 GOTO 2040
2010 PRINT TAB(24);J
2020 IF X$<>"Y" THEN 2040
2024 IF J<>1 THEN 2030
2025 PRINT# PT,SPC(24);
2030 PRINT# PT,J
2040 NEXT J
2050 PRINT
2060 IF X$<>"Y" THEN 2080
2070 PRINT# PT
2080 NEXT I
```

```
DEC / 1984
------------------------------
SU  MO  TU  WE  TH  FR  SA
                        1
2   3   4   5   6   7   8
9   10  11  12  13  14  15
16  17  18  19  20  21  22
23  24  25  26  27  28  29
30  31

JAN / 1920
------------------------------
SU  MO  TU  WE  TH  FR  SA
                1   2   3
4   5   6   7   8   9   10
11  12  13  14  15  16  17
18  19  20  21  22  23  24
25  26  27  28  29  30  31
```

```
2100 GOTO 230
2110 J$=STR$(J)
2120 LJ=LEN(J$)
2130 IF LJ>2 THEN 2150
2140 PRINT# PT,SPC(1);
2150 RETURN
2180 IF PX$="3" THEN 2200
2190 CLOSE PT
2200 END
```

DIVMULT1

```
100 REM ************************
110 REM *          DIVMULT1          *
120 REM *                            *
130 REM *      COPYRIGHT 1983        *
140 REM *    DONALD C. KREUTNER      *
150 REM ************************
160 PRINT CHR$(147):POKE 53280,14:POKE
    53281,6:PRINT CHR$(5)
170 REM DIVMULT1
200 PRINT CHR$(147):REM CLR HOME
210 INPUT "WITH BORDER (Y/N)";YN$
220 INPUT "TOP # FROM 1 TO (2/999)";T1
230 IF T1<2 THEN 220
240 IF T1>999 THEN 220
250 INPUT "BOTTOM # 1 TO (2/999)";B1
260 IF B1<2 THEN 250
270 IF B1>999 THEN 250
280 ERRS=0
290 C1=0
300 INPUT "DIV, MULT, OR BOTH
    (D/M/B)";DMB$
310 IF DMB$="D" THEN 350
320 IF DMB$="M" THEN 350
330 IF DMB$="B" THEN 350
340 GOTO 300
350 PRINT CHR$(147):IF YN$="N" THEN 450
355 R=8
360 FOR C=12 TO 25
365 PT=1024+C+40*R:POKE PT,102
370 PT=55296+C+40*R:POKE PT,1
375 NEXT C
380 R=18
385 FOR C=13 TO 26
390 PT=1024+C+40*R:POKE PT,102
395 PT=55296+C+40*R:POKE PT,1
400 NEXT C
```

DIVMULT1 is very similar to ADDSUB1, but the skills DIVMULT1 improves are division and multiplication. The screen layout and program logic are much the same as those described in ADDSUB1.

Again, you can have a border around the problem, if desired. You can have only multiplication or division, or both (line 300).

The top and bottom numbers are selected randomly in lines 450 and 460, as in the addition/subtraction program. In lines 520-580 the operation (division or multiplication) is determined.

The method of displaying the two numbers is the same as in ADDSUB1, moving one character at a time to the two rows in the center of the screen and asking for the answer at the bottom of the display.

This program is particularly good for drilling a young child on the multiplication tables, since you can select the ending ranges for both the top and bottom numbers. For instance, you can start with a top value of 1 to 9 and a bottom value of 1 to 2, and then gradually work up to 1 to 12 on top and bottom, constantly reviewing already learned material every day.

DIVMULT1 can also sharpen the skills of an adult who tries to respond as quickly and accurately as possible. And remember that both top and bottom numbers can range up to 999.

See the sample screens below.

```
405 C=12
410 FOR R=8 TO 18
415 PT=1024+C+40*R:POKE PT,102
420 PT=55296+C+40*R:POKE PT,1
425 PT=1024+26+40*R:POKE PT,102
430 PT=55296+26+40*R:POKE PT,1
435 NEXT R
450 N1=INT(T1*RND(1))+1
460 N2=INT(B1*RND(1))+1
520 IF DMB$="D" THEN 580
530 IF DMB$="M" THEN 560
540 O1=INT(2*RND(1))+1
550 GOTO 590
560 O1=1
570 GOTO 590
580 O1=2
590 IF O1=1 THEN 600
595 N1=N1*N2
600 N1$=STR$(N1)
610 N2$=STR$(N2)
620 IF O1=1 THEN 650
630 OP$="/"
640 GOTO 660
650 OP$="X"
655 OP$=CHR$(24):REM PUT X SCREEN
    CODE IN OP$
660 L1=LEN(N1$)
670 L2=LEN(N2$)
680 J=21
690 FOR I=L1 TO 1 STEP -1
700 J=J-1
705 V=ASC(MID$(N1$,I,1))
710 PT=1024+J+40*12:POKE PT,V
720 PT=55296+J+40*12:POKE PT,1
730 NEXT I
740 J=21
750 FOR I=L2 TO 1 STEP -1
760 J=J-1
770 V=ASC(MID$(N2$,I,1))
780 PT=1024+J+40*13:POKE PT,V
```

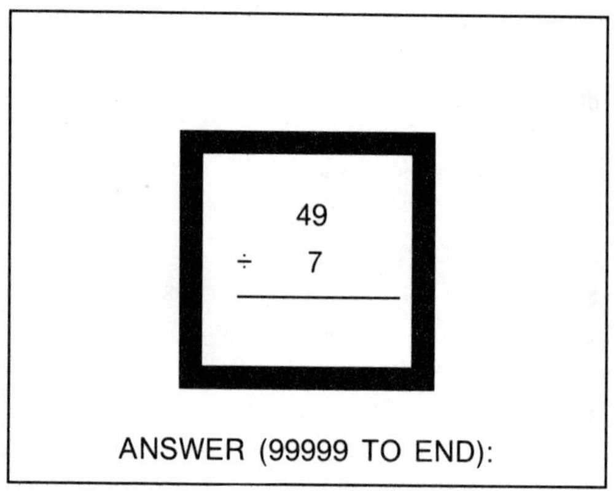

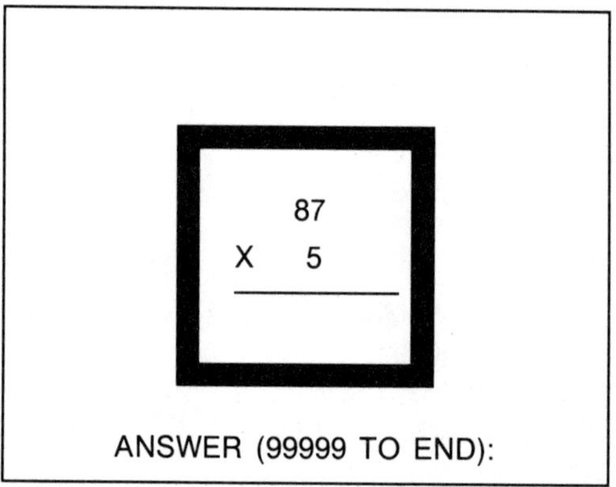

```
790 PT=55296+J+40*13:POKE PT,1
795 NEXT I
800 O2=ASC(OP$)
810 PT=1024+16+13*40:POKE PT,O2
815 PT=55296+16+13*40:POKE PT,1
820 FOR I=17 TO 20
830 PT=1024+I+14*40:POKE PT,67
835 PT=55296+I+14*40:POKE PT,1
840 NEXT I
845 INPUT "ANSWER (99999 TO END)";X
847 IF X=99999 THEN 1000
850 IF O1=2 THEN 880
860 IF X=N1*N2 THEN 960
870 GOTO 890
880 IF X=N1/N2 THEN 960
890 PRINT CHR$(147)
900 IF O1=2 THEN 930
910 PRINT "INCORRECT ";N1;" X ";
    N2;" = ";N1*N2
920 GOTO 940
930 PRINT "INCORRECT ";N1;" / ";N2;" = ";N1/N2
940 ERRS=ERRS+1
950 GOTO 980
960 C1=C1+1
970 GOTO 350
980 INPUT X$
990 GOTO 350
1000 PRINT CHR$(147):REM CLEAR SCREEN
1010 PRINT "************************"
1020 PRINT "*";TAB(23);"*"
1030 PRINT "*CORRECT=";C1;TAB(23);"*"
1040 PRINT "*";TAB(23);"*"
1050 PRINT "*ERRORS=";ERRS;TAB(23);"*"
1060 PRINT "*";TAB(23);"*"
1070 IF C1>0 THEN 1100
1080 IF ERRS>0 THEN 1100
1090 ERRS=1
1100 PRINT "*SCORE=";INT(C1/(C1+ERRS)*100);
     "%";TAB(23);"*"
1110 PRINT "*";TAB(23);"*"
1120 PRINT "************************"
1130 PRINT
1140 PRINT
1150 END
```

GRAPH1

```
100 REM   **************************
120 REM   *         GRAPH1         *
130 REM   *                        *
140 REM   *     COPYRIGHT 1983     *
150 REM   *   DONALD C. KREUTNER   *
160 REM   **************************
162 PRINT CHR$(147):POKE 53280,14:POKE
    53281,6:PRINT CHR$(5)
165 INPUT "1525 PRTR(1), RS232(2), NONE(3)";P$
170 IF P$="3" THEN 215
175 IF P$="1" THEN 190
180 IF P$="2" THEN 190
185 GOTO 165
190 PT=VAL(P$)
195 PT=126+PT
200 IF PT=127 THEN 210
205 OPEN PT,2,0,CHR$(8):PT=128:P$="2":
    GOTO 215
210 OPEN PT,4
215 DIM V(10)
220 DIM N$(10)
230 PRINT CHR$(147):REM CLR SCREEN
240 CTR=0
250 INPUT "MAX VALUE";MAX
260 IF MAX=0 THEN 830
270 INPUT "GRAPH NAME (18 CHARS)";GN$
280 IF LEN(GN$)>18 THEN 270
290 PYN$="N"
300 IF P$="3" THEN 320
310 INPUT "PRINTER (Y/N)";PYN$
320 IF PYN$="Y" THEN 350
330 IF PYN$<>"N" THEN 310
350 PRINT CHR$(147)
370 FOR I=1 TO 10
380 PRINT "ELEMENT #; ";I
390 INPUT "ELEMENT TITLE (9 CHAR)";N$(I)
```

GRAPH1 will draw a horizontal bar graph for any set of figures. Each bar to be drawn is given a name, which is printed to the left of the bar. The name can contain up to 9 characters (the "element title" in line 390).

At the beginning of the program, you are asked for a "graph name," which will be the title for the graph. This title can have up to 18 characters (lines 270-280). You also need to identify the maximum value that you want the graph to be able to chart (line 250). Notice that by entering a maximum value of zero, you will end the program (line 260). You can have up to 10 bars displayed on any chart.

Once you have set up the maximum value, you begin entering values for elements 1 to the number of elements desired. You keep on entering values until you enter **END** for the element name, at which time the entry portion (lines 370-460) terminates. The maximum value previously keyed is then divided by 12 to get the value of one "square" or block in the graph (see line 470). In other words, if any element has a maximum value (they all can have lesser values or the same, but not greater), the length of that element's bar would be 12 blocks.

Lines 490-670 then display the graph on the screen and/or on the printer (if you answered **Y** in line 310). The title is printed at the top, and the name of each graph element precedes the bar for its value. If

```
400 IF LEN(N$(I))>9 THEN 390
410 IF N$(I)="END" THEN 470
420 CTR=CTR+1
430 INPUT "VALUE OF ELEMENT";V(I)
440 IF V(I)>MAX THEN 430
450 IF V(I)<0 THEN 430
460 NEXT I
470 BLOCK=INT(MAX/12)
480 PRINT CHR$(147)
490 FOR I=1 TO CTR
500 PRINT N$(I);TAB(10);
510 IF PYN$<>"Y" THEN 530
520 PRINT# PT,N$(I);SPC(10-LEN(N$(I)));
530 V2=INT(V(I)/BLOCK)
540 IF V2=0 THEN 600
550 FOR J=1 TO V2
560 PRINT CHR$(113);
570 IF PYN$<>"Y" THEN 590
580 PRINT# PT,"O";
590 NEXT J
600 PRINT
610 PRINT TAB(10);V(I)
620 PRINT
630 IF PYN$<>"Y" THEN 670
640 PRINT# PT
650 PRINT# PT,SPC(10);V(I)
660 PRINT# PT
670 NEXT I
680 PRINT
690 PRINT CHR$(113);" =";BLOCK;TAB(10);GN$
700 IF PYN$<>"Y" THEN 720
710 PRINT# PT,"O =";BLOCK;SPC(5);GN$
720 PRINT
730 IF PYN$<>"Y" THEN 750
740 PRINT# PT
750 INPUT "Q=QUIT/P=PRT/RETURN=CONT";E$
755 IF E$="Q" THEN 830
760 IF P$="3" AND E$="P" THEN 750
765 IF E$="P" THEN PYN$="Y"
775 IF E$="P" THEN 480
```

"drawn" also on the printer, O's are used instead of the shaded blocks on the screen. When the graph is completed, the options are to quit (**Q**), print the same graph (**P**), or continue with a new graph (**RETURN**).

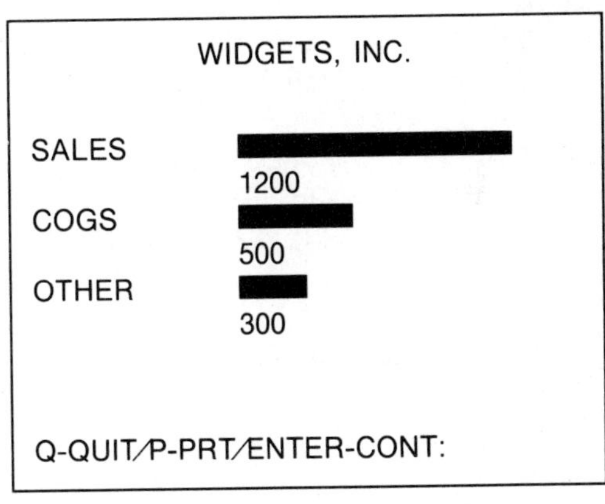


```
780 GOTO 230
830 PRINT CHR$(147)
840 IF PYN$<>"Y" THEN 860
850 CLOSE PT
860 END
```

MORTGAGE

```
100 REM  **************************
110 REM  *        MORTGAGE        *
120 REM  *                        *
130 REM  *     COPYRIGHT 1983     *
140 REM  *   DONALD C. KREUTNER   *
150 REM  **************************
152 PRINT CHR$(147):POKE 53280,14:
    POKE 53281,6:PRINT CHR$(5)
154 INPUT "1525 PRTR(1), RS232(2), NONE(3)";P$
156 IF P$="3" THEN 165
157 IF P$="1" THEN 160
158 IF P$="2" THEN 160
159 GOTO 154
160 PT=VAL(P$)
161 PT=126+PT
162 IF PT=127 THEN 164
163 OPEN PT,2,0,CHR$(8):PT=128:P$="2":
    GOTO 165
164 OPEN PT,4
165 PRINT CHR$(147)
170 INPUT "PRINCIPLE              ";PRIN
180 IF PRIN<=0 THEN 880
190 INPUT "YEARLY INTEREST%       ";IY
200 IY=IY/100
210 INPUT "MONTHS OF LOAN         ";N
220 IM=IY/12
230 P=PRIN*IM*(1+IM)^N/(((1+IM)^N)-1)
240 P2=P*100
250 P3=INT(P2)+.5
260 IF P2>=P3 THEN 290
270 P2=INT(P2)
280 GOTO 300
290 P2=INT(P2)+1
300 PAMT=P2/100
310 PRINT "MONTHLY PAYMENT IS: ";PAMT
320 INPUT "DETAILED SCHEDULE (Y/N)";YN$
```

Back in 1973 a loan amortization table book had interest rates from 6% to 10%. Obviously, times have changed—oh, to find such interest rates today! About the only use this book has now is to check the accuracy of a loan amortization program.

MORTGAGE will give you the monthly payment amount needed to amortize a loan over any number of months at any desired interest rate. In line 170 the principal amount of the loan is input, and lines 190-210 obtain the yearly interest rate and the number of months for the loan to be paid off. The monthly interest rate is computed as the yearly rate divided by 12 in line 220. As you will notice, line 200 has divided the interest rate entered (say 12, for example) by 100, giving .12 for calculations. The payment amount is then derived from the formula in line 230, and lines 240-300 round the payment off to the nearest whole cent.

At this time you are asked whether you want to see a detailed schedule of payments with the declining loan balance. If you just want to compare the difference in payments between various interest rates and/or payoff periods, you may not want to see the detailed payoff schedule. However, if you want to obtain an idea of the amount of interest paid each year for tax purposes, or if you would like to know how much equity you will have in your home at any time in the future, you may want to see those exact payments and balances.

```
330 IF YN$="N" THEN 160
340 IF YN$="Y" THEN 360
350 GOTO 320
360 INPUT "PRINTER (Y/N)";PYN$
370 IF P$="3" THEN 380
375 GOTO 390
380 PYN$="N"
390 INPUT "CALCULATED AMOUNT(Y/N)";YN$
400 IF YN$="Y" THEN 440
410 IF YN$="N" THEN 430
420 GOTO 390
430 INPUT "DESIRED MONTHLY AMOUNT";PAMT
440 IF PYN$<>"Y" THEN 520
450 PRINT# PT,"PRINCIPLE:";PRIN
460 PRINT# PT,"YEARLY INT:";IY
470 PRINT# PT,"PAYMENT AMT:";PAMT
480 PRINT# PT
490 PRINT# PT,"PRINCIPLE";SPC(6);"INTEREST";
    SPC(7);
500 PRINT# PT,"TO PRINCIPLE";SPC(6);
    "PAY AMT"
510 PRINT# PT
520 CTRP=0
530 FOR I=1 TO N
540 I1=PRIN*IM
550 I2=I1*100
560 I3=INT(I2)+.5
570 IF I2>=I3 THEN 600
580 I2=INT(I2)
590 GOTO 610
600 I2=INT(I2)+1
610 I1=I2/100
620 IF I<N THEN 650
640 PAMT=PRIN+I1
650 TPRIN=PAMT-I1
660 PRIN=PRIN-TPRIN
670 IF PRIN>=0 THEN 720
680 PRIN=PRIN+TPRIN
690 PAMT=PRIN
700 TPRIN=PAMT-I1
```

Furthermore, you can see the schedule of payments and balances on the screen with the display stopping when each screen is filled. (You hit **RETURN** to continue to the next screen.) Or you can obtain a printout of the same information if you have a printer. When the schedule is completed, you can then continue with another schedule or end the program. (The program can be terminated by entering **0** to the principal amount prompt in line 170.)

```
710 PRIN=0
715 PRIN=INT(PRIN*100):PRIN=PRIN/100
720 TPRIN=INT(TPRIN*100)/100
728 PRINT "P=";PRIN;TAB(16);"INT=";I1
730 PRINT "TO P=";TPRIN;TAB(16);"PAY=";PAMT
740 PRINT "***************PAYMENT#";I
750 CTRP=CTRP+1
760 IF PYN$="Y" THEN 810
770 IF CTRP<7 THEN 800
780 INPUT "ENTER TO CONINUE";X$
790 CTRP=0
800 IF PYN$<>"Y" THEN 830
810 PRINT# PT,PRIN;SPC(15-LEN(STR$(PRIN)));
    I1;SPC(15-LEN(STR$(I1)));TPRIN;
820 PRINT# PT,SPC(15-LEN(STR$(TPRIN)));
    PAMT;SPC(15-LEN(STR$(PAMT)));I
830 NEXT I
860 INPUT "CONTINUE (Y/N)";YN$
865 IF YN$<>"Y" THEN 880
870 GOTO 165
880 IF PYN$<>"Y" THEN 900
890 CLOSE PT
900 END
```

PRINCIPAL: 5000
YEARLY INT: .12
PAYMENT AMT: 166.07

PRINCIPAL	INTEREST	TO PRINCIPAL	PAY AMT	
4883.93	50	116.07	166.07	1
4766.7	48.84	117.23	166.07	2
4648.3	47.67	118.4	166.07	3
4528.71	46.48	119.59	166.07	4
4407.93	45.29	120.78	166.07	5
4285.94	44.08	121.99	166.07	6
4162.73	42.86	123.21	166.07	7
4038.29	41.63	124.44	166.07	8
3912.6	40.38	125.69	166.07	9
3785.66	39.13	126.94	166.07	10
3657.45	37.86	128.21	166.07	11
3527.95	36.57	129.5	166.07	12
3397.16	35.28	130.79	166.07	13
3265.06	33.97	132.1	166.07	14
3131.64	32.65	133.42	166.07	15
2996.89	31.32	134.75	166.07	16
2860.79	29.97	136.1	166.07	17
2723.33	28.61	137.46	166.07	18
2584.49	27.23	138.84	166.07	19
2444.26	25.84	140.23	166.07	20
2302.63	24.44	141.63	166.07	21
2159.59	23.03	143.04	166.07	22
2015.12	21.6	144.47	166.07	23
1869.2	20.15	145.92	166.07	24
1721.82	18.69	147.38	166.07	25
1572.97	17.22	148.85	166.07	26
1422.63	15.73	150.34	166.07	27
1270.79	14.23	151.84	166.07	28
1117.43	12.71	153.36	166.07	29
962.53	11.17	154.9	166.07	30
806.09	9.63	156.44	166.07	31
648.08	8.06	158.01	166.07	32
488.49	6.48	159.59	166.07	33
327.3	4.88	161.19	166.07	34
164.5	3.27	162.8	166.07	35
0	1.65	164.5	166.15	36

SAVE1

```
100 REM **************************
110 REM *          SAVE1         *
120 REM *                        *
130 REM *     COPYRIGHT 1983     *
140 REM *   DONALD C. KREUTNER   *
150 REM **************************
155 PRINT CHR$(147):POKE 53280,14:
    POKE 53281,6:PRINT CHR$(5)
156 POKE 53282,7
165 INPUT "1525 PRINTER(1), RS232(2),
    NONE(3)";P$
170 IF P$="3" THEN 215
175 IF P$="1" THEN 190
180 IF P$="2" THEN 190
185 GOTO 165
190 PT=VAL(P$)
195 PT=126+PT
200 IF PT=127 THEN 210
205 OPEN PT,2,0,CHR$(8):PT=128:P$="2":
    GOTO 215
210 OPEN PT,4
215 PRTR$="N"
220 PRINT CHR$(147):REM CLR SCREEN
225 PRINT SPC(5);"$$$$$$$$$$$$$$$$"
230 PRINT SPC(5);"SAVINGS ANALYSIS"
235 PRINT SPC(5);"$$$$$$$$$$$$$$$$"
240 PRINT
245 PRINT
250 PRINT "IM   INVESTMENT COMPOUNDED
                MO"
260 PRINT "IY   INVESTMENT COMPOUNDED
                YR"
270 PRINT "MAO MO ANNUITY (ORDINARY)"
280 PRINT "YAO YR ANNUITY (ORDINARY)"
290 PRINT "MAD MO ANNUITY DUE"
300 PRINT "YAD YR ANNUITY DUE"
```

SAVE1 allows you to analyze various savings and investments that you can make. Basically, two major types of investments are analyzed: the investment of a lump sum, and an annuity payment that adds to a savings account on a regular basis. There are two kinds of annuities: one is the ordinary annuity, and the other is an annuity due. In an ordinary annuity, the deposits are made at the end of the period, which means that no interest is received on the last payment amount. In an annuity due, deposits are made at the beginning of each period, and interest is received on the last payment made. The difference between the two annuities is essentially a difference of timing.

The menu screen in lines 225-360 describes the possible commands that can be used:

1. IM (a lump INVESTMENT compounded MONTHLY) will analyze how much an investment of, say $500, would amount to in a certain number of months.
2. IY (a lump INVESTMENT compounded YEARLY) does the same thing over a period of years.
3. MAO (a MONTHLY ANNUITY, ORDINARY type) tells you how much you would have if you had invested, say $50, every month for a period of 36 months.

```
310 PRINT "ON    TURN PRINTER ON"
320 PRINT "OFF  TURN PRINTER OFF"
330 PRINT "END  END PROGRAM"
340 PRINT
350 PRINT
360 PRINT
370 REM ORDINARY ANNUITIES BEAR NO
380 REM INTEREST ON THE LAST PAYMENT
390 REM BECAUSE THE PAYMENTS ARE DUE
400 REM AT THE END OF THE PERIOD
410 REM ****************************
420 INPUT "SELECTION";S$
430 IF S$="END" THEN 2540
440 IF S$="IM" THEN 640
450 IF S$="IY" THEN 1070
460 IF S$="MAO" THEN 1460
470 IF S$="MAD" THEN 1460
480 IF S$="YAO" THEN 2030
490 IF S$="YAD" THEN 2030
500 IF S$="ON" THEN 540
510 IF S$="OFF" THEN 590
520 GOTO 220
530 REM ****************************
540 IF PRTR$="Y" THEN 570
545 IF P$="3" THEN 570
550 PRTR$="Y"
570 GOTO 220
580 REM ****************************
590 IF PRTR$="N" THEN 620
600 PRTR$="N"
620 GOTO 220
630 REM ****************************
640 PRINT CHR$(147)
650 PRINT "INVESTMENT COMPOUNDED
    MONTHLY"
660 INPUT "INVESTMENT AMOUNT";IV
670 INPUT "YEARLY INTEREST RATE";YI
680 IF YI>=1 THEN 710
690 PRINT "ENTER 12% AS 12"
700 GOTO 670
```

4. YAO (a YEARLY ANNUITY, ORDI—NARY type) analyzes an annuity payment made yearly for a certain number of years.
5. MAD (MONTHLY ANNUITY DUE) does the same as MAO, but the payments are made at the beginning of every interest period, so more interest is earned.
6. YAD (YEARLY ANNUITY DUE) is similar to YAO, but again the payments are made at the beginning of an interest period.

Each of these six different commands will ask you for a dollar amount of investment or payment (depending on whether it is for an investment or annuity). In addition, an interest rate must be keyed. For example, a yearly interest rate of 12.75% would be entered as **12.75**, and 13% would be **13**. The value after the time period requested is then displayed. If you want a detailed breakdown, you can obtain a month-by-month (or year-by-year) summary.

Specific commands of note include lines 1150-1210, which are a simple investment computation, based on the financial formula: future value = principal times (1 + the interest rate) to the number-of-payments power. The future value is then rounded off to the nearest cent in lines 1160-1200. The annuity formulas are in lines 1820-1940 and lines 2150-2220.

SAVE1, like many other programs in this book, can utilize a printer. If you have one, you can print out analyses of savings and annuity schedules. This is accomplished by

```
710 MI=YI/1200
720 INPUT "MONTHS OF INVESTMENT";MO
730 FV=IV*(1+MI)^MO
740 FV=FV*100
750 ITF=INT(FV)
760 IF ITF+.5>FV THEN 780
770 ITF=ITF+1
780 FV=ITF/100
790 PRINT "VALUE AFTER ";MO;" MOS: ";FV
800 PRINT
810 IF PRTR$<>"Y" THEN 880
820 PRINT# PT
830 PRINT# PT,"INVESTMENT COMPOUNDED
    MONTHLY"
840 PRINT# PT,"INVESTMENT AMOUNT: ";IV
850 PRINT# PT,"YEARLY INT RATE: ";YI
860 PRINT# PT,"VALUE AFTER ";MO;" MOS: ";FV
870 PRINT# PT
880 INPUT "PRINT MONTHLY DETAILS";YN$
890 IF YN$<>"Y" THEN 1030
900 FOR I=1 TO MO
910 FV=IV*(1+MI)
920 FX=FV
930 FV=FV*100
940 ITF=INT(FV)
950 IF ITF+.5>FV THEN 970
960 ITF=ITF+1
970 FV=ITF/100
980 PRINT "MONTH ";I;TAB(18);FV
990 IF PRTR$<>"Y" THEN 1010
1000 PRINT# PT,"MONTH ";I;
     SPC(12-LEN(STR$(I)));FV
1010 IV=FX
1020 NEXT I
1030 PRINT
1040 INPUT "RETURN TO CONTINUE";X$
1050 GOTO 220
1060 REM ***************************
1070 PRINT CHR$(147)
1080 INPUT "INVESTMENT AMOUNT";IV
```

keying the commands **ON** or **OFF**, as described in the menu lines.

```
        $$$$$$$$$$$$$$$$$$
        SAVINGS ANALYSIS
        $$$$$$$$$$$$$$$$$$

IM      INVSTMT COMPOUNDED MO
IY      INVSTMT COMPOUNDED YR
MAO     MO ANNUITY (ORDINARY)
YAO     YR ANNUITY (ORDINARY)
MAD     MO ANNUITY DUE
YAD     YR ANNUITY DUE
ON      TURN PRTR ON
OFF     TURN PRTR OFF
END     END PROGRAM

        SELECTION:
```

```
YEARLY ANNUITY DUE
YEARLY ANNUITY AMT: 1000
YEARLY INT RATE:    .1
ANNUITY AMOUNT:     108181.77

YEAR   1          1100
YEAR   2          2310
YEAR   3          3641
YEAR   4          5105.1
YEAR   5          6715.61
YEAR   6          8487.17
YEAR   7          10435.89
YEAR   8          12579.48
YEAR   9          14937.42
YEAR   10         17531.17
YEAR   11         20384.28
YEAR   12         23522.71
YEAR   13         26974.98
YEAR   14         30772.48
YEAR   15         34949.73
YEAR   16         39544.7
YEAR   17         44599.17
YEAR   18         50159.09
YEAR   19         56275
YEAR   20         63002.5
YEAR   21         70402.75
YEAR   22         78543.02
YEAR   23         87497.33
YEAR   24         97347.06
YEAR   25         108181.77
```

```
1090 INPUT "YEARLY INT RATE";YI
1100 IF YI>1 THEN 1130
1110 PRINT "ENTER 12% AS 12"
1120 GOTO 1090
1130 YI=YI/100
1140 INPUT "YEARS OF INVESTMENT";YR
1150 FV=IV*(1+YI)^YR
1160 FV=FV*100
1170 ITF=INT(FV)
1180 IF ITF+.5>FV THEN 1200
1190 ITF=ITF+1
1200 FV=ITF/100
1210 PRINT "VALUE AFTER ";YR;" YRS: ";FV
1220 IF PRTR$<>"Y" THEN 1270
1230 PRINT# PT,"INVESTMENT AMOUNT: ";IV
1240 PRINT# PT,"YEARLY INT RATE:  ";YI
1250 PRINT# PT,"VALUE AFTER ";YR;" YRS: ";FV
1260 PRINT# PT
1270 INPUT "PRINT YEARLY DETAILS";YN$
1280 IF YN$<>"Y" THEN 1420
1290 FOR I=1 TO YR
1300 FV=IV*(1+YI)
1310 FX=FV
1320 FV=FV*100
1330 ITF=INT(FV)
1340 IF ITF+.5>FV THEN 1360
1350 ITF=ITF+1
1360 FV=ITF/100
1370 PRINT "YEAR ";I;TAB(18);FV
1380 IF PRTR$<>"Y" THEN 1400
1390 PRINT# PT,"YEAR ";I;SPC(13-LEN(STR$(I)));FV
1400 IV=FX
1410 NEXT I
1420 PRINT
1430 INPUT "RETURN TO CONTINUE";X$
1440 GOTO 220
1450 REM ***********************
1460 PRINT CHR$(147)
1470 IF S$="MAO" THEN 1500
1480 PRINT "MONTHLY ANNUITY DUE"
```

```
INVESTMENT COMPOUNDED MONTHLY
INVESTMENT AMOUNT:  1000
YEARLY INT RATE:    13
VALUE AFTER 24 MOS: 1295.12

MONTH  1          1010.83
MONTH  2          1021.78
MONTH  3          1032.85
MONTH  4          1044.04
MONTH  5          1055.35
MONTH  6          1066.79
MONTH  7          1078.34
MONTH  8          1090.02
MONTH  9          1101.83
MONTH  10         1113.77
MONTH  11         1125.84
MONTH  12         1138.03
MONTH  13         1150.36
MONTH  14         1162.82
MONTH  15         1175.42
MONTH  16         1188.15
MONTH  17         1201.03
MONTH  18         1214.04
MONTH  19         1227.19
MONTH  20         1240.48
MONTH  21         1253.92
MONTH  22         1267.51
MONTH  23         1281.24
MONTH  24         1295.12
```

```
MONTHLY ORDINARY ANNUITY
MONTHLY ANNUITY AMT: 200
YEARLY INT RATE:     13
ANNUITY AMOUNT:      2548.29

MONTH  1          200
MONTH  2          402.17
MONTH  3          606.52
MONTH  4          813.09
MONTH  5          1021.9
MONTH  6          1232.97
MONTH  7          1446.33
MONTH  8          1662
MONTH  9          1880
MONTH  10         2100.37
MONTH  11         2323.12
MONTH  12         2548.29
```

```
1490 GOTO 1510
1500 PRINT "MONTHLY ORDINARY ANNUITY"
1510 INPUT "MONTHLY ANNUITY AMOUNT";PAY
1520 INPUT "YEARLY INTEREST RATE";YI
1530 IF YI>=1 THEN 1560
1540 PRINT "ENTER 12% AS 12"
1550 GOTO 1520
1560 MI=YI/1200
1570 INPUT "MONTHS OF PAYS";MO
1580 AMT=(PAY/MI)*((1+MI)^MO-1)
1590 IF S$="MAO" THEN 1610
1600 AMT=AMT*(1+MI)
1610 AMT=AMT*100
1620 IAMT=INT(AMT)
1630 IF IAMT+.5>AMT THEN 1650
1640 IAMT=IAMT+1
1650 AMT=IAMT/100
1660 PRINT "ANNUITY AMOUNT";AMT
1670 PRINT
1680 IF PRTR$<>"Y" THEN 1770
1690 IF S$="MAO" THEN 1720
1700 PRINT# PT,"MONTHLY ANNUITY DUE"
1710 GOTO 1730
1720 PRINT# PT,"MONTHLY ORDINARY ANNUITY"
1730 PRINT# PT,"MONTHLY ANNUITY AMOUNT:
     ";PAY
1740 PRINT# PT,"YEARLY INT RATE:        ";YI
1750 PRINT# PT,"ANNUITY AMOUNT:         ";AMT
1760 PRINT# PT
1770 INPUT "PRINT MONTHLY DETAILS";YN$
1780 IF YN$<>"Y" THEN 1990
1790 AMT=0
1800 FOR I=1 TO MO
1810 IF S$="MAO" THEN 1830
1820 AMT=AMT+PAY
1830 FV=AMT*(1+MI)
1840 FX=FV
1850 FV=FV*100
1860 ITF=INT(FV)
1870 IF ITF+.5>FV THEN 1890
```

```
INVESTMENT AMOUNT:  1500
YEARLY INT RATE:    .128
VALUE AFTER 10 YRS: 5002.44

YEAR   1          1692
YEAR   2          1908.58
YEAR   3          2152.87
YEAR   4          2428.44
YEAR   5          2739.28
YEAR   6          3089.91
YEAR   7          3485.42
YEAR   8          3931.55
YEAR   9          4434.79
YEAR   10         5002.44
```

```
1880 ITF=ITF+1
1890 FV=ITF/100
1900 IF S$="MAD" THEN 1940
1910 FV=FV+PAY
1920 AMT=FX+PAY
1930 GOTO 1950
1940 AMT=FVX
1950 PRINT "MONTH ";I;TAB(18);FV
1960 IF PRTR$<>"Y" THEN 1980
1970 PRINT# PT,"MONTH ";I;
     SPC(12-LEN(STR$(I)));FV
1980 NEXT I
1990 PRINT
2000 INPUT "RETURN TO CONTINUE";X$
2010 GOTO 220
2020 REM ***********************
2030 PRINT CHR$(147)
2040 IF S$="YAO" THEN 2070
2050 PRINT "YEARLY ANNUITY DUE"
```

```
2060 GOTO 2080
2070 PRINT "YEARLY ORDINARY ANNUITY"
2080 INPUT "YEARLY ANNUITY AMOUNT";PAY
2090 INPUT "YEARLY INT RATE";YI
2100 IF YI>1 THEN 2130
2110 PRINT "ENTER 12% AS 12"
2120 GOTO 2090
2130 YI=YI/100
2140 INPUT "YEARS OF PAYS";YR
2150 AMT=(PAY/YI)*((1+YI)^YR-1)
2160 IF S$="YAO" THEN 2180
2170 AMT=AMT*(1+YI)
2180 AMT=AMT*100
2190 IAMT=INT(AMT)
2200 IF IAMT+.5>AMT THEN 2220
2210 IAMT=IAMT+1
2220 AMT=IAMT/100
2230 PRINT "ANNUITY AMOUNT: ";AMT
2240 PRINT
2250 IF PRTR$<>"Y" THEN 2340
2260 IF S$="YAO" THEN 2290
2270 PRINT# PT,"YEARLY ANNUITY DUE"
2280 GOTO 2300
2290 PRINT# PT,"YEARLY ORDINARY ANNUITY"
2300 PRINT# PT,"YEARLY ANNUITY AMT: ";PAY
2310 PRINT# PT,"YEARLY INT RATE:    ";YI
2320 PRINT# PT,"ANNUITY AMOUNT:     ";AMT
2330 PRINT# PT
2340 INPUT "PRINT YEARLY DETAILS";YN$
2350 IF YN$<>"Y" THEN 2510
2360 AMT=0
2370 FOR I=1 TO YR
2372 IF S$="YAO" THEN 2380
2375 AMT=AMT+PAY
2380 FV=AMT*(1+YI)
2390 FX=FV
2400 FV=FV*100
2410 ITF=INT(FV)
2420 IF ITF+.5>FV THEN 2440
2430 ITF=ITF+1
2440 FV=ITF/100
2445 IF S$="YAD" THEN 2465
2450 FV=FV+PAY
2460 AMT=FX+PAY
2462 GOTO 2470
2465 AMT=FX
2470 PRINT "YEAR ";I;TAB(18);FV
2480 IF PRTR$<>"Y" THEN 2500
2490 PRINT# PT,"YEAR ";I;TAB(18);FV
2500 NEXT I
2510 PRINT
2520 INPUT "RETURN TO CONTINUE";X$
2530 GOTO 220
2540 IF PRTR$<>"Y" THEN 2560
2550 CLOSE PT
2560 END
```

SCORE1

```
100 REM **************************
120 REM *          SCORE1          *
130 REM *                          *
140 REM *      COPYRIGHT 1983      *
150 REM *    DONALD C. KREUTNER    *
160 REM **************************
162 PRINT CHR$(147):POKE 53280,14:
    POKE 53281,6:PRINT CHR$(5)
165 INPUT "1525 PRTR(1), RS232(2), NONE(3)";P$
170 IF P$="3" THEN 215
175 IF P$="1" THEN 190
180 IF P$="2" THEN 190
185 GOTO 165
190 PT=VAL(P$)
195 PT=126+PT
200 IF PT=127 THEN 210
205 OPEN PT,2,0,CHR$(8):PT=128:P$="2":
    GOTO 215
210 OPEN PT,4
215 DIM N(50)
220 DIM N$(50)
225 DIM SL(50)
230 DIM SN(50)
235 DIM NWTTL(50)
240 FOR I=1 TO 50
250 N$(I)="@"
260 SL(I)=0
270 SN(I)=0
280 N(I)=I
290 NWTTL(I)=0
300 NEXT I
310 DATA "01 DIRK & SUSAN MULLENGER"
320 DATA "02 DON & JANET KREUTNER"
330 DATA "03 RON & MARY BROWN"
340 DATA "04 JACK & CAROL MASON"
350 DATA "05 SCOTT & SHARON MCALLISTER"
```

SCORE1 can perform a variety of scorekeeping applications, ranging from keeping track of a bridge club's monthly and cumulative scores, to accumulating a team's scores in various games, to keeping a rudimentary general-ledger total of money spent on certain categories of expenses and money received from certain sources.

Obviously, the program name implies that it was designed for scorekeeping purposes, but it can keep track of many different totals. The categories used by the program are defined in the **DATA** statements in lines 310-390. You are not limited to this number of items, since you can have up to 50 classes with which to "score" totals. You can have several copies of this program with different **DATA** statements. Then you can save various team totals on tape or disk and later add to them either regularly or irregularly.

The following five arrays are used to accumulate the data:

1. The number (must be 1 to 50) of the team or group (N)
2. The name of the category or group (N$)
3. The last score or total of the category (SL)
4. The new score to be added to the SL(SN)

```
360 DATA "06 ROGER & BARBARA HOWARD"
370 DATA "07 BOB & SALLY BARD"
380 DATA "08 TONY & HARRIET HUGHES"
390 DATA "END"
400 CTR=0
410 FOR I=1 TO 50
420 READ NAME$
430 IF NAME$="END" THEN 470
440 CTR=CTR+1
450 N$(I)=NAME$
460 NEXT I
470 FOR I=1 TO CTR
480 PRINT "ENTRY #";I
490 PRINT N$(I)
500 INPUT "LAST TOTAL";SL(I)
510 INPUT "NEW SCORE";SN(I)
520 NWTTL(I)=SL(I)+SN(I)
530 NEXT I
540 REM *******************
550 INPUT "TITLE OF REPORT";T$
555 PYN$="N":IF P$="3" THEN 590
560 INPUT "PRINTER (Y/N)";PYN$
590 T2$="NUMERICAL SEQUENCE"
600 FLAG$="N"
610 FOR I=1 TO CTR-1
620 IF N(I)<=N(I+1) THEN 640
630 GOSUB 880
640 NEXT I
650 IF FLAG$="Y" THEN 600
660 GOSUB 1050
670 FLAG$="N"
680 FOR I=1 TO CTR-1
690 IF NWTTL(I)>=NWTTL(I+1) THEN 710
700 GOSUB 880
710 NEXT I
720 IF FLAG$="Y" THEN 670
730 T2$="NEW TOTAL SEQUENCE"
740 GOSUB 1050
750 FLAG$="N"
760 FOR I=1 TO CTR-1
```

5. The new total or accumulation of SL and SN(NWTTL)

The **DIM** statements in lines 215-235 set up these arrays, and the loop in lines 240-300 initializes the numeric values to zero and the names to "@" for all names. Line 400 sets the counter CTR to zero. This variable keeps track of how many items are entered, so that the sorts and printouts that follow "know" how many items are to be evaluated. (Remember that up to 50 are possible as the program has been set up.) If you have more than 50 items, you can enter the data in two or more groups, using programs with different **DATA** statements. In the lines 410-530, you enter the applicable input information. You must key a previous score and the new score for each as you are prompted (even if both are zero). The program will ask for an old and new total for each number from 1 to CTR (the total number of **DATA** statements numbered from 01 to 50, or as high a number as you want).

Line 550 asks for the name of the report, which you key in (no commas, unless you enclose the title in quotation marks). Then you are asked if you have a printer. (If you do not, the report will be displayed on the screen.) Three orders will be printed: numerical sequence by number (01 through 50), descending order by total scores, and descending order by the current score only. Each report is preceded by a bubble sort (see the description in the program BSKTSTAT) to arrange the data in the proper sequence for the desired report. Each report is performed by the same subroutine **GOSUB** 1050, which prints a

```
770 IF SN(I)>=SN(I+1) THEN 790
780 GOSUB 880
790 NEXT I
800 IF FLAG$="Y" THEN 750
810 T2$="CURRENT SCORE SEQUENCE"
820 GOSUB 1050
830 INPUT "REPEAT (Y/N)";RYN$
840 IF RYN$="Y" THEN 590
850 IF PYN$<>"Y" THEN 870
860 CLOSE 1
870 GOTO 1390
880 NXTTL=NWTTL(I)
890 NWTTL(I)=NWTTL(I+1)
900 NWTTL(I+1)=NXTTL
910 NZ=N(I)
920 N(I)=N(I+1)
930 N(I+1)=NZ
940 NX$=N$(I)
950 N$(I)=N$(I+1)
960 N$(I+1)=NX$
970 SXL=SL(I)
980 SL(I)=SL(I+1)
990 SL(I+1)=SXL
1000 XSN=SN(I)
1010 SN(I)=SN(I+1)
1020 SN(I+1)=XSN
1030 FLAG$="Y"
1040 RETURN
1050 INPUT "HIT RETURN TO CONTINUE";X$
1060 C2=0
1070 PRINT CHR$(147)
1080 PRINT T$
1090 PRINT T2$
1100 PRINT
1110 IF PYN$<>"Y" THEN 1220
1120 PRINT# PT,"*******************
     ***********";
1130 PRINT# PT,"*******************
     ***********";
1140 PRINT# PT,"************************"
```

different subtitle based on the value of T2$ (assigned in lines 590, 730, and 810).

If the report is displayed on the screen only, the scrolling is stopped by keeping track of how many totals have been printed (C2 in lines 1230-1260). In this manner, when a screen fills up, the program will wait for you to hit **RETURN** before it rolls the previous information off the screen. Furthermore, you can repeat the report again and again by answering **Y** to the input statement in line 830.

Notice that in the sort routines, the same subroutine, **GOSUB** 880, is used to switch elements if they are out of order.

```
1150 PRINT# PT
1160 PRINT# PT,T$
1170 PRINT# PT,T2$
1180 PRINT# PT
1190 PRINT# PT,SPC(40);"OLD TOT";SPC(5);
     "NEW TOT";
1200 PRINT# PT,SPC(5);"CURRENT"
1210 PRINT# PT
1220 FOR I=1 TO CTR
1230 C2=C2+1
1240 IF C2<5 THEN 1270
1250 C2=1
1260 INPUT "RETURN TO CONTINUE";X$
1270 PRINT I;N$(I)
1280 PRINT "OLD TOTAL: ";SL(I)
```

```
1290 PRINT "NEW TOTAL: ";NWTTL(I)
1300 PRINT "CURRENT: ";SN(I)
1310 PRINT "******************************"
1320 IF PYN$<>"Y" THEN 1360
1330 PRINT# PT,I;"- ";N$(I);SPC(36-LEN(N$(I)));SL(I);
1340 PRINT# PT,SPC(12-LEN(STR$(SL(I))));
     NWTTL(I);
1350 PRINT# PT,SPC(12-LEN(STR$(NWTTL(I))));
     SN(I)
1360 NEXT I
1365 IF PYN$<>"Y" THEN 1380
1370 PRINT# PT
1380 RETURN
1390 IF PYN$<>"Y" THEN 1410
1400 CLOSE PT
1410 END
```

```
*******************************************************************************

SAMPLE ACCUMULATED SCORES
NUMERICAL SEQUENCE

                                           OLD TOT      NEW TOT      CURRENT

 1 - 01 DIRK & SUSAN MULLENGER              21124        22222        1098
 2 - 02 DON & JANET KREUTNER                20013        21012        999
 3 - 03 RON & MARY BROWN                    18900        19605        705
 4 - 04 JACK & CAROL MASON                  20996        22196        1200
 5 - 05 SCOTT & SHARON MCALLISTER           18002        19025        1023
 6 - 06 ROGER & BARBARA HOWARD              19072        20195        1123
 7 - 07 BOB & SALLY BARD                    19201        20501        1300
 8 - 08 TONY & HARRIET HUGHES               20100        20997        897

*******************************************************************************

SAMPLE ACCUMULATED SCORES
NEW TOTAL SEQUENCE

                                           OLD TOT      NEW TOT      CURRENT

 1 - 01 DIRK & SUSAN MULLENGER              21124        22222        1098
 2 - 04 JACK & CAROL MASON                  20996        22196        1200
 3 - 02 DON & JANET KREUTNER                20013        21012        999
 4 - 08 TONY & HARRIET HUGHES               20100        20997        897
 5 - 07 BOB & SALLY BARD                    19201        20501        1300
 6 - 06 ROGER & BARBARA HOWARD              19072        20195        1123
 7 - 03 RON & MARY BROWN                    18900        19605        705
 8 - 05 SCOTT & SHARON MCALLISTER           18002        19025        1023

*******************************************************************************

SAMPLE ACCUMULATED SCORES
CURRENT SCORE SEQUENCE

                                           OLD TOT      NEW TOT      CURRENT

 1 - 07 BOB & SALLY BARD                    19201        20501        1300
 2 - 04 JACK & CAROL MASON                  20996        22196        1200
 3 - 06 ROGER & BARBARA HOWARD              19072        20195        1123
 4 - 01 DIRK & SUSAN MULLENGER              21124        22222        1098
 5 - 05 SCOTT & SHARON MCALLISTER           18002        19025        1023
 6 - 02 DON & JANET KREUTNER                20013        21012        999
 7 - 08 TONY & HARRIET HUGHES               20100        20997        897
 8 - 03 RON & MARY BROWN                    18900        19605        705
```

2

Games and Miscellaneous Programs

BEEP1

```
100 REM  **************************
110 REM  *          BEEP1         *
120 REM  *                        *
130 REM  *     COPYRIGHT 1983     *
140 REM  *   DONALD C. KREUTNER   *
150 REM  **************************
160 VOL=54296:WAVE=54276:ATTACK=54277:
    HI=54273:LO=54272
180 PRINT CHR$(147):REM CLR SCREEN
190 FOR I=1 TO 20
200 POKE VOL,15:POKE WAVE,17:POKE
    ATTACK,100:POKE HI,34:POKE LO,75
205 FOR J=1 TO 50:NEXT J
220 POKE WAVE,0
225 NEXT I
230 INPUT "WHAT TO SAY";X$
240 IF X$="SAME" THEN 330
250 IF X$="XX" THEN 440
260 L$=X$
270 INPUT "HOW MANY BEEPS";B
280 INPUT "CLEAR SCREEN";YN$
290 INPUT "FREQUENCY (34-72)";F
300 GOTO 340
330 X$=L$
340 FOR I= 1 TO B
```

BEEP1 is a "fun" program that allows you to key any message you want repeated over and over on the screen. At the same time the message is displayed, you can have a beep or tone sounded at any pitch, at any level of loudness, and for any duration.

When the message has been selected in line 230, you are then prompted for the number of beeps in line 270. If you want the display to last a long time, just enter a high number. The screen is cleared after each beep if you select the clear-screen feature (line 280). And if you want to repeat the same message on completion, you need to key only **SAME** to the "WHAT TO SAY?" prompt. If you do, you are not asked for information about duration, pitch, and loudness.

Note that at program startup and before the "WHAT TO SAY?" prompt, a loop of 20 tones is sounded to catch your attention.

```
360 POKE VOL,15:POKE WAVE,17:POKE
    ATTACK,100:POKE HI,F:POKE LO,F*2
370 FOR J=1 TO 25:NEXT J
380 IF YN$<>"Y" THEN 400
390 PRINT CHR$(147)
400 PRINT I;TAB(6);X$
410 POKE WAVE,0
420 NEXT I
430 GOTO 180
440 END
```

BIRTHDAY

```
100 REM ***************************
105 REM *          BIRTHDAY       *
110 REM *                         *
115 REM *      COPYRIGHT 1983     *
120 REM *    DONALD C. KREUTNER   *
125 REM ***************************
130 PRINT CHR$(147):POKE 53280,14:POKE
    53281,6:PRINT CHR$(5)
135 INPUT "1525 PRINTER(1), RS232(2), OR
    NONE(3)";PX$
140 IF PX$="3" THEN 170
145 IF PX$="1" THEN 154
150 IF PX$="2" THEN 154
152 GOTO 135
154 PR=VAL(PX$)+126
156 IF PX$="1" THEN 160
158 OPEN PR,2,0,CHR$(8):PX$="2":PR=128:
    GOTO 170
160 OPEN PR,4
170 DATA 01/03/71 ROBERT JAY
180 DATA 08/08/45 BARD JANET
185 DATA 11/19/18 BARD SALLY
190 DATA 06/07/69 SEAN DEREK
195 DATA 12/21/19 BARD ROBERT
200 DATA 10/11/37 DEXTER EARL
210 DATA 03/14/59 SANDLIN DONNA
220 DATA 01/23/63 BEYL ANDREW
230 DATA 12/23/58 STIDHAM DEBRA
240 DATA 09/28/57 FORD JUDY
250 DATA 06/29/59 MEYER DIANE
260 DATA 08/03/42 ANN CAROL
270 DATA 12/03/56 WHITSITT DEBBIE
280 DATA 06/25/45 CHARLES DON
290 DATA 03/19/55 MAY SUSAN
300 DATA 03/15/15 JOHN ALBERT
310 DATA 01/26/19 KREUTNER PAULINE
```

BIRTHDAY is a very useful program that can (1) tell you all your acquaintances who have birthdays in any given month, or (2) provide you with an alphabetical list of people with their birthdays.

This program also can be used for many other purposes. For example, it can give you a calendar of events for any given month or let you keep an alphabetical list of event names. On January 10th, for example, you may have ten things listed for you to remember, whereas on the 11th, you may have three. If you want to see all the appointments you have with a certain firm, you can obtain a sorted list (provided, of course, that you were careful to enter the "names" of those appointments in the same way each time).

BIRTHDAY can be used, then, in a variety of ways to keep a calendar of events so that you don't have to keep track of all of them in your head. With BIRTHDAY you won't forget an anniversary, a birthday, or an important appointment.

The **DATA** statements in lines 170 to 440 can be replaced by your own statements, and you can have multiple copies of this program to serve multiple purposes (a birthday version, an anniversary version, a personal calendar version, or a combination of these). To do so, just key your own **DATA** statements instead of the ones in the listing (unless you want to remember my birthday list). Note that a final **DATA** state-

```
320 DATA 12/29/56 WYNE GREG
330 DATA 11/11/36 LONGEST NORMAN
340 DATA 05/19/21 MCKNIGHT MARTHA
350 DATA 02/01/49 JOHNSON BARBARA
351 DATA 02/25/71 MASON KEVIN
352 DATA 08/29/78 MASON ANDREA
353 DATA 04/28/44 MASON JACK
354 DATA 04/15/71 HEALY CHRIS
355 DATA 08/18/73 HEALY KARA
356 DATA 03/23/69 HEALY MARJAN
360 DATA 07/05/53 WHITE JAMES
370 DATA 10/31/58 WEST KEVIN
380 DATA 02/19/41 CAPITO BETTY
390 DATA 10/26/70 HOWARD TODD
400 DATA 05/15/70 THOM BILLY
410 DATA 02/23/71 GOLDMAN JOHN
420 DATA 12/26/70 STRIEGEL JOHN
430 DATA 11/06/67 ASBERRY SHAWN
440 DATA 99/99/99 ZZZZZ
450 DIM X$(200)
460 FOR I=1 TO 200
470 READ X$(I)
480 IF MID$(X$(I),1,2)="99" THEN 500
490 NEXT I
500 CTR=I
510 FOR J=1 TO I
520 PRINT X$(J)
530 NEXT J
540 PRINT CHR$(147)
550 PRINT "##    BIRTHDAYS IN MONTH ##"
560 PRINT "      (13=ALL MONTHS)"
570 PRINT "A     BIRTHDAYS (ALPH ORDER"
580 PRINT "END  END PROGRAM"
590 PRINT
600 INPUT "SELECTION";S$
610 IF S$="A" THEN 1030
620 IF S$="END" THEN 1350
630 S1$=MID$(S$,1,1)
640 S2$=MID$(S$,2,1)
650 IF S1$<"0" THEN 540
```

ment of "99/99/99 ZZZZZ" is needed to indicate to the data **READ** statement of line 470 that all of the input data has been read. You can add or delete input data by adding or taking away **DATA** statements.

Now let's look at some of the program statements that are of interest. After the **DATA** statements have been read into the X$ array in lines 460-490, your choices are as follows:

1. List all the birthdays or appointments in any month number (01 through 12).
2. List in alphabetical order all names or appointment descriptions.
3. End the program.

These choices are given in lines 540-600.

If you key **A** (for an alphabetical list), control passes to line 1030 from line 610. **END** causes the program to end, going to statement 1350 from line 620. Any other selection is analyzed by lines 610-710 to make certain a two-digit number was keyed. This check is accomplished by looking at S1$ (the first character) and S2$ (the second character) to make sure they are between 0 and 9. The check is not quite perfect, since months higher than 12 could be requested. The result of such a request, however, would not be disastrous.

If a month number is keyed, the next step that the program accomplishes is a sort of the data to rearrange it in order of the first 5 characters (the month, a slash, and the day). This sorting is done by a bubble sort in lines 720-830. Note that each time you request a month's appointments (or other

```
660 IF S1$>"9" THEN 540
670 IF S2$<"0" THEN 540
680 IF S2$>"9" THEN 540
690 M$=S1$+S2$
700 PASS=0
710 IF LEN(M$)<>2 THEN 540
720 SW$="N"
730 PASS=PASS+1
740 PRINT CHR$(147)
750 PRINT "SORT PASS ";PASS
760 FOR I=1 TO CTR-1
770 IF MID$(X$(I),1,5)<=MID$(X$(I+1),1,5) THEN 820
780 Y$=X$(I)
790 X$(I)=X$(I+1)
800 X$(I+1)=Y$
810 SW$="Y"
820 NEXT I
830 IF SW$="Y" THEN 720
840 CX=0
850 INPUT "PRINTER (Y/N)";PYN$
860 IF PX$="3" THEN PYN$="N"
880 FOR I=1 TO CTR
890 IF M$="13" THEN 910
900 IF MID$(X$(I),1,2)<>M$ THEN 980
910 PRINT X$(I)
920 IF PYN$<>"Y" THEN 940
930 PRINT# PR,X$(I)
940 CX=CX+1
950 IF CX<20 THEN 980
960 CX=0
970 INPUT "ENTER TO CONTINUE";E$
980 NEXT I
1010 INPUT "ENTER TO CONTINUE";E$
1020 GOTO 540
1030 PASS=0
1040 SW$="N"
1050 PASS=PASS+1
1060 PRINT CHR$(147)
1070 PRINT "SORT PASS ";PASS
1080 FOR I=1 TO CTR-1
```

information), you will "re-sort" the data. You may think this process is rather inefficient. However, if the data is already in month/day order, the sort pass checks only one time through the data to verify that the elements are already in sequence. Remember from previous examples that in a bubble sort a flag is kept to see if any elements were out of order and switched. If not, the sort is terminated. The flag is SW$ in lines 720, 810, and 830.

Next, you are asked if you want a listing on a printer or only on the screen. (See lines 850-860.) Only the data from the month selected will be displayed because the first two characters must be equal to the month selected. (See line 900.) Notice also that if you key **13** as the month selected, all data is displayed in month/day sequence. Now you can see that if you key a number higher than 13, the data is sorted (or re-sorted) in month/day sequence, but no detail data is displayed—unless, of course, you actually chose to key into your **DATA** statements "months" higher than 12.

If you select an alphabetical list, a sort of the data in alphabetical order is accomplished by lines 1040-1170. The sort key used is from the tenth position of the data (after the space following the eight-character date) to the end of each data element. Lines 1090-1100 analyze the names by using the **MID$** function. Again, a printout in alphabetical order can be obtained. If you do not have a printer, 20 items at a time are displayed on the screen. After each display, you must hit **RETURN** to continue the screen listing.

```
1090 S1$=MID$(X$(I),10,LEN(X$(I))-9)
1100 S2$=MID$(X$(I+1),10,LEN(X$(I+1))-9)
1110 IF S1$<=S2$ THEN 1160
1120 SW$="Y"
1130 Y$=X$(I)
1140 X$(I)=X$(I+1)
1150 X$(I+1)=Y$
1160 NEXT I
1170 IF SW$="Y" THEN 1040
1180 CX=0
1190 INPUT "PRINTER (Y/N)";PYN$
1200 IF PX$="3" THEN PYN$="N"
1220 FOR I=1 TO CTR
1230 PRINT X$(I)
1240 IF PYN$<>"Y" THEN 1260
1250 PRINT# PR,X$(I)
1260 CX=CX+1
1270 IF CX<20 THEN 1300
1280 CX=0
1290 INPUT "RETURN TO CONTINUE";E$
1300 NEXT I
1330 INPUT "RETURN TO CONTINUE";E$
1340 GOTO 540
1350 IF PX$="3" THEN 1370
1360 CLOSE PR
1370 END
```

```
01/03/71 ROBERT JAY
01/23/63 BEYL ANDREW
01/26/19 KREUTNER PAULINE
02/01/49 JOHNSON BARBARA
02/19/41 CAPITO BETTY
02/23/71 GOLDMAN JOHN
02/25/71 MASON KEVIN
03/14/59 SANDLIN DONNA
03/15/15 JOHN ALBERT
03/19/55 MAY SUSAN
03/23/69 HEALY MARJAN
04/15/71 HEALY CHRIS
04/28/44 MASON JACK
05/15/70 THOM BILLY
05/19/21 MCKNIGHT MARTHA
06/07/69 SEAN DEREK
06/25/45 CHARLES DON
06/29/59 MEYER DIANE
```

```
07/05/53 WHITE JAMES
08/03/42 ANN CAROL
08/08/45 BARD JANET
08/18/73 HEALY KARA
08/29/78 MASON ANDREA
09/28/57 FORD JUDY
10/11/37 DEXTER EARL
10/26/70 HOWARD TODD
10/31/58 WEST KEVIN
11/06/67 ASBERRY SHAWN
11/11/36 LONGEST NORMAN
11/19/18 BARD SALLY
12/03/56 WHITSITT DEBBIE
12/21/19 BARD ROBERT
12/23/58 STIDHAM DEBRA
12/26/70 STRIEGEL JOHN
12/29/56 WYNE GREG
99/99/99 ZZZZZ
```

```
08/03/42 ANN CAROL
11/06/67 ASBERRY SHAWN
08/08/45 BARD JANET
12/21/19 BARD ROBERT
11/19/18 BARD SALLY
01/23/63 BEYL ANDREW
02/19/41 CAPITO BETTY
06/25/45 CHARLES DON
10/11/37 DEXTER EARL
09/28/57 FORD JUDY
02/23/71 GOLDMAN JOHN
04/15/71 HEALY CHRIS
08/18/73 HEALY KARA
03/23/69 HEALY MARJAN
10/26/70 HOWARD TODD
03/15/15 JOHN ALBERT
02/01/49 JOHNSON BARBARA
01/26/19 KREUTNER PAULINE
```

DRAW1

```
100 REM  **************************
110 REM  *          DRAW1         *
120 REM  *                        *
130 REM  *     COPYRIGHT 1983     *
140 REM  *   DONALD C. KREUTNER   *
150 REM  **************************
165 DIM X(20,30)
170 INPUT "* OR C FOR CIRCLE";A$
200 FOR I=1 TO 20
210 FOR J=1 TO 30
220 PRINT "ROW ";I;" POSITION ";J
230 PRINT "(0 = ADVANCE TO NEXT ROW)"
240 PRINT "(999 = DRAW THE DIAGRAM)"
250 PRINT "(998 = END PROGRAM)"
260 PRINT "(## = COL IN ROW TO USE)"
270 INPUT N
280 X(I,J)=N
290 IF N=0 THEN 330
300 IF N=999 THEN 340
310 IF N=998 THEN 610
320 NEXT J
330 NEXT I
340 PRINT CHR$(147)
350 INPUT "# OF TIMES";N2
360 N3=0
370 PRINT CHR$(147)
380 FOR I=1 TO 20
390 FOR J=1 TO 30
400 IF X(I,J)=0 THEN 470
410 IF X(I,J)=999 THEN 510
420 N=X(I,J)
430 IF A$<>"C" THEN 460
440 POKE 1024+X(I,J)+40*(I+4),81
445 POKE 55296+X(I,J)+40*(I+4),1
450 GOTO 470
460 PRINT TAB(N);"*";
```

DRAW1 enables you to "draw" any picture or diagram you want on the screen, using circles or asterisks. If you first lay out your picture on graph paper by filling in some blocks and leaving others blank, you can then duplicate your drawing on the screen.

Your picture can be up to 20 rows deep (up and down) and 30 columns wide (across the screen). Line 170 asks you if you want to use circles or asterisks to draw the diagram. You must answer either **C** or *.

Then you need to tell your Commodore 64 what columns in each row are to be "filled in." The program will start out with ROW 1 and POSITION 1. You key the first column (a number from 1 to 30) in which you want a circle. Then you are asked for ROW 1, POSITION 2, to which you key the second column where you want a circle. This process is repeated for ROW 1 until you type **0** (zero) to advance to the next row, **998** to end the program, or **999** to draw the picture.

The actual drawing takes place in lines 350-570. You are asked in line 350 how many times you want to draw the picture, have it erased, and then have it redrawn. If you selected circles, the **POKE** statements of lines 440 and 445 are used to put the circles in the proper rows and columns. (See the discussion about putting characters anywhere on the screen, using the formulas of these two lines, in Chapter 4, under **POKE**.) Or if you selected asterisks, **PRINT**s and **TAB**s to columns are used.

```
470 NEXT J
480 IF A$="C" THEN 500
490 PRINT
500 NEXT I
510 IF A$="C" THEN 550
520 PRINT:PRINT:PRINT
550 N3=N3+1
560 IF N3>=N2 THEN 580
570 GOTO 370
580 INPUT "REPEAT (Y/N)";YN$
590 IF YN$="Y" THEN 340
600 GOTO 170
610 PRINT
620 PRINT
630 PRINT
640 END
```

When the number of repetitions you requested has been displayed, you can repeat the same diagram (line 580), or you can key in a new one.

EDIT1

```
100 REM ************************
110 REM *          EDIT1           *
120 REM *      COPYRIGHT 1983      *
130 REM *   DONALD C. KREUTNER     *
140 REM ************************
142 PRINT CHR$(147):REM CLR SCREEN
144 INPUT "1525 PRTR(1), RS232(2),
    NONE(3)";PX$
146 IF PX$="3" THEN 170
148 IF PX$="1" THEN 154
150 IF PX$="2" THEN 154
152 GOTO 144
154 PR=126+1
156 IF PX$="1" THEN 162
158 OPEN PR,2,0,CHR$(8):PX$="2":PR=128
160 GOTO 170
162 OPEN PR,4
170 DIM E$(300)
175 QUOT$=CHR$(34)
180 E$(1)="END"
200 PRINT "W/R/C/E/L/P/S (WRITE/READ/CK
    TAPE/EDIT/LIST/PRINT/STOP)":INPUT WR$
210 IF WR$="W" THEN 290
220 IF WR$="R" THEN 450
230 IF WR$="L" THEN 760
240 IF WR$="E" THEN 950
250 IF WR$="P" THEN 1050
260 IF WR$="C" THEN 630
270 IF WR$="S" THEN 1140
280 GOTO 200
290 INPUT "CASSETTE OR DISK (C/D)";CD$
300 IF CD$="C" THEN 350
310 IF CD$<>"D" THEN 290
320 INPUT "FILE NAME";D$
330 OPEN 2,8,2,"@0:"+D$+",S,W"
340 GOTO 360
```

EDIT1 is one of two programs (EDIT2 is the other) in this book that can create a multipurpose file to be saved on disk or tape. When you use either of these two programs, files can be read back, and lines can be deleted or added to correct a file to the condition you want. You can use these files to keep any important details or records you may later want to review.

Both programs write data in the same format so that files created by one can be modified by the other. In addition, several programs in this book have been written so that they can read data created by EDIT1 and EDIT2. You can easily create files, add to them, or modify them. In this chapter the programs that use files created by either EDIT1 or EDIT2 include LABEL1, RECIPE1, and SORT1.

In the EDIT1 program the commands available are the following: **READ** a file; **WRITE** a file; **EDIT** a file that has been **READ** in; **LIST** a file the way it has been **READ** or **EDIT**ed; **PRINT** a file; **CHECK** a tape file for accuracy; or **STOP** the program. Lines 200-270 select the appropriate actions based on the response you key in line 200.

The **READ** (**R**) action is implemented by lines 450-750. You are given two suboptions (to read from tape or disk). If you request disk, you are then prompted for the disk file name in line 480. Otherwise, the cassette tape is read. Any file that you input from tape or disk will replace a previous file

```
350 OPEN 2,1,2:REM OPEN TAPE FOR OUTPUT
360 FOR I=1 TO 300
370 A$=E$(I)
380 PRINT I;"***WRITE TO FILE***"
390 PRINT A$
400 PRINT# 2,QUOT$+A$+QUOT$
410 IF A$="END" THEN 430
420 NEXT I
430 CLOSE 2
440 GOTO 200
450 INPUT "CASSETTE OR DISK (C/D)";CD$
460 IF CD$="C" THEN 510
470 IF CD$<>"D" THEN 450
480 INPUT "FILE NAME";D$
490 OPEN 2,8,2,"0:"+D$+",S,R"
500 GOTO 520
510 OPEN 2,1,0:REM OPEN TAPE FOR INPUT
520 I=0
530 INPUT# 2,X$
540 A$=X$
550 I=I+1
560 E$(I)=X$
570 PRINT I;"***READ FROM FILE***"
580 PRINT A$
590 IF A$="END" THEN 610
600 GOTO 530
610 CLOSE 2
620 GOTO 200
630 OPEN 2,1,0:REM OPEN TAPE FOR INPUT
    VERIFICATION
640 I=0
650 E=0
660 INPUT 2,X$
670 I=I+1
680 IF E$(I)=X$ THEN 700
690 E=E+1
700 IF X$="END" THEN 730
710 IF I>300 THEN 730
720 GOTO 660
730 CLOSE 2
```

that you had read in or entered. Each record is read into the array E$, starting from position 1 (line 520 sets the subscript to 0) and continuing until a record is read containing the word "END" only, which marks the end of the file (see line 590).

You can **EDIT** (function **E**) the file in memory; or if you desire to create a new file, you can start putting new lines or records into memory, beginning at position 1 and using the **E** command. Line 950 asks you for the line # you desire to edit. If you select line number 1, you can erase all records with the same record sequence number you are keying.

It is important to note that how you terminate the edit mode can affect what lines are left intact in memory. You can key **//** to stop editing (or replacing) lines, thus leaving alone the lines following. However, be sure that some record later on has only the word "END" in it since the END record is the signal to the **WRITE** command that the end of the file has been reached. Besides using **//**, you can key a record with "END" only to terminate the edit mode. This method will erase any records following the END record, as far as the **WRITE** command is concerned. Keying **STOP** to end the edit mode has the same effect as keying **//**. Then succeeding records are left intact.

For a brief example, let's suppose you **READ** in from cassette a file containing the following records:

```
This is record number 1
And this is # 2
This is the third record
END
```

```
740 PRINT "ERRORS = ";E
750 GOTO 200
760 INPUT "BEG LINE#";B
770 INPUT "END LINE#";EN
780 INPUT "DELAY (200-1000)";DELAY
790 INPUT "LIST LINE #'S";YN$
800 IF B<1 THEN 760
810 IF B>300 THEN 760
820 IF EN<B THEN 760
830 IF EN<1 THEN 760
840 IF EN>300 THEN 760
850 FOR I=B TO EN
860 IF YN$<>"Y" THEN 880
870 PRINT I;"***"
880 PRINT E$(I)
890 IF E$(I)="END" THEN 200
900 REM *** NEXT 2 LINES FOR DELAY
    TO SCREEN***
910 IF DELAY<200 THEN 930
915 FOR J=1 TO DELAY
920 NEXT J
930 NEXT I
940 GOTO 200
950 INPUT "LINE TO EDIT";E
960 IF E>300 THEN 200
970 PRINT E;"***EDIT***"
980 A$=" ":INPUT A$
990 IF A$="STOP" THEN 200
1000 IF A$="//" THEN 200
1010 E$(E)=A$
1020 IF A$="END" THEN 200
1030 E=E+1
1040 GOTO 960
1050 IF PX$="3" THEN 200
1060 INPUT "BEG LINE";B
1070 INPUT "END LINE";EN
1080 FOR I=B TO EN
1090 IF E$(I)="END" THEN 1120
1100 PRINT# PR,E$(I)
1110 NEXT I
```

Now if you key **E** to edit, answer record number 1, then key

This was record # 1
//

The file will now contain

This was record # 1
And this is # 2
This is the third record
END

If you had, however, keyed

This was record # 1
END

then the file would now contain

This was record # 1
END
This is the third record
END

In this latter entry, when the file is rewritten back to tape or disk, only two records will be written—the first one and the END record (since the **WRITE** command stops when an END record is encountered).

Action **W**, as mentioned earlier, will write the memory file to disk or tape in lines 290-440. Again, a disk file name is requested if the file is a disk file.

Action **L** lists from a beginning to an ending line number (lines 760-770) and delays by requiring a count from 1 to any number between 200 to 1000 before the next line is displayed. You can experiment with various delays to slow down or speed up the listing to the screen. Note that when an END record is found (line 890), the listing terminates as if the end of the file had been

```
1120 GOTO 200
1140 IF PX$="3" THEN 1160
1150 CLOSE PR
1160 END
```

found. If you know, however, that there are more records that you have "cut off" by keying an END record, you could replace that END with whatever you want by using the **E** command, and following it with **//** or **STOP**, as described earlier.

The **P** command does the same thing as the **LIST** command, but prints the records to a printer instead of displaying them on the screen.

The **C** command will check a file you have just written to cassette to verify that what is read back is the same as what is contained in memory.

Finally, the **S** command stops the program, obviously erasing whatever file has been stored in memory. Be sure that you have saved your file to disk or tape, using the **W** command, unless you don't care whether the data is saved or not.

EDIT2

```
10 REM ************************
20 REM *          EDIT2          *
30 REM *                         *
40 REM *     COPYRIGHT 1983      *
50 REM *   DONALD C. KREUTNER    *
60 REM ************************
70 PRINT CHR$(147):POKE 53280,14:POKE
   53281,6:PRINT CHR$(5)
75 INPUT "1525 PRTR(1), RS232(2),
   NONE(3)";PX$
80 IF PX$="3" THEN 120
85 IF PX$="1" THEN 100
90 IF PX$="2" THEN 100
95 GOTO 75
100 PR=126
105 IF PX$="1" THEN 115
110 PR=PR+2:OPEN PR,2,0,CHR$(8):PR=128:
    PX$="2":GOTO 120
115 PR=PR+1:OPEN PR,4
120 PRINT CHR$(147)
130 QUOT$=CHR$(34)
180 DIM A$(500)
190 DIM A2$(500)
200 FOR I= 1 TO 500
210 A$(I)="@"
220 NEXT I
230 LAST1=1
235 GOTO 390
240 REM *****COMMANDS*****
250 INPUT B$
260 IF B$="HELP" THEN 390
270 IF B$="C" THEN 200
280 IF B$="A" THEN 530
290 IF B$="D" THEN 780
300 IF B$="T" THEN 890
310 IF B$="L" THEN 1080
```

EDIT2 creates the same type of file as EDIT1. EDIT2, however, uses a different manner of manipulating the data, thus giving you a choice of "tools" to use in creating or altering data files.

Perhaps the principal difference is that EDIT2 adds records, using "steps" of record numbers. With this method, you can add records, starting at record number 120 and adding in steps of 5—that is, record number 125, then 130, 135, etc. Thus, gaps are left for adding records that need to be inserted later.

EDIT2 also can renumber records. For example, you can renumber the entire file in memory from record number 1 to 500 in any desired step (such as 1, 5, 9, etc., in steps of 4).

Two arrays are used to keep track of the data and renumber it (A$ and A2$ in lines 180-190). Notice that the **FOR-NEXT** loop in lines 200-230 puts an @ in every position of A$ so that any data added later can be easily identified from "empty" lines (ones that contain an @).

The different commands are listed on the menu screen (lines 240-500).

To add lines the **A** command branches to line number 520, where you specify the beginning line number and the step for incrementing line numbers. If the step is given as 1, then there will be no gaps between each record, unless you later

```
320 IF B$="K" THEN 1150
330 IF B$="LU" THEN 1300
340 IF B$="R" THEN 1370
350 IF B$="P" THEN 1550
360 IF B$="PU" THEN 1650
370 IF B$="E" THEN 1730
380 REM *****HELP SCREEN*****
390 PRINT "HELP PRINT THESE INSTRUCTIONS"
400 PRINT "A     ADD LINES"
410 PRINT "C     CLEAR WORKFILE"
420 PRINT "D     DELETE LINES"
430 PRINT "T     TEXT IN A FILE"
440 PRINT "L     LIST WORKFILE"
450 PRINT "K     KEEP A FILE"
460 PRINT "LU    LIST WORKFILE
                 UNNUMBERED"
470 PRINT "R     RENUMBER WORKFILE"
480 PRINT "P     PRINT WORKFILE"
490 PRINT "PU    PRINT WORKFILE
                 UNNUMBERED"
500 PRINT "E     END PROGRAM"
510 GOTO 250
520 REM *****ADD LINES*****
530 INPUT "LINE #";A
540 INPUT "STEP #";S1
550 IF S1<>0 THEN 570
560 S1=5
570 IF A$(A)<>"@" THEN 740
580 IF A<10 THEN 620
590 IF A<100 THEN 640
600 IF A<1000 THEN 650
610 PRINT A;
615 GOTO 680
620 PRINT "    ";A;
625 REM FOUR SPACES ABOVE
630 GOTO 680
640 PRINT "   ";A;
645 REM THREE SPACES ABOVE
650 PRINT " ";A;
660 GOTO 680
```

renumber the file. One major difference between this program and EDIT1 is that if you try to add a record on top of a record (or line) number that already has data in it, you are warned about the condition, and the program returns to the menu. Your options then are to renumber the data, leaving gaps, or to delete lines that you meant to get rid of.

You should note that when the program is **RUN**, a **/** prompt comes up on the screen. If you key **HELP** or any unacceptable command, the program will print a menu of commands available.

By keying **C** after the **/** prompt, you will clear the work file in memory, wiping out any file you may have "texted" (or read) in using the **T** command, or entered through the **A** command, as described earlier.

The **D** command will delete any desired lines from a beginning line number to an ending line number (lines 770-860). As mentioned earlier, you can delete lines within a specified range or from a certain line number to the end. (500 is the maximum line number.)

To "read in" a file from disk or tape, the **T** or **TEXT** command is used (lines 890-1060). You are asked for the step to be used in adding the new records to the work file.

Another major difference between EDIT1 and EDIT2 is that in EDIT2, records added from a file will not automatically erase previously existing data. The program keeps track of where the last record was and continues from that point. Of course, you can **CLEAR** the work file at any time by

```
665 REM ONE SPACE ABOVE
670 GOTO 680
680 INPUT C$
681 IF A<LAST1 THEN 700
690 LAST1=A
700 IF C$="END" THEN 760
710 A$(A)=C$
720 A=A+S1
730 GOTO 570
740 PRINT "THIS LINE ALREADY EXISTS"
750 PRINT A$(A)
760 GOTO 250
770 REM *****DELETE LINES*****
780 INPUT "BEG LINE #";B
790 INPUT "END LINE #";E
791 IF E<LAST1 THEN 800
792 LAST1=B
793 A$(B)="END"
800 IF E>500 THEN 790
810 FOR I=B TO E
820 IF A$(I)="@" THEN 860
830 REM ***SAME AS ABOVE LINES***
840 PRINT " ";A$(I)
850 A$(I)="@"
860 NEXT I
870 GOTO 250
880 REM *****TEXT IN FILE*****
890 INPUT "CASSETTE OR DISK (C/D)";CD$
900 IF CD$="D" THEN 940
910 IF CD$<>"C" THEN 890
915 OPEN 2,1,0:REM OPEN TAPE FOR INPUT
920 GOTO 960
940 INPUT "FILE NAME";F$
950 OPEN 2,8,2,"0:"+F$+",S,R"
960 INPUT "STEP #";S1
970 IF S1<>0 THEN 990
980 S1=5
990 FOR I=LAST1 TO 500 STEP S1
1000 INPUT# 2,X$
1005 A$(I)=X$
```

using the **C** command before texting in a file.

Two commands will list the records in the work file: the **L** and the **LU** commands. The **L** command will list the data immediately following the line number, whereas the **LU** command will list the data only. You can use the **L** command to determine what line numbers are available for your use.

The **P** and the **PU** commands are similar to **L** and **LU**, but print the data on a printer if you have one.

The **K** command "keeps" the work file in a disk or tape file, whereas the **E** command ends the program.

```
                EDIT2

HELP      PRT INSTRUCTIONS
A         ADD LINES
C         CLEAR WORKFILE
D         DELETE LINES
T         TEXT IN FILE
L         LIST WORKFILE
K         KEEP A FILE
LU        LIST UNNUMBERED
R         RENUMBER WORKFILE
P         PRINT WORKFILE
PU        PRINT UNNUMBERED
E         END PROGRAM
```

```
1010 IF A$(I)="END" THEN 1040
1020 LAST1=I
1030 NEXT I
1040 CLOSE 2
1045 IF I>500 THEN I=500
1050 A$(I)="@"
1060 GOTO 250
1070 REM *****LIST WORKFILE*****
1080 FOR I=1 TO 500
1090 IF I>LAST1 THEN 1130
1100 IF A$(I)="@" THEN 1120
1110 PRINT I;A$(I)
1120 NEXT I
1130 GOTO 250
1140 REM *****KEEP AS A FILE*****
1150 INPUT "CASSETTE OR DISK (C/D)";CD$
1160 IF CD$="D" THEN 1190
1170 OPEN 2,1,2:REM OPEN TAPE FOR OUTPUT
1180 GOTO 1210
1190 INPUT "OUTPUT FILE NAME";F$
1200 OPEN 2,8,2,"@0:"+F$+",S,W"
1210 FOR I=1 TO 500
1220 IF I>LAST1 THEN 1260
1230 IF A$(I)="@" THEN 1250
1240 PRINT# 2,QUOT$+A$(I)+QUOT$
1250 NEXT I
1260 PRINT# 2,"END"
1270 CLOSE 2
1280 GOTO 250
1290 REM *****LIST WORKFILE
     UNNUMBERED*****
1300 FOR I=1 TO 500
1310 IF I>LAST1 THEN 1350
1320 IF A$(I)="@" THEN 1340
1330 PRINT A$(I)
1340 NEXT I
1350 GOTO 250
1360 REM *****RENUMBER WORKFILE*****
1370 INPUT "STEP #";S1
1380 J=0
1390 IF STP1<>0 THEN 1410
1400 S1=5
1410 FOR I=1 TO 500
1420 A2$(I)="@"
1430 NEXT I
1440 FOR I=1 TO 500
1450 IF I>LAST1 THEN 1500
1460 IF A$(I)="@" THEN 1490
1470 J=J+S1
1480 A2$(J)=A$(I)
1490 NEXT I
1500 FOR I=1 TO 500
1510 A$(I)=A2$(I)
1515 IF A$(I)="@" THEN 1520
1516 LAST1=I
1520 NEXT I
1530 GOTO 250
1540 REM *****PRINT WORKFILE*****
1550 FOR I=1 TO 500
1570 IF I>LAST1 THEN 1620
1580 IF A$(I)="@" THEN 1610
1590 REM *****VARIOUS LINES FOR
     LENGTH OF A*****
1600 PRINT# PR,I;TAB(5);A$(I)
1610 NEXT I
1620 GOTO 250
1640 REM *****PRINT WORKFILE
     UNNUMBERED*****
1650 FOR I=1 TO 500
1660 IF I>LAST1 THEN 1710
1680 IF A$(I)="@" THEN 1700
1690 PRINT# PR,A$(I)
1700 NEXT I
1710 GOTO 250
1730 IF PX$="3" THEN 1750
1740 CLOSE PR
1750 END
```

EDITMASK

```
10 REM  **************************
20 REM  *        EDITMASK        *
30 REM  *                        *
40 REM  *     COPYRIGHT 1983     *
50 REM  *   DONALD C. KREUTNER   *
60 REM  **************************
170 INPUT "ENTER # TO EDIT";N1
180 IF N1<>INT(N1) THEN 170
190 IF N1=9 THEN 580
200 NUMED=N1
210 MASK$="XX,XXX,XXX.XX-"
220 GOSUB 270
230 PRINT MASK$
240 GOTO 170
270 REM ***EDITING SUBROUTINE****
280 REM ***MASK$=MASK FOR EDITED RESULT
290 REM ***EXAMPLE: XXX,XXX.XX-
300 REM ***NUMED=NUMBER TO EDIT
    (INTEGER FORMAT)
310 N2=NUMED
320 NUMED=ABS(NUMED)
330 LMASK=LEN(MASK$)
340 NUMED$=STR$(NUMED)
350 LNUMED=LEN(NUMED$)
360 CN=LNUMED+1
370 FOR CTM=LMASK TO 1 STEP -1
380 CN=CN-1
390 IF CN<2 THEN 550
400 IF MID$(MASK$,CTM,1)<>"-" THEN 480
410 IF N2>0 THEN 450
420 MASK$=MID$(MASK$,1,CTM-1)+"-"
430 CN=CN+1
440 GOTO 470
450 MASK$=MID$(MASK$,1,CTM-1)+" "
460 CN=CN+1
470 GOTO 560
```

EDITMASK is a fairly simple program that takes any number which you key (for example, 1200050) and edits it, putting in commas, a decimal point, and a minus sign, if needed. For the example just given, the edited result would be 12,000.50.

The importance of EDITMASK is to show how a formatted result can be obtained using regular Commodore 64 BASIC, which does not have the **PRINT USING** option of the **PRINT** command. With this subroutine any program can take a number, such as N1 in line 170, put it into NUMED, supply an editing "mask," such as MASK$ in line 210, and get the result in MASK$ by stating simply **GOSUB** 270, which means to perform the subroutine in line 270 until a **RETURN** statement is found.

The subroutine looks from right to left through the editing mask and substitutes digits from the number NUMED. Zeros to the left are suppressed, along with unneeded commas, to obtain the result.

```
480 IF MID$(MASK$,CTM,1)="," THEN 510
490 IF MID$(MASK$,CTM,1)="." THEN 510
500 GOTO 530
510 CN=CN+1
515 IF CTM=2 THEN CN=CN-1
520 GOTO 560
530 M$=MID$(MASK$,1,CTM-1)+MID$
    (NUMED$,CN,1)+MID$(MASK$,CTM+1,
    LMASK-(CTM-1)-1)
535 MASK$=M$
540 GOTO 560
550 MASK$=MID$(MASK$,1,CTM-1)+" "+MID$
    (MASK$,CTM+1,(LMASK-(CTM-1)-1))
560 REM PRINT CTM;MASK$
565 NEXT CTM
570 RETURN
580 END
```

FIGURE1

```
10 REM ***************************
20 REM *            FIGURE1           *
30 REM *                              *
40 REM *        COPYRIGHT 1983        *
50 REM *     DONALD C. KREUTNER       *
60 REM ***************************
70 PRINT CHR$(147):POKE 53280,14:
   POKE 53281,6:PRINT CHR$(5)
80 BL=098:LL=097:RL=225:TL=226
90 DL=123:UL=126:UR=124:DR=108
100 C1=5:C2=19:C3=33
110 POKE 54296,15
180 INPUT "DELAY";DELAY
190 IF DELAY<0 THEN 180
200 IF DELAY=0 THEN 660
660 PRINT CHR$(147)
670 PRINT TAB(16);"*FIGURE1*"
680 R=11
690 C=C2
700 GOSUB 990
710 R=11
720 C=C1
730 GOSUB 990
740 R=11
750 C=C3
760 GOSUB 990
770 R=2
780 C=C1
790 GOSUB 990
830 R=2
840 C=C3
850 GOSUB 990
860 R=20
870 C=C1
880 GOSUB 990
882 R=20:C=C2
```

FIGURE1 is a program that uses graphics to draw some very interesting patterns. Line 660 clears the screen. Then, in the center of the screen, a small circle is drawn clockwise. Next, a square is drawn around the circle. Finally, a second square is drawn around the inner square.

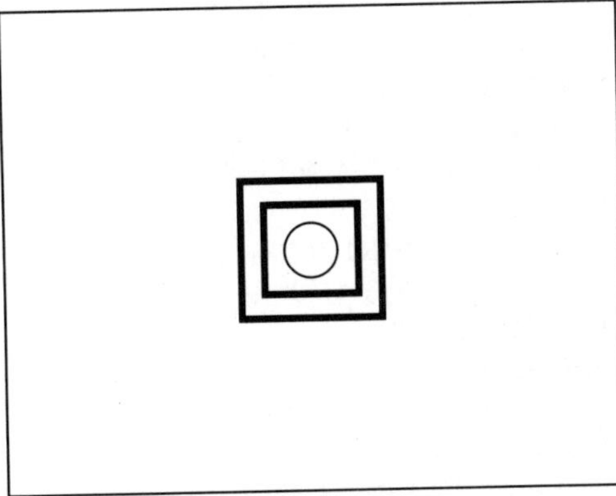

And yet that's not all. The figure of two squares and a circle is repeated seven more times in symmetrical locations on the screen. Next, each group is "shot" in the middle with a solid dark square, and each square is then wiped out, with appropriate sound effects. The pattern is repeated over and over, creating an entertaining display for a computer show or just serving as a demonstration of what the Commodore 64 can do with graphics.

Lines 680-910 repeat the squares-and-circle patterns eight times with different coordinates designating rows (R) and columns (C). Special characters have been

```
884 GOSUB 990
890 R=20
900 C=C3
910 GOSUB 990
920 CHA=160
930 GOSUB 1540
940 CHA=32
950 GOSUB 1540
960 FOR I=1 TO 2000
970 NEXT I
980 GOTO 660
990 POKE 1024+C+0+40*(R+0),85:
    POKE 55296+C+0+40*(R+0),1
1000 GOSUB 1470
1010 POKE 1024+C+1+40*(R+0),73:
     POKE 55296+C+1+40*(R+0),1
1020 GOSUB 1470
1030 POKE 1024+C+1+40*(R+1),75:
     POKE 55296+C+1+40*(R+1),1
1040 GOSUB 1470
1050 POKE 1024+C+0+40*(R+1),74:
     POKE 55296+C+0+40*(R+1),1
1060 GOSUB 1470
1070 POKE 1024+C+0+40*(R-1),BL:
     POKE 55296+C+0+40*(R-1),1
1080 GOSUB 1470
1090 POKE 1024+C+1+40*(R-1),BL:
     POKE 55296+C+1+40*(R-1),1
1100 GOSUB 1470
1105 POKE 1024+C+2+40*(R-1),DL:
     POKE 55296+C+2+40*(R-1),1
1110 POKE 1024+C+2+40*(R+0),LL:
     POKE 55296+C+2+40*(R+0),1
1120 GOSUB 1470
1130 POKE 1024+C+2+40*(R+1),LL:
     POKE 55296+C+2+40*(R+1),1
1140 GOSUB 1470
1145 POKE 1024+C+2+40*(R+2),UL:
     POKE 55296+C+2+40*(R+2),1
```

defined by the **POKE** statements in lines 990, etc. The number following the comma after the **POKE 1024** statement represents the graphic segment to be placed at a particular location on the screen.

Lines 920-950 shoot the squares into and out of the centers, and lines 960-970 delay the erasure before repeating the diagram.

At the beginning of the program, you are asked to supply a delay (to which the program must count after each portion is painted to the screen).

```
1150 POKE 1024+C+1+40*(R+2),TL:
     POKE 55296+C+1+40*(R+2),1
1160 GOSUB 1470
1170 POKE 1024+C+0+40*(R+2),TL:
     POKE 55296+C+0+40*(R+2),1
1180 GOSUB 1470
1185 POKE 1024+C-1+40*(R+2),UR:
     POKE 55296+C-1+40*(R+2),1
1190 POKE 1024+C-1+40*(R+1),RL:
     POKE 55296+C-1+40*(R+1),1
1200 GOSUB 1470
1210 POKE 1024+C-1+40*(R+0),RL:
     POKE 55296+C-1+40*(R+0),1
1220 GOSUB 1470
1225 POKE 1024+C-1+40*(R-1),DR:
     POKE 55296+C-1+40*(R-1),1
1230 REM ************************
1260 POKE 1024+C-1+40*(R-2),BL:
     POKE 55296+C-1+40*(R-2),1:GOSUB 1470
```

```
1270 POKE 1024+C+0+40*(R-2),BL:
     POKE 55296+C+0+40*(R-2),1:GOSUB 1470
1280 POKE 1024+C+1+40*(R-2),BL:
     POKE 55296+C+1+40*(R-2),1:GOSUB 1470
1290 POKE 1024+C+2+40*(R-2),BL:
     POKE 55296+C+2+40*(R-2),1:GOSUB 1470
1295 POKE 1024+C+3+40*(R-2),DL:
     POKE 55296+C+3+40*(R-2),1:GOSUB 1470
1300 POKE 1024+C+3+40*(R-1),LL:
     POKE 55296+C+3+40*(R-1),1:GOSUB 1470
1310 POKE 1024+C+3+40*(R+0),LL:
     POKE 55296+C+3+40*(R+0),1:GOSUB 1470
1320 POKE 1024+C+3+40*(R+1),LL:
     POKE 55296+C+3+40*(R+1),1:GOSUB 1470
1330 POKE 1024+C+3+40*(R+2),LL:
     POKE 55296+C+3+40*(R+2),1:GOSUB 1470
1335 POKE 1024+C+3+40*(R+3),UL:
     POKE 55296+C+3+40*(R+3),1:GOSUB 1470
1340 POKE 1024+C+2+40*(R+3),TL:
     POKE 55296+C+2+40*(R+3),1:GOSUB 1470
1350 POKE 1024+C+1+40*(R+3),TL:
     POKE 55296+C+1+40*(R+3),1:GOSUB 1470
1360 POKE 1024+C+0+40*(R+3),TL:
     POKE 55296+C+0+40*(R+3),1:GOSUB 1470
1370 POKE 1024+C-1+40*(R+3),TL:
     POKE 55296+C-1+40*(R+3),1:GOSUB 1470
1375 POKE 1024+C-2+40*(R+3),UR:
     POKE 55296+C-2+40*(R+3),1:GOSUB 1470
1380 POKE 1024+C-2+40*(R+2),RL:
     POKE 55296+C-2+40*(R+2),1:GOSUB 1470
1390 POKE 1024+C-2+40*(R+1),RL:
     POKE 55296+C-2+40*(R+1),1:GOSUB 1470
1400 POKE 1024+C-2+40*(R+0),RL:
     POKE 55296+C-2+40*(R+0),1:GOSUB 1470
1410 POKE 1024+C-2+40*(R-1),RL:
     POKE 55296+C-2+40*(R-1),1:GOSUB 1470
1415 POKE 1024+C-2+40*(R-2),DR:
     POKE 55296+C-2+40*(R-2),1:GOSUB 1470
1430 RETURN
1470 REM * * * * * * * * * * * * * * * * * * * *
1475 POKE 54277,9:POKE 54276,17:POKE 54296,10
1480 FOR T=1 TO 002:NEXT T
1485 POKE 54273,17:POKE 54272,37:
     POKE 54276,17
1490 FOR T=1 TO 002:NEXT T
1500 POKE 54276,16
1502 IF DELAY<1 THEN 1510
1505 FOR I=1 TO DELAY:NEXT I
1510 RETURN
1520 FOR I=5 TO 0 STEP-1:POKE 54296,I:
     POKE 54276,129:POKE 54277,15
1525 POKE 54273,40:POKE 54272,200:NEXT I
1530 POKE 54276,0
1535 RETURN
1540 R=11:C=C2:GOSUB 1730
1550 R=11:C=C1:GOSUB 1730
1560 R=11:C=C3:GOSUB 1730
1570 R=02:C=C1:GOSUB 1730
1590 R=02:C=C3:GOSUB 1730
1600 R=20:C=C1:GOSUB 1730
1610 R=20:C=C2:GOSUB 1730
1620 R=20:C=C3:GOSUB 1730
1630 RETURN
1730 POKE 1024+C+0+40*(R+0),CHA:
     POKE 55296+C+0+40*(R+0),1:GOSUB 1520
1740 POKE 1024+C+1+40*(R+0),CHA:
     POKE 55296+C+1+40*(R+0),1:GOSUB 1520
1750 POKE 1024+C+1+40*(R+1),CHA:
     POKE 55296+C+1+40*(R+1),1:GOSUB 1520
1760 POKE 1024+C+0+40*(R+1),CHA:
     POKE 55296+C+0+40*(R+1),1:GOSUB 1520
1770 RETURN
1790 END
```

GAMBLE

```
10 REM **************************
20 REM *          GAMBLE        *
30 REM *                        *
40 REM *      COPYRIGHT 1983    *
50 REM *    DONALD C. KREUTNER  *
60 REM **************************
180 DIM P(10)
190 DIM P$(10)
210 D1=INT(RND(1)*6)+1
220 D2=INT(RND(1)*6)+1
230 PRINT CHR$(147)
240 INPUT "# OF PLAYERS (1 TO 10)";NP
250 IF NP<1 THEN 240
260 IF NP>10 THEN 240
270 INPUT "PLAY TO SCORE";PT
280 IF PT<1 THEN 270
290 REM ********************
300 REM THIS GAME ALLOWS THE PLAYER
310 REM TO SHAKE THE DICE - THEN HE
320 REM HAS THE OPTION TO TRY TO
330 REM GET A DOUBLE - IF HE SHAKES
350 REM THE HIGHER DIE, HE HAS A
360 REM 1 IN 2 CHANCE OF GETTING A
370 REM DOUBLE - BUT IF THE LOWER
380 REM DIE IS RESHAKEN, HE HAS A
390 REM 1 IN 3 CHANCE
400 REM ********************
410 REM SCORING:
420 REM NO DOUBLE - DICE TOTAL
430 REM DOUBLE - TWICE DICE TOTAL
440 REM FAILED DOUBLE - 0
450 REM ********************
460 FOR I=1 TO NP
470 PRINT "PLAYER #";I;"NAME";
480 INPUT P$(I)
490 P(I)=0
```

GAMBLE is a dice game that allows up to ten players to compete. The remarks in lines 290-440 briefly summarize the game's rules. Notice that after you shake the two dice, if you choose to reshake either die in an attempt to get a double, and you fail, you will get zero for your score on that attempt. The unique thing about this game is that it cannot be duplicated "as is" without a computer. To have one chance out of two to get a double with a real die, you would need to have three opportunities to try to match the other die. Similarly, to have one chance out of three, you would be allowed two reshakes, using real dice.

With GAMBLE, however, all you need is to tell the program you want to reshake die 1 or die 2 (line 710), or answer **N** to decline a rethrow. Then the program automatically determines whether you are rethrowing the higher or lower die, and computes your result, giving you the appropriate odds (lines 810 and 910). If you rethrow the lower die, line 810 selects a random number between 1 and 3. If the number 1 comes up, you have a double. The same logic applies to one chance out of two, except that you get a random result of 1 or 2.

In the program, lines 460-500 obtain the player names in the array P$ for as many players as are specified in line 240.

Each round of the game begins in line 550, and each player gets his turn in a long **FOR-NEXT** loop from line 560 to line 1450. When

```
500 NEXT I
510 ROUND=0
520 REM FLAGD=0 MEANS NO
    DOUBLE ATTEMPT
530 REM FLAGD=1 MEANS LOW DIE
    ATTEMPT
540 REM FLAGD=2 MEANS HIGH DIE ATTEMPT
550 ROUND=ROUND+1
560 FOR I=1 TO NP
570 PRINT CHR$(147)
580 PRINT "***************************"
590 PRINT "ROUND #";ROUND
600 PRINT "PLAYER #";I;
610 PRINT "(";P$(I);")"
620 PRINT
630 D2=INT(6*RND(1))+1
640 IF D1<>0 THEN 660
650 D1=1
660 IF D2<>0 THEN 680
670 D2=1
680 FLAGD=0
690 PRINT "DIE1=";D1;"  DIE2=";D2
700 PRINT
710 INPUT "RETHROW (N/1/2)";N12$
720 IF N12$="N" THEN 1240
730 IF N12$="1" THEN 760
740 IF N12$="2" THEN 1010
750 GOTO 710
760 IF D1<=D2 THEN 790
770 FLAGD=2
780 GOTO 910
790 FLAGD=1
800 REM ********************
810 D1=INT(RND(1)*3)+1
820 IF D1=1 THEN 880
830 IF D2=1 THEN 860
840 D1=D2-1
850 GOTO 870
860 D1=D2+1
870 GOTO 1240
```

all players have had their turns, for one round, control returns from line 1460 to line 550, where the number of the round is incremented and another **FOR-NEXT** loop is started for a new round. This continues until one player reaches the goal for a specified number of points, selected in line 270.

Lines 590-700, using random number selections between 1 and 6, obtain the original results of throwing two dice.

Lines 810-990 allow an attempt to get a double using a rethrow of die 1. Line 760 analyzes whether that die is less than or equal to the other die. If you decide (stupidly) to reshake and you already have a double, you will have one chance out of two of getting the same double again. You should just answer **N** in line 710 if you get a double right away. (Remember that you get 10 points for any double whose point total doubled is less than 10.)

Lines 1000-1230 do the same thing for a reshake of die #2.

Lines 1240-1380 then figure your score. Lines 1260-1274 and lines 1310-1324 give you 10 points for a double that would otherwise score less than 10 points.

After each player's turn, the players' cumulative totals are displayed before the next player's turn (lines 1380-1450). If, however, any player's score exceeds the "play-to" score (PT), line 1390 transfers program control to line 1470, where the final scores are displayed.

```
880 D1=D2
890 GOTO 1240
900 REM ********************
910 D1=INT(RND(1)*2)+1
920 IF D1=1 THEN 980
930 IF D2=1 THEN 960
940 D1=D2-1
950 GOTO 970
960 D1=D2+1
970 GOTO 1240
980 D1=D2
990 GOTO 1240
1000 REM ********************
1010 IF D1<=D2 THEN 1040
1020 FLAGD=2
1030 GOTO 1160
1040 FLAGD=1
1050 REM ********************
1060 D2=INT(RND(1)*3)+1
1070 IF D2=1 THEN 1130
1080 IF D1=1 THEN 1110
1090 D2=D1-1
1100 GOTO 1120
1110 D2=D1+1
1120 GOTO 1240
1130 D2=D1
1140 GOTO 1240
1150 REM ********************
1160 D2=INT(RND(1)*2)+1
1170 IF D2=1 THEN 1230
1180 IF D1=1 THEN 1210
1190 D2=D1-1
1200 GOTO 1220
1210 D2=D1+1
1220 GOTO 1240
1230 D2=D1
1240 IF FLAGD=1 THEN 1310
1250 IF FLAGD=2 THEN 1310
1260 IF D1<>D2 THEN 1290
1270 TTL=2*(D1+D2)
1272 IF TTL>9 THEN 1280
1274 TTL=10
1280 GOTO 1350
1290 TTL=D1+D2
1300 GOTO 1350
1310 IF D1<>D2 THEN 1340
1320 TTL=2*(D1+D2)
1322 IF TTL>9 THEN 1330
1324 TTL=10
1330 GOTO 1350
1340 TTL=0
1350 P(I)=P(I)+TTL
1360 PRINT CHR$(147)
1370 PRINT "DIE1=";D1;"  DIE2=";D2;TAB(23);P(I)
1380 PRINT "***************************"
1390 IF P(I)>=PT THEN 1470
1400 PRINT "****TOTALS****"
1410 FOR J=1 TO NP
1420 PRINT "PLAYER #";J;P$(J);TAB(23);P(J)
1430 NEXT J
1440 INPUT "RETURN TO CONTINUE";E$
1450 NEXT I
1460 GOTO 550
1470 PRINT CHR$(147)
1480 PRINT "****FINAL SCORE****"
1490 FOR J=1 TO NP
1500 PRINT "PLAYER #";J;P$(J);TAB(23);P(J)
1510 NEXT J
1520 PRINT
1530 INPUT "PLAY AGAIN (Y/N)";YN$
1540 IF YN$="Y" THEN 240
1550 END
```

GUESS3

```
10 REM   **************************
20 REM   *         GUESS3         *
30 REM   *                        *
40 REM   *     COPYRIGHT 1983     *
50 REM   *   DONALD C. KREUTNER   *
60 REM   **************************
70 PRINT CHR$(147):POKE 53280,14:
   POKE 53281,6:PRINT CHR$(5)
190 PRINT TAB(10);"**********"
200 PRINT TAB(10);"**GUESS3**"
210 PRINT TAB(10);"**********"
220 PRINT
230 PRINT
240 PRINT
250 PRINT
260 PRINT
270 PRINT
280 INPUT "PLAY OR QUIT (P/Q)";PQ$
290 IF PQ$="Q" THEN 920
300 PRINT CHR$(147)
310 X=INT(RND(1)*999)+1
320 X$=STR$(X)
330 CTR=0
340 LX=LEN(X$)-1:X$=MID$(X$,2,LX)
350 ON LX GOTO 380,400,410
360 PRINT LX
370 GOTO 280
380 X$="00"+X$
390 GOTO 410
400 X$="0"+X$
410 X1$=MID$(X$,1,1)
420 X2$=MID$(X$,2,1)
430 X3$=MID$(X$,3,1)
440 CTR=CTR+1
450 PRINT "ATTEMPT #";CTR
460 INUT "GUESS MY 3 DIGIT #";Y$
```

GUESS3 is a logic analysis game that allows you to try to guess a three-digit number based on the clues you obtain from previous guesses.

First, a random number is selected by the program from 1 to 999 (line 310). In lines 320-400, a one- or two-digit number has leading zeros added to the string representation of the number (X$ in line 320). Thus, the number 9 is 009, and 98 is 098. X1$, X2$, and X3$ contain the first, second, and third digits to be used in comparing to the guessed numbers. The number of guesses you make is incremented in line 440 prior to the three-digit guess of line 460.

If you failed to enter three digits, line 480 returns you to line 460 to reenter a new guess. (To guess the number 3, you must key **003**.) Then Y1$, Y2$, and Y3$ are given the values of the three guessed digits to be compared to the actual digits. Lines 570-640 check for the right numbers being in the right positions. If all three numbers are correct, you've guessed the random number, and control transfers from line 630 to line 740.

Otherwise, lines 650-700 check each digit you guessed against each digit of the number and tell you how many digits of your guess were correct (but not necessarily in the right position). From the accumulated information, you should try to guess the number in as few guesses as possible.

```
470 LY=LEN(Y$)
480 IF LY<>3 THEN 460
490 Y1$=MID$(Y$,1,1)
500 Y2$=MID$(Y$,2,1)
510 Y3$=MID$(Y$,3,1)
520 CNUM=0
530 CP=0
540 X1F=0
550 X2F=0
560 X3F=0
570 IF X1$<>Y1$ THEN 590
580 CP=CP+1
590 IF X2$<>Y2$ THEN 610
600 CP=CP+1
610 IF X3$<>Y3$ THEN 650
620 CP=CP+1
630 IF CP=3 THEN 740
640 REM IF CP=3 YOU GOT IT!
650 Z$=Y1$
660 GOSUB 770
670 Z$=Y2$
680 GOSUB 770
690 Z$=Y3$
700 GOSUB 770
710 PRINT "YOU HAVE";CP;" (RIGHT POSITION)"
720 PRINT "AND....";CNUM;" (RIGHT DIGITS)"
730 GOTO 440
740 PRINT "RIGHT!!!";CHR$(7);" IT'S ";X$
750 PRINT "**************************"
760 GOTO 280
770 IF X1F=1 THEN 820
780 IF Z$<>X1$ THEN 820
790 X1F=1
800 CNUM=CNUM+1
810 GOTO 910
820 IF X2F=1 THEN 870
830 IF Z$<>X2$ THEN 870
840 X2F=1
850 CNUM=CNUM+1
860 GOTO 910
870 IF X3F=1 THEN 910
880 IF Z$<>X3$ THEN 910
890 X3F=1
900 CNUM=CNUM+1
910 RETURN
920 END
```

```
ATTEMPT NUMBER 1
GUESS MY 3 DIGIT NUMBER: 123
YOU HAVE 0 RIGHT POSITION
AND... 1 RIGHT DIGITS
ATTEMPT NUMBER 2
GUESS MY 3 DIGIT NUMBER: 145
YOUR HAVE 1 RIGHT POSITION
AND... 2 RIGHT DIGITS
ATTEMPT NUMBER 3
GUESS MY 3 DIGIT NUMBER:
```

GUESS4

```
10 REM **************************
20 REM *         GUESS4         *
30 REM *                        *
40 REM *     COPYRIGHT 1983     *
50 REM *   DONALD C. KREUTNER   *
60 REM **************************
70 PRINT CHR$(147):POKE 53280,14:
   POKE 53281,6:PRINT CHR$(5)
190 PRINT TAB(10);"**********"
200 PRINT TAB(10);"**GUESS4**"
210 PRINT TAB(10);"**********"
220 PRINT
230 PRINT
240 PRINT
250 PRINT
260 PRINT
270 PRINT
280 INPUT "PLAY OR QUIT (P/Q)";PQ$
290 IF PQ$="Q" THEN 1050
300 PRINT CHR$(147)
310 X=INT(RND(1)*9999)+1
320 X$=STR$(X)
330 CTR=0
340 LX=LEN(X$)-1:X$=MID$(X$,2,LX)
350 ON LX GOTO 380,400,420,430
360 PRINT LX
370 GOTO 280
380 X$="000"+X$
390 GOTO 430
400 X$="00"+X$
410 GOTO 430
420 X$="0"+X$
430 X1$=MID$(X$,1,1)
440 X2$=MID$(X$,2,1)
450 X3$=MID$(X$,3,1)
460 X4$=MID$(X$,4,1)
```

Although similar to GUESS3, GUESS4 requires you to guess a four-digit number instead of one with three digits.

In line 310 a random number between 1 and 9999 is selected. Leading zeros are added to numbers less than 1000 in lines 340-420.

The number you guess in line 490 is compared to the number to be guessed, just as in GUESS3. Obviously, you will need more guesses to discover a four-digit number than a three-digit number.

```
ATTEMPT NUMBER 1
GUESS MY 4 DIGIT NUMBER: 1234
YOU HAVE 0 RIGHT POSITION
AND... 2 RIGHT DIGITS
ATTEMPT NUMBER 2
GUESS MY 4 DIGIT NUMBER: 2156
YOUR HAVE 1 RIGHT POSITION
AND... 1 RIGHT DIGITS
ATTEMPT NUMBER 3
GUESS MY 4 DIGIT NUMBER:
```

```
470 CTR=CTR+1
480 PRINT "ATTEMPT #";CTR
490 INPUT "GUESS MY 4 DIGIT #";Y$
500 LY=LEN(Y$)
510 IF LY<>4 THEN 460
520 Y1$=MID$(Y$,1,1)
530 Y2$=MID$(Y$,2,1)
540 Y3$=MID$(Y$,3,1)
550 Y4$=MID$(Y$,4,1)
560 CNUM=0
570 CP=0
580 X1F=0
590 X2F=0
600 X3F=0
610 X4F=0
620 IF X1$<>Y1$ THEN 640
630 CP=CP+1
640 IF X2$<>Y2$ THEN 660
650 CP=CP+1
660 IF X3$<>Y3$ THEN 680
670 CP=CP+1
680 IF X4$<>Y4$ THEN 720
690 CP=CP+1
700 IF CP=4 THEN 830
710 REM IF CP=4 YOU GOT IT!
720 Z$=Y1$
730 GOSUB 860
740 Z$=Y2$
750 GOSUB 860
760 Z$=Y3$
770 GOSUB 860
780 Z$=Y4$
790 GOSUB 860
800 PRINT "YOU HAVE";CP;" (RIGHT POSITION)"
810 PRINT "AND....";CNUM;" (RIGHT DIGITS)"
820 GOTO 470
830 PRINT "RIGHT!!! ";CHR$(7);"IT'S ";X$
840 PRINT "**************************"
850 GOTO 280
860 IF X1F=1 THEN 910
870 IF Z$<>X1$ THEN 910
880 X1F=1
890 CNUM=CNUM+1
900 GOTO 1040
910 IF X2F=1 THEN 960
920 IF Z$<>X2$ THEN 960
930 X2F=1
940 CNUM=CNUM+1
950 GOTO 1040
960 IF X3F=1 THEN 1000
970 IF Z$<>X3$ THEN 1000
980 X3F=1
990 CNUM=CNUM+1
1000 IF X4F=1 THEN 1040
1010 IF Z$<>X4$ THEN 1040
1020 X4F=1
1030 CN=CN+1
1040 RETURN
1050 END
```

HANGMAN

```
10 REM **************************
20 REM *         HANGMAN        *
30 REM *                        *
40 REM *      COPYRIGHT 1983    *
50 REM *    DONALD C. KREUTNER  *
60 REM **************************
70 PRINT CHR$(147):POKE 53280,14:
   POKE 53281,6:PRINT CHR$(5)
180 DIM X$(200)
190 DIM G1$(30)
200 DIM G2$(30)
210 REM HANGMAN
220 DATA LOUSY,WORDS,ANIMAL
230 DATA STRATEGY,PRODUCT,SYSTEM
240 DATA PROVIDE,FUTURE,DIFFICULT
250 DATA STORAGE,LIMITED,CLOSED
260 DATA IRON,STOVE,WASHER
270 DATA SWEATER,TABLE,COMPUTER
280 DATA USEFUL,MACHINE,SUBTRACT
290 DATA BASEBALL,ONIONS,WATERMELON
300 DATA LANTERN,PRIMARY,AWFUL
310 DATA FOREST,COUNTRY,BEAUTIFUL
320 DATA FOWL,ALPHABET,TEENAGER
330 DATA ELEPHANT,TELEVISION,REVISION
340 DATA TELEPHONE,TOASTER,FATHER
350 DATA END
360 REM YOU CAN USE THE WORDS SUPPLIED
370 REM OR REKEY NEW ONES IN DIFFERENT
380 REM DATA STATEMENTS - OR YOU CAN
390 REM KEY EACH OTHERS' WORDS
400 REM *********************
610 PRINT CHR$(147)
620 FOR I=1 TO 200
630 READ X$(I)
640 IF X$(I)="END" THEN 660
650 NEXT I
```

HANGMAN is a game for one or two players. With one player the words to be used are taken from the **DATA** statements in lines 220-350. With two players these preprogrammed words may be used, or you can make up your own words. When the preprogrammed words are used, the game randomly selects one or two of them, depending on the number of players. If you want, you can replace the words in the **DATA** statements with your own. Lines 2040-2255 draw the rope and body parts for each player, depending on the number of errors in the variable E.

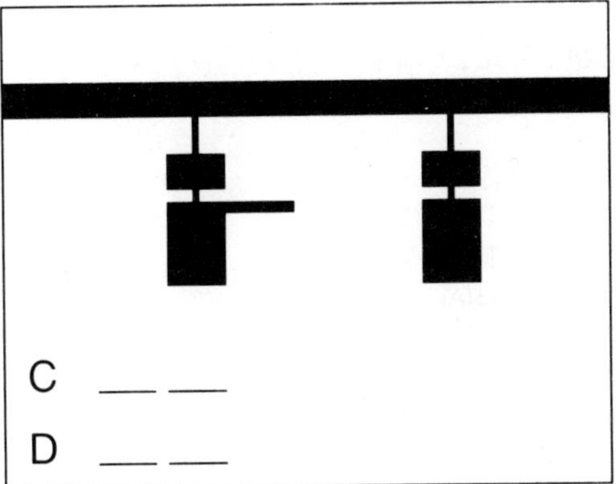

The two string arrays G1$ and G2$, defined in lines 190 and 200, are used to accumulate the past guesses of each person. With this feature you don't need to write down your guesses; the program remembers for you and tells you on each turn what guesses you have made so far.

```
660 CTR=I-1
670 INPUT "1 OR 2 PLAYERS (99 TO QUIT)";P
680 G1=0
690 G2=0
700 P1$=" "
710 P2$=" "
720 YN$=" "
725 REM ALL THREE STRINGS ABOVE
    CONTAIN ONE SPACE
730 IF P=99 THEN 2480
740 IF P<1 THEN 670
750 IF P>2 THEN 670
760 IF P<>2 THEN 840
770 INPUT "PLAYER1'S NAME";P1$
780 INPUT "PLAYER2'S NAME";P2$
790 INPUT "KEY EACH OTHER'S WORDS
    (Y/N)";YN$
800 IF YN$<>"Y" THEN 840
810 INPUT "PLAYER1 KEY PLAYER2'S WORD";
    W2$
820 PRINT CHR$(147)
830 INPUT "PLAYER2 KEY PLAYER1'S WORD";
    W$
840 IF YN$="Y" THEN 900
850 A=INT(CTR*RND(1))+1
860 B=INT(CTR*RND(1))+1
870 W$=X$(A)
880 W2$=X$(B)
890 IF A=B THEN 860
900 Y$=CHR$(100):REM CHR$(100)
    IS AN UNDERSCORE
910 Y2$=CHR$(100)
920 E1=0
930 E2=0
940 LW=LEN(W$)
950 L2=LEN(W2$)
960 FOR I=1 TO LW
970 Y$=Y$+CHR$(100)
980 NEXT I
990 FOR I=1 TO L2
```

If you choose the two-player game in line 670, the players' names are requested in lines 770 and 780. You can key each others' words or let the computer choose words at random (lines 790-890). Lines 900-1010 then create two strings of underscores, one for each letter in the two selected words.

Next, player 1 chooses a letter. If the letter "fits" for any letter(s) of the word selected for player 1 (W$), that letter replaces the underscore(s) in Y$, which is displayed after each turn to allow the players to see what letters they have correctly guessed so far. If a player guesses a letter in the hidden word, a switch (SW$) is set. If the switch is **Y**, ERR1 is not added to. Later, when the hangman is drawn, the number of errors made determines how "complete" a figure is—in other words, how completely a figure is hanging.

This process takes place for player 1 in lines 1030-1230, and for player 2 in lines 1240-1430. Both players have certain displays performed by the same routines, but each player is given different row and column coordinates. For instance, GOSUB 2040 in lines 1500 and 1780 draws the two hangmen, with the number of parts dependent on the number of errors made. Lines 1470-1490 and 1750-1770 define the base row and column, and the number of errors (R, C, and E). The guesses are displayed by lines 1510-1530 and lines 1790-1810. The players' names are printed by lines 1540-1560 and lines 1820-1840.

HANGMAN continues until one of the players is "hung" or until one player has guessed all the letters in his word. Note that

```
1000 Y2$=Y2$+CHR$(100)
1010 NEXT I
1020 PRINT CHR$(147)
1030 INPUT "GUESS A LETTER (PLAYER1)";L$
1040 IF LEN(L$)=LW THEN 2280
1050 G1=G1+1
1060 G1$(G1)=L$
1070 IF LEN(L$)<>1 THEN 1030
1080 IF L$<"A" THEN 1030
1090 IF L$>"Z" THEN 1030
1100 SW$=" "
1110 FOR I=1 TO LW
1120 IF L$<>MID$(W$,I,1) THEN 1180
1130 IF I<>1 THEN 1160
1140 Y$=MID$(W$,I,1)+MID$(Y$,I+1,LW-1)
1150 GOTO 1170
1160 Y$=MID$(Y$,1,I-1)+MID$(W$,I,1)
     +MID$(Y$,I+1,LW-1)
1170 SW$="Y"
1180 NEXT I
1190 PRINT CHR$(147)
1200 IF SW$="Y" THEN 1220
1210 E1=E1+1
1220 GOSUB 1460
1230 IF P<>2 THEN 1020
1240 INPUT "GUESS A LETTER (PLAYER2)";L$
1250 IF LEN(L$)=L2 THEN 2260
1260 G2=G2+1
1270 G2$(G2)=L$
1280 IF LEN(L$)<>1 THEN 1240
1290 IF L$<"A" THEN 1240
1300 IF L$>"Z" THEN 1240
1310 SW$=" "
1320 FOR I=1 TO L2
1330 IF L$<>MID$(W2$,I,1) THEN 1390
1340 IF I<>1 THEN 1370
1350 Y2$=MID$(W2$,I,1)+MID$(Y2$,I+1,L2-1)
1360 GOTO 1380
1370 Y2$=MID$(Y2$,1,I-1)+MID$(W2$,I,1)
     +MID$(Y2$,I+1,L2-1)
```

at any time you may spell out what you think your word is, but if you are wrong—you lose!

```
1380 SW$="Y"
1390 NEXT I
1400 PRINT CHR$(147)
1410 IF SW$="Y" THEN 1430
1420 E2=E2+1
1430 GOSUB 1460
1440 GOTO 1020
1450 PRINT CHR$(147)
1460 FOR I=0 TO 39:R=4:C=I:
     POKE 1024+C+40*R,160
1465 POKE 55296+C+40*R,1:NEXT I
1470 RX=5
1480 CX=7
1490 E=E1
1500 GOSUB 2040
1510 FOR I=1 TO G1
1515 V=ASC(G1$(I))
1520 R=13:C=I+2:V=V-64:GOSUB 2472:
     REM SUBROUTINE TO MOVE IN LETTERS
     TO SCREEN
1530 NEXT I
1540 FOR I=1 TO LEN(P1$)
1545 V=ASC(MID$(P1$,I,1)):IF V=32 THEN V=96
1550 V=V-64:R=12:C=I+2:GOSUB 2472
1560 NEXT I
1570 IF E1>9 THEN 2310
1580 C=1
1590 F1$="N"
1600 FOR I=1 TO LW
1610 C=C+2
1615 V=ASC(MID$(Y$,I,1)):IF V<>100 THEN V=V-64
```

```
1620 R=19:GOSUB 2472
1630 IF MID$(Y$,I,1)<>CHR$(100) THEN 1650
1640 F1$="Y"
1650 NEXT I
1660 V=ASC("P")-64:R=21:C=3:GOSUB 2472
1670 V=ASC("L")-64:C=4:GOSUB 2472
1680 V=ASC("A")-64:C=5:GOSUB 2472
1690 V=ASC("Y")-64:C=6:GOSUB 2472
1700 V=ASC("E")-64:C=7:GOSUB 2472
1710 V=ASC("R")-64:C=8:GOSUB 2472
1720 V=ASC("1"):C=9:GOSUB 2472
1730 IF F1$="N" THEN 2420
1740 IF P=1 THEN 2020
1750 RX=5
1760 CX=25
1770 E=E2
1780 GOSUB 2040
1785 IF G2<1 THEN 1940
1790 FOR I=1 TO G2
1795 V=ASC(G2$(I))
1800 R=16:C=I+2:V=V-64:GOSUB 2472
1810 NEXT I
1820 FOR I=1 TO LEN(P2$)
1825 V=ASC(MID$(P2$,I,1)):IF V=32 THEN V=96
1830 V=V-64:R=15:C=I+2:GOSUB 2472
1840 NEXT I
1850 IF E2>9 THEN 2390
1860 C=1
1870 F1$="N"
1880 FOR I=1 TO L2
1890 C=C+2
1895 V=ASC(MID$(Y2$,I,1)):IF V<>100 THEN V=V-64
1900 R=22:GOSUB 2472
1910 IF MID$(Y2$,I,1)<>CHR$(100) THEN 1930
1920 F1$="Y"
1930 NEXT I
1940 V=ASC("P")-64:R=24:C=3:GOSUB 2472
1950 V=ASC("L")-64:C=4:GOSUB 2472
1960 V=ASC("A")-64:C=5:GOSUB 2472
1970 V=ASC("Y")-64:C=6:GOSUB 2472
1980 V=ASC("E")-64:C=7:GOSUB 2472
1990 V=ASC("R")-64:C=8:GOSUB 2472
2000 V=ASC("2"):C=9:GOSUB 2472
2010 IF F1$="N" THEN 2450
2020 INPUT "RETURN TO CONTINUE";C$
2030 RETURN
2040 V=93:R=RX:C=CX:GOSUB 2472:REM ROPE
2050 IF E<1 THEN 2255
2060 V=81:R=RX+1:C=CX:GOSUB 2472:REM HEAD
2070 IF E<2 THEN 2255
2080 V=160:R=RX+2:C=CX:GOSUB 2472:
     REM BODY
2090 R=RX+3:GOSUB 2472
2100 IF E<3 THEN 2255
2110 V=119:R=RX+2:C=CX+1:GOSUB 2472:
     REM RIGHT ARM
2120 IF E<4 THEN 2255
2130 V=119:R=RX+2:C=CX-1:GOSUB 2472:
     REM LEFT ARM
2140 IF E<5 THEN 2255
2150 V=116:R=RX+4:C=CX+1:GOSUB 2472:
     REM RIGHT LEG
2160 IF E<6 THEN 2255
2170 V=106:R=RX+4:C=CX-1:GOSUB 2472:
     REM LEFT LEG
2180 IF E<7 THEN 2255
2190 V=126:R=RX+2:C=CX+2:GOSUB 2472:
     REM RIGHT HAND
2200 IF E<8 THEN 2255
2210 V=124:R=RX+2:C=CX-2:GOSUB 2472:
     REM LEFT HAND
2220 IF E<9 THEN 2255
2230 V=126:R=RX+5:C=CX+1:GOSUB 2472:
     REM RIGHT FOOT
2240 IF E<10 THEN 2255
2250 V=124:R=RX+5:C=CX-1:GOSUB 2472:
     REM LEFT FOOT
2255 RETURN
2260 IF L$=W2$ THEN 2450
2270 GOTO 2390
```

```
2280 IF L$=W$ THEN 2420
2290 GOTO 2320
2310 REM
2320 PRINT CHR$(147)
2325 PRINT "***********************"
2330 PRINT "*P L A Y E R 1* LOSES*"
2340 PRINT "***********************"
2350 PRINT W$
2360 PRINT W2$
2370 INPUT "RETURN TO CONTINUE";C$
2380 GOTO 670
2390 PRINT CHR$(147)
2395 PRINT "***********************"
2400 PRINT "*P L A Y E R 2* LOSES*"
2410 GOTO 2370
2420 PRINT CHR$(147)
2425 PRINT "***********************"
2430 PRINT "*P L A Y E R 1*WINS*"
2440 GOTO 2340
2450 PRINT CHR$(147)
2455 PRINT "***********************"
2460 PRINT "*P L A Y E R 2*WINS*"
2470 GOTO 2340
2472 REM ****************
2474 POKE 1024+C+40*R,V:POKE 55296+C+40*R,1
2475 RETURN
2480 END
```

LABEL1

```
10 REM  *************************
20 REM  *        LABEL1          *
30 REM  *                        *
40 REM  *    COPYRIGHT 1983      *
50 REM  *  DONALD C. KREUTNER    *
60 REM  *************************
70 PRINT CHR$(147):POKE 53280,14:POKE
   53281,6:PRINT CHR$(5)
75 INPUT "1525 PRTR(1), RS232(2)";PX$
85 IF PX$="1" THEN 100
90 IF PX$="2" THEN 100
95 GOTO 75
100 PR=126
105 IF PX$="1" THEN 115
110 PR=PR+2:OPEN PR,2,0,CHR$(8):
    PR=128:PX$="2":GOTO 120
115 PR=PR+1:OPEN PR,4
120 REM *************************
170 REM EACH LABEL WILL BE PRINTED
180 REM FROM A SET OF 6 RECORDS
190 PRINT CHR$(147)
200 PRINT "RC    READ CASSETTE FILE"
210 PRINT "RD    READ DISK FILE"
220 PRINT "END   END PROGRAM"
230 PRINT
240 INPUT "ACTION";A$
250 IF A$="RC" THEN 280
260 IF A$="RD" THEN 300
270 IF A$="END" THEN 440
280 OPEN 2,2,0:REM OPEN TAPE FOR INPUT
290 GOTO 320
300 INPUT "FILE NAME";D$
310 OPEN 2,8,2,"0:"+D$+",S,R"
320 CTR=0
330 INPUT "START WITH RECORD #";NUM1
```

LABEL1 is one of the programs that uses input from either of the two edit programs, EDIT1 or EDIT2. Other programs in this chapter that also use EDIT1 or EDIT2 are SORT1 and RECIPE1. The two label programs and PRTRCMDS are the only programs in this book that require a printer. If you have a printer now or plan to get one soon, then these programs will be quite useful.

In this program, each label is printed on sticker or gummed labels. LABEL1 must read exactly six records for each label printed. When you key the data to be written to a file in EDIT1 or EDIT2, keep in mind that even if an address has less than six lines, you must still add blank records to "pad" each label to six records. The program allows you to start printing from a certain record in the file. Using the edit programs, you will know exactly which record number to start with if you do not want to print the entire file of labels.

```
340 IF NUM1<1 THEN 330
360 INPUT# 2,X$
370 CTR=CTR+1
380 IF X$="END" THEN 410
390 PRINT# PR,X$
400 GOTO 360
410 CLOSE 2
430 GOTO 190
440 CLOSE PR
450 END
```

LABELP

```
10 REM  **************************
20 REM  *        LABELP          *
30 REM  *                        *
40 REM  *     COPYRIGHT 1983     *
50 REM  *   DONALD C. KREUTNER   *
60 REM  **************************
70 PRINT CHR$(147):POKE 53280,14:POKE
   53281,6:PRINT CHR$(5)
75 INPUT "1525 PRTR(1), RS232(2),";PX$
85 IF PX$="1" THEN 100
90 IF PX$="2" THEN 100
95 GOTO 75
100 PR=126
105 IF PX$="1" THEN 115
110 PR=PR+2:OPEN PR,2,0,CHR$(8):
    PR=128:PX$="2":GOTO 120
115 PR=PR+1:OPEN PR,4
120 REM *************************
180 REM LABELP - PRINTS LABELS USING
190 REM UP TO 6 LINES AND REPEATS
200 REM ANY NUMBER OF LABELS FOR
210 REM THAT ADDRESS
220 REM **************************
230 N1$=" ":N2$=" ":N3$=" ":N4$=" ":N5$=" ":
    N6$=" "
235 INPUT "NAME1 (XXXX TO QUIT)";N1$
240 IF N1$="XXXX" THEN 420
250 INPUT "NAME2";N2$
260 INPUT "NAME3";N3$
270 INPUT "NAME4";N4$
280 INPUT "NAME5";N5$
290 INPUT "NAME6";N6$
300 INPUT "# OF LABELS";N1
320 FOR I=1 TO N1
330 PRINT# PR,N1$
340 PRINT# PR,N2$
```

LABELP is similar to LABEL1, but instead of reading a file of label input data, in LABELP you key the six lines of address information as the program requests it (lines 230-290). You are then asked how many labels you want with this keyed address. If you want 500 return address labels with your own address, you can easily accomplish this task with LABELP. If you want to send information to several addresses, you can make two labels of each, sending one and keeping the other to remind yourself of where you sent the information. Or if you do not need a record, you can simply request one label for each address keyed.

JOHN Q. DOE
1234 ANYROAD AVENUE
ANYTOWN, U.S.A. 99999

JOHN Q. DOE
1234 ANYROAD AVENUE
ANYTOWN, U.S.A. 99999

```
            LABEL P


NAME1 (XXXX TO QUIT):
NAME2:
NAME3:
NAME4:
NAME5:
NAME6:
NUMBER OF LABELS:
```

```
350 PRINT# PR,N3$
360 PRINT# PR,N4$
370 PRINT# PR,N5$
380 PRINT# PR,N6$
390 NEXT I
400 GOTO 230
420 CLOSE PR
430 END
```

PRTRCMDS

```
10 REM  *************************
20 REM  *        PRTRCMDS       *
30 REM  *                       *
40 REM  *     COPYRIGHT 1983    *
50 REM  *   DONALD C. KREUTNER  *
60 REM  *************************
70 PRINT CHR$(147):POKE 53280,14:
   POKE 53281,6:PRINT CHR$(5)
75 INPUT "1525 PRTR(1), RS232(2)";PX$
85 IF PX$="1" THEN 100
90 IF PX$="2" THEN 100
95 GOTO 75
100 PR=126
105 IF PX$="1" THEN 115
110 PR=PR+2:OPEN PR,2,0,CHR$(8):
    PR=128:PX$="2":GOTO 120
115 PR=PR+1:OPEN PR,4
120 REM ************************
180 PRINT CHR$(147)
190 PRINT "CQ    CORRESPONDENCE QUALITY"
200 PRINT "REG   REGULAR QUALITY"
210 PRINT "6LPI  6 LINES PER INCH"
220 PRINT "8LPI  8 LINES PER INCH"
230 PRINT "10CPI 10 CHARACTERS PER INCH"
240 PRINT "12CPI 12 CHARACTERS PER INCH"
250 PRINT "17CPI 17 CHARACTERS PER INCH"
260 PRINT "DOUB DOUBLE WIDTH
                CHARACTERS"
270 PRINT "FF    FORMFEED (TOP OF PAGE)"
280 PRINT "##PG  DESIGNATE PAGE LENGTH"
290 PRINT "PAGE  DEFAULT PAGE LENGTH"
295 PRINT "TYPE  TYPEWRITER MODE"
300 PRINT "END   END PROGRAM"
310 PRINT
320 INPUT "SELECTION";S$
```

PRTRCMDS is a program that enables a printer to enter and leave certain modes of printing. When you use the TYPE command in PRTRCMDS, the printer also will perform like a typewriter. You can select many different print styles and then "type" the desired lines to your printer. PRTRCMDS has been designed for the control codes used on an Okidata Microline 92 printer, but some of the commands will work on many different models of printers.

Before you run PRTRCMDS, look in your printer's manual to see what character sequences cause your printer to do the things you want it to do. As stated in the Introduction, the printer statements used in this book assume a 1200-baud setting, but any other baud rate from 50 to 19,200 is supported by the Commodore 1011A RS-232 interface. To adapt a program for use with a different printer, you may only need to change **CHR$(8)** for 1200 baud to **CHR$(14)** for 9600 baud or to some other setting.

In checking your printer's manual, you should find a control code reference section. Almost all printers use the FF (formfeed) character to align the top of the page with the print head. In this program, FF is given in line 800. The ASCII code for FF is 12, so printing the function **CHR$(12)** to the printer will cause a form feed. Some commands that contain only one character being sent to the printer include FF; the

```
330 IF S$="CQ" THEN 460
340 IF S$="REG" THEN 510
350 IF S$="6LPI" THEN 550
360 IF S$="8LPI" THEN 590
370 IF S$="10CPI" THEN 630
380 IF S$="12CPI" THEN 670
390 IF S$="17CPI" THEN 710
400 IF S$="DOUB" THEN 750
410 IF S$="FF" THEN 790
420 IF S$="PAGE" THEN 850
425 IF S$="TYPE" THEN 930
430 IF MID$(S$,3,2)="PG" THEN 820
440 IF S$="END" THEN 970
450 GOTO 180
460 REM *****CORR QUALITY*****
470 GOSUB 880
480 PRINT# PR,CHR$(27);"1"
490 GOSUB 900
500 GOTO 180
510 REM *****REGULAR QUALITY*****
520 GOSUB 880
530 GOSUB 900
540 GOTO 180
550 REM *****6 LPI*****
560 PRINT# PR,CHR$(27);"6"
570 GOSUB 900
580 GOTO 180
590 REM *****8 LPI*****
600 PRINT# PR,CHR$(27);"8"
610 GOSUB 900
620 GOTO 180
630 REM *****10 CPI*****
640 PRINT# PR,CHR$(30)
650 GOSUB 900
660 GOTO 180
670 REM *****12 CPI*****
680 PRINT# PR,CHR$(28)
690 GOSUB 900
700 GOTO 180
710 REM *****17 CPI*****
```

10CPI (10 characters per inch) command RS (ASCII 30); the 12CPI command FS (ASCII 28); and the 17CPI command GS (ASCII 29). Printing of regular quality is caused by the CAN character (ASCII 24), which returns the printer to its default values.

Double-width characters are started by sending the US (ASCII 31) code to the printer.

Many printer commands are called "escape sequences." In other words, the printer escapes from its printing responsibility to perform a setup function.

Escape functions used in PRTRCMDS include the following:

1. Correspondence-quality printing is obtained by printing the escape sequence ESC-1 (ASCII 27, or escape; followed by ASCII 49, the ASCII number for the character "1").
2. 6LPI (6 lines per inch) is designated by ESC-6 (ASCII 27, or escape, and the character "6").
3. 8LPI is caused by the ESC-8 sequence.
4. A different page length is caused by sending the sequence ESC-F, followed by a two-digit number that represents the page length.

After many of these commands have been given to the printer, two lines of X's and a test pattern can be printed in lines 900-910 to demonstrate what mode the printer is now in. You can, for example, run this program to cause better quality printing

```
720 PRINT# PR,CHR$(29)
730 GOSUB 900
740 GOTO 180
750 REM *****DOUBLE WIDTH*****
760 PRINT# PR,CHR$(31)
770 GOSUB 900
780 GOTO 180
790 REM *****TOP OF FORM*****
800 PRINT# PR,CHR$(12)
810 GOTO 180
820 REM *****NEW PAGE LENGTH*****
830 PRINT# PR,CHR$(27);"F";MID$(S$,1,1)
840 GOTO 790
850 REM *****DEFAULT PAGE LENGTH*****
860 PRINT# PR,CHR$(27);"F";"66"
870 GOTO 790
880 PRINT# PR,CHR$(24)
890 RETURN
900 INPUT "PRINT TEST PATTERN (Y/N)";TPYN$
902 IF TPYN$<>"Y" THEN 920
904 PRINT# PR,"XXXXXXXXXXXXXXXXXXXX"
906 PRINT# PR,"XXXXXXXXXXXXXXXXXXXX"
908 PRINT# PR,"ABCDEFGHIJKLMNOPQRSTUVW
    XYZ0123456789"
910 PRINT# PR,"!@#$%^&*()+=-/:;<,>.[]?'"
920 RETURN
930 PRINT "TYPE LINE (END TO STOP):"
935 INPUT I$
940 IF I$="END" THEN 180
950 PRINT# PR,I$
960 GOTO 930
970 CLOSE PR
980 END
```

before running another program that uses the printer. Or the program that does the printing can send the printer the appropriate codes immediately after opening the printer file.

```
CQ      CORRESPONDENCE QUALITY
REG     REGULAR QUALITY
6LPI    6 LINES PER INCH
8LPI    8 LINES PER INCH
10CPI   10 CHARS PER INCH
12CPI   12 CHARS PER INCH
17CPI   17 CHARS PER INCH
DOUB    DOUBLE WIDTH CHARS
FF      FORMFEED (TOP OF PAGE)
##PG    DESIGNATE PAGE LENGTH
PAGE    DEFAULT PAGE LENGTH
END     END PROGRAM
```

```
XXXXXXXXXXXXXXXXXXXX
XXXXXXXXXXXXXXXXXXXX
ABCDEFGHIJKLMNOPQRSTUVWXYZ0123456789
!@#$%^&*()+=-/:;<,>.~[]_?'|{}\`
THE ABOVE IS REGULAR QUALITY
```

```
XXXXXXXXXXXXXXXXXXXX
XXXXXXXXXXXXXXXXXXXX
ABCDEFGHIJKLMNOPQRSTUVWXYZ0123456789
!@#$%^&*()+=-/:;<,>.~[]_?'|{}\`
AND THIS IS CORRESPONDENCE
QUALITY; REMEMBER THE
TEST PATTERN IS OPTIONAL
WHEN CHANGING PRTR CMDS

XXXXXXXXXXXXXXXXXXXX
XXXXXXXXXXXXXXXXXXXX
ABCDEFGHIJKLMNOPQRSTUVWXYZ0123456789
!@#$%^&*()+=-/:;<,>.~[]_?'|{}\`
THIS IS 10CPI (CHARS PER INCH)

XXXXXXXXXXXXXXXXXXXX
XXXXXXXXXXXXXXXXXXXX
ABCDEFGHIJKLMNOPQRSTUVWXYZ0123456789
!@#$%^&*()+=-/:;<,>.~[]_?'|{}\`
AND THIS IS 12CPI

AND DOUBLE WIDTH
ABCDEFGHIJKLMNOPQR
STUVWXYZ0123456789

XXXXXXXXXXXXXXXXXXXX
XXXXXXXXXXXXXXXXXXXX
ABCDEFGHIJKLMNOPQRSTUVWXYZ0123456789
!@#$%^&*()+=-/:;<,>.~[]_?'|{}\`
17CPI WORKS ONLY IN REGULAR MODE

XXXXXXXXXXXXXXXXXXXX
XXXXXXXXXXXXXXXXXXXX
ABCDEFGHIJKLMNOPQRSTUVWXYZ0123456789
!@#$%^&*()+=-/:;<,>.~[]_?'|{}\`
ABOVE IS 6LPI (LINES PER INCH)

XXXXXXXXXXXXXXXXXXXX
XXXXXXXXXXXXXXXXXXXX
ABCDEFGHIJKLMNOPQRSTUVWXYZ0123456789
!@#$%^&*()+=-/:;<,>.~[]_?'|{}\`
AND 8LPI...
```

RECIPE1

```
10 REM * * * * * * * * * * * * * * * * * * * * * * * * *
20 REM *              RECIPE1              *
30 REM *                                   *
40 REM *          COPYRIGHT 1983           *
50 REM *        DONALD C. KREUTNER         *
60 REM * * * * * * * * * * * * * * * * * * * * * * * * *
70 PRINT CHR$(147):POKE 53280,14:
   POKE 53281,6:PRINT CHR$(5)
120 REM ************************
170 DIM N$(300)
180 CTR=0
190 DATA 01. CHOCOLATE CAKE
200 DATA CHOPPED WALNUTS/1/C
210 DATA FLOUR/2/C
220 DATA CHOCOLATE/.5/C
230 DATA SUGAR/1/C
240 DATA BLEND FLOUR WATER & SUGAR
250 DATA WATER/1/C
260 DATA END RECIPE
270 DATA 02. SUGAR COOKIES
280 DATA FLOUR/2/C
290 DATA SUGAR/1/C
300 DATA WATER/1/C
310 DATA END RECIPE
320 DATA END
330 PRINT CHR$(147)
340 INPUT "DATA FROM PROGRAM OR FILE
   (P/F)";PF$
350 IF PF$="P" THEN 380
360 IF PF$="F" THEN 430
370 GOTO 180
380 READ NAME$
390 CTR=CTR+1
400 N$(CTR)=NAME$
410 IF NAME$="END" THEN 590
420 GOTO 350
```

RECIPE1 is a simple, yet versatile program that can be used to save ingredients and their quantities, as well as detailed preparation instructions for recipes or other types of "formula" applications, such as paint blending or chemical mixing.

With RECIPE1 you can also specify any multiple of the original recipe and thus obtain the amounts required for its ingredients.

Two basic functions are available: (1) to list the menu of recipes that can be displayed in detail, and (2) to print the specific ingredients and instructions for one recipe at a time.

The information can come from **DATA** statements contained within the program (lines 190-320). You can have different programs with different menus using different **DATA** statements.

Perhaps a more practical way to save your recipe information is to have only one program version (with certain frequently used recipes "built in" to **DATA** statements), and to read any desired file containing recipes. With this method, you can specify in line 340 whether you want to use the data in the program or in a file. Then, if you select a file, line 430 asks you whether the file is on cassette tape or disk. If the program data is chosen, lines 380-410 read the information from the **DATA** statements into the array N$, which can hold up to 300 lines of data. If a file is chosen, lines 510-

```
430 INPUT "CASSETTE OR DISK (C/D)";CD$
440 IF CD$="C" THEN 470
450 IF CD$="D" THEN 490
460 GOTO 430
470 OPEN 2,2,0:REM OPEN TAPE FOR INPUT
480 GOTO 510
490 INPUT "FILE NAME";D$
500 OPEN 2,8,2,"0:"+D$+",S,R"
510 FOR I=1 TO 300
520 INPUT# 2,NAME$
530 CTR=I
540 N$(I)=NAME$
550 IF NAME$="END" THEN 570
560 NEXT I
570 CLOSE 2
590 PRINT "M      MENU OF RECIPES"
600 PRINT "##.    PRINT RECIPE ##"
610 PRINT "END  END PROGRAM"
620 PRINT
630 PRINT
640 PRINT
650 INPUT "SELECTION";S$
660 IF S$="M" THEN 700
670 IF MID$(S$,3,1)="." THEN 760
680 IF S$="END" THEN 1150
690 GOTO 650
700 PRINT CHR$(147)
710 FOR I=1 TO CTR
720 IF MID$(N$(I),3,1)<>"." THEN 740
730 PRINT N$(I)
740 NEXT I
750 GOTO 590
760 FOR I=1 TO CTR
770 IF S$<>MID$(N$(I),1,3) THEN 800
780 REC$=N$(I)
790 GOTO 830
800 NEXT I
810 PRINT "RECIPE#: ";S$;" NOT FOUND"
820 GOTO 590
830 INPUT "MULTIPLE OF RECIPE: ";MU
```

570 read the data from the selected file into the same N$ array.

Once the data has been stored in the array, its manipulation by the program is a simple matter. To list a menu of the available recipes loaded, just key **M** to the menu screen, and lines 700-740 read through the array, looking for lines that have a period in the third position. These lines are then listed (the "title" lines for the recipe records that follow them).

If you request a printout for a specific recipe, the program looks through the file for the title record, starting with the same ## and period (.) that you requested. The multiple you specify in line 830 is then multiplied by the quantities of each ingredient to get the totals needed.

Remember that in the programs EDIT1 and EDIT2, RECIPE1 was mentioned as one of the programs that could use data keyed by either of these two programs. Just make certain when you create a file (or **DATA** statements) that you begin each recipe with a **##.** and follow the period with a space and then the title of the recipe.

Then records for ingredients or preparation instructions can follow in any order since the RECIPE1 program "knows" which record is which. If there is no slash (/) in the line, the record is an instruction line, whereas ingredient lines have slashes separating the ingredient from the quantity and the quantity from the "unit of measure" field (for example, C for cup, T for tablespoon, or any other measurements you may want to use).

```
840 PRINT CHR$(147)
850 PRINT REC$;" ";MU;"(MULT)"
860 FOR J=I+1 TO CTR
870 IF N$(J)="END RECIPE" THEN 1130
880 LS=LEN(N$(J))
890 L1=0
900 L2=0
905 REM L1 AND L2 ARE THE LOCATIONS
    OF SLASH 1 AND SLASH 2
910 FOR L=1 TO LS
920 IF MID$(N$(J),L,1)<>"/" THEN 970
930 IF L1<>0 THEN 960
940 L1=L
950 GOTO 970
960 L2=L
970 NEXT L
980 IF L1=0 THEN 1110
990 INGRED$=MID$(N$(J),1,L1-1)
1000 IF L1<>0 THEN 1050
1010 IF L2<>0 THEN 1050
1020 QTY=0
1030 MEAS$=" "
1040 GOTO 1090
1050 QTY$=MID$(N$(J),L1+1,L2-L1-1)
1060 QTY=VAL(QTY$)
1070 MEAS$=MID$(N$(J),L2+1,LS-L2)
1080 QTY=QTY*MU
1090 PRINT INGRED$;TAB(20);QTY;TAB(25);MEAS$
1100 GOTO 1120
1110 PRINT N$(J)
1120 NEXT J
1130 INPUT "CONTINUE (Y/N)";YN$
1140 IF YN$="Y" THEN 590
1150 END
```

Each recipe must end with an "END RECIPE" line to tell the program when to stop listing the recipe. This **DATA** statement is necessary to tell the program when to stop reading data. If reading from a file, the EDIT1/EDIT2 programs automatically put an "END" record at the end of the file.

```
RECIPE1

01. ROAST BEEF AU GRATIN
02. BARBEQUED CHICKEN
03. SWEDISH MEATBALLS
04. PIZZA
05. BEEF STROGANOFF
```

SCREEN1

```
10 REM  **************************
20 REM  *          SCREEN1          *
30 REM  *                           *
40 REM  *       COPYRIGHT 1983      *
50 REM  *     DONALD C. KREUTNER    *
60 REM  **************************
70 PRINT CHR$(147):POKE 53280,14:
   POKE 53281,6:PRINT CHR$(5)
190 INPUT "REPEAT 1 LINE OR 5 (1/5)";R$
200 IF R$="1" THEN 230
210 IF R$="5" THEN 440
220 GOTO 170
230 INPUT "MSG";A$
240 X=LEN(A$)
250 IF X>38 THEN 230
260 INPUT "# OF LINES";REPS
270 INPUT "SCREENS";S
280 FOR K=1 TO S
290 PRINT CHR$(147)
300 FOR J=1 TO REPS
310 FOR I=1 TO X
315 ROW=J+1:COL=I+1
320 V=ASC(MID$(A$,I,1)):IF V>63 AND V<95
    THEN V=V-64
325 POKE 1024+COL+40*ROW,V
330 POKE 55296+COL+40*ROW,1
335 NEXT I
340 NEXT J
350 FOR J=REPS TO 1 STEP -1
360 FOR I=X TO 1 STEP-1
370 ROW=J+1:COL=I+1
375 POKE 1024+COL+40*ROW,32
377 POKE 55296+COL+40*ROW,1
380 NEXT I
390 NEXT J
400 NEXT K
```

SCREEN1 is an interesting message program. If you have to leave at 4:45 p.m., and a family member is coming home at 5:00 p.m., just start up this program. Your relative can read a message (of up to five lines) that fills and clears the screen repeatedly.

Two variations are available: to repeat one line any number of times or to repeat five lines any number of times. If you select the one liner, the screen will fill up with that line, one character at a time, and then erase, one character at a time, from right to left and bottom to top—unusual, to say the least!

The one-line variation is in lines 230-400, while the five-line message is in lines 440-920. The **POKE** statement is used to move one character at a time from the string(s) you keyed as messages to be displayed.

```
SCREEN1 WILL DISPLAY
A MSG ON THE SCREEN OF UP TO
5 LINES 1 CHARACTER AT A TIME
AND THEN ERASE THE SCREEN
AND REPEAT THE MSG DISPLAY
```

```
410 INPUT "MORE (Y/N)";YN$
420 IF YN$="Y" THEN 170
430 GOTO 930
440 INPUT "MSGA";A$
450 XA=LEN(A$)
460 IF XA>38 THEN 440
470 INPUT "MSGB";B$
480 XB=LEN(B$)
490 IF XB>38 THEN 470
500 INPUT "MSGC";C$
510 XC=LEN(C$)
520 IF XC>38 THEN 500
530 INPUT "MSGD";D$
540 XD=LEN(D$)
550 IF XD>38 THEN 530
560 INPUT "MSGE";E$
570 XE=LEN(E$)
580 IF XE>38 THEN 560
590 INPUT "CONTINUE (Y/N)";Y2$
600 IF Y2$<>"Y" THEN 190
610 INPUT "DELAY (0-1000)";DELAY
620 INPUT "# OF REPETITIONS";R2
630 FOR K=1 TO R2
640 PRINT CHR$(147)
650 IF XA<1 THEN 690
660 FOR I=1 TO XA
670 ROW=2:COL=I+1:V=ASC(MID$(A$,I,1)):
    IF V>63 AND V<95 THEN V=V-64
675 POKE 1024+COL+40*ROW,V:
    POKE 55296+COL+40*ROW,1
680 NEXT I
690 IF XB<1 THEN 730
700 FOR I=1 TO XB
710 ROW=3:COL=I+1:V=ASC(MID$(B$,I,1)):
    IF V>63 AND V<95 THEN V=V-64
715 POKE 1024+COL+40*ROW,V:
    POKE 55296+COL+40*ROW,1
720 NEXT I
730 IF XC<1 THEN 770
740 FOR I=1 TO XC
750 ROW=4:COL=I+1:V=ASC(MID$(C$,I,1)):
    IF V>63 AND V<95 THEN V=V-64
755 POKE 1024+COL+40*ROW,V:
    POKE 55296+COL+40*ROW,1
760 NEXT I
770 IF XD<1 THEN 810
780 FOR I=1 TO XD
790 ROW=5:COL=I+1:V=ASC(MID$(D$,I,1)):
    IF V>63 AND V<95 THEN V=V-64
795 POKE 1024+COL+40*ROW,V:
    POKE 55296+COL+40*ROW,1
800 NEXT I
810 IF XE<1 THEN 850
820 FOR I=1 TO XE
830 ROW=6:COL=I+1:V=ASC(MID$(E$,I,1)):
    IF V>63 AND V<95 THEN V=V-64
835 POKE 1024+COL+40*ROW,V:
    POKE 55296+COL+40*ROW,1
840 NEXT I
850 FOR I=7 TO 10
860 FOR J=2 TO 38
870 ROW=I:COL=J
880 POKE 1024+COL+40*ROW,42:
    POKE 55296+COL+40*ROW,1
895 NEXT J
900 NEXT I
905 IF DELAY<1 THEN 920
910 FOR I=1 TO DELAY:NEXT I
920 NEXT K
925 GOTO 410
930 END
```

SORT1

```
10 REM **************************
20 REM *          SORT1         *
30 REM *                        *
40 REM *      COPYRIGHT 1983    *
50 REM *   DONALD C. KREUTNER    *
60 REM **************************
70 PRINT CHR$(147):POKE 53280,14:
   POKE 53281,6:PRINT CHR$(5)
75 INPUT "1525 PRTR(1), RS232(2),
   NONE(3)";PX$
80 IF PX$="3" THEN 120
85 IF PX$="1" THEN 100
90 IF PX$="2" THEN 100
95 GOTO 75
100 PR=126
105 IF PX$="1" THEN 115
110 PR=PR+2:OPEN PR,2,0,CHR$(8):PR=128:
    PX$="2":GOTO 120
115 PR=PR+1:OPEN PR,4
120 REM *************************
180 DIM BEG(19)
190 DIM LNG(19)
200 DIM X$(500)
210 PRINT CHR$(147)
220 PRINT "R    READ FILE"
230 PRINT "S    SORT FILE"
240 PRINT "W    WRITE FILE"
250 PRINT "L    LIST FILE"
260 PRINT "E    END PROGRAM"
270 PRINT
280 INPUT "ACTION";A$
290 IF A$="R" THEN 340
300 IF A$="S" THEN 500
310 IF A$="W" THEN 1090
320 IF A$="L" THEN 890
330 IF A$="E" THEN 1220
```

SORT1 is a versatile tool that can sort any file entered or modified by EDIT1 or EDIT2. In using SORT1 you can specify a sort key composed of up to ten fields in any positions of the record.

For example, let's consider a record composed of an account number of four digits; a name field of 20 positions, with last name first; a telephone number field of ten positions, with hyphens included; and an outstanding balance field, with leading zeros and a total of eight digits. Let's say that each field is separated from the previous field by a space. The record layout can be described as follows:

Pos. 01-04 Acct Number
Pos. 06-25 Last-First Name
Pos. 27-36 Telephone #
Pos. 38-45 Balance Due

Although this record provides a very simple example, you can use many more fields in the records keyed by EDIT1 or EDIT2. But even with records as short as this one, SORT1 enables you to sort, resort, and print (on the screen or a printer) data from this kind of record in many ways:

By account number only
By balance due by account number
By last name by account number
By telephone number

Note one final caution about entering the data: be sure to include the appropriate spaces in every field of every record. In the example above, all account numbers are

```
340 PRINT CHR$(147):REM CLR SCREEN
350 INPUT "READ FROM CASSETTE OR DISK
    (C/D)";CD$
360 IF CD$="C" THEN 420
370 IF CD$="D" THEN 390
380 GOTO 340
390 INPUT "FILE NAME";D$
400 OPEN 2,8,2,"0:"+D$+",S,R"
410 GOTO 430
420 OPEN 2,2,0:REM OPEN TAPE FOR INPUT
430 FOR I=1 TO 498
440 INPUT# 2,X$(I)
450 IF X$(I)="END" THEN 470
460 NEXT I
470 CTR=I-1
480 CLOSE 2
490 GOTO 210
500 J=0
510 INPUT "ASCENDING OR DESCENDING
    (A/D)";AD$
520 J=J+1
530 PRINT "SORT KEY # ";J
540 INPUT "BEG LOC OF FIELD
    (999 TO STOP)";B
550 IF B=999 THEN 600
560 INPUT "LENGTH OF FIELD";L
570 BEG(J)=B
580 LNG(J)=L
590 GOTO 520
600 CS=J-1
610 PASS1=0
620 SW$="N"
630 PASS1=PASS1+1
640 PRINT CHR$(147)
650 PRINT "SORT PASS ";PASS1
660 FOR I=1 TO CTR-1
670 S1$=" "
680 S2$=" ":REM S1$ AND S2$ CONTAIN
    ONE SPACE
690 FOR J=1 TO CS
```

four characters in length, followed by a space; all name fields are 20 characters long (even if the field requires ten or more trailing spaces), followed by a space; and so on. In short, each record keyed by the edit program should have fields located directly beneath the corresponding fields of the last record.

When you run the SORT1 program, the following options will appear on the menu screen: **READ** a file, **SORT** a file, **WRITE** a sorted file, **LIST** a sorted file to the screen or to a printer, or **END** the program. These functions are accomplished in lines 280-330 by keying **R**, **S**, **W**, **L**, or **E**.

The file can be read in from cassette or disk in lines 350-480.

A sort is accomplished by lines 500-870. Line 510 allows you to specify whether you want the sort to be in ascending or descending sequence. If you sort by amount due, you may want the largest amounts to appear first. Then lines 520-590 allow you to describe the beginning location of each sort field and the length of each. For example, to sort by Last Name by Account Number, you specify position 27 for the starting location of sort field 1, with a length of 20; and position 1 for the location of sort field 2, with a length of 4. Then you key **999** in line 540 for the third sort field (to indicate that there are no more fields).

The actual sorting takes place in lines 620-860. Lines 690-720 "construct" the sort field from the subsort fields you defined. Then lines 730-840 switch the data elements if they are out of sequence (for ascending or descending sequences).

```
700 S1$=S1$+MID$(X$(I),BEG(J),LNG(J))
710 S2$=S2$+MID$(X$(I+1),BEG(J),LNG(J))
720 NEXT J
730 IF AD$="D" THEN 800
740 IF S1$<=S2$ THEN 850
750 X1$=X$(I)
760 X$(I)=X$(I+1)
770 X$(I+1)=X1$
780 SW$="Y"
790 GOTO 850
800 IF S1$>=S2$ THEN 850
810 X1$=X$(I)
820 X$(I)=X$(I+1)
830 X$(I+1)=X1$
840 SW$="Y"
850 NEXT I
860 IF SW$="Y" THEN 620
870 PRINT "SORT COMPLETE"
880 GOTO 210
890 PRINT CHR$(147)
900 INPUT "PRINTER (Y/N)";PYN$
905 INPUT "TITLE";T$
910 IF PX$="3" THEN PYN$="N"
930 INPUT "PAUSE (Y/N)";PA$
940 CP=0
944 PRINT T$
945 PRINT
946 IF PYN$<>"Y" THEN 950
947 PRINT# PR,T$
948 PRINT# PR
950 FOR I=1 TO CTR
960 PRINT X$(I)
970 CP=CP+1
980 IF PA$<>"Y" THEN 1020
990 IF CP<20 THEN 1020
1000 INPUT "RETURN TO CONTINUE";E$
1010 CP=0
1020 IF PYN$<>"Y" THEN 1040
1030 PRINT# PR,X$(I)
1040 NEXT I
```

Lines 900-1040 display the sorted data on the screen and/or to a printer.

Finally, in lines 1090-1200 the sorted file can be saved to a new file or to the same file as was input, if desired.

SORT1 can be a most powerful tool.

```
1070 INPUT "RETURN TO CONTINUE";E$
1080 GOTO 210
1090 INPUT "CASSETTE OR DISK (C/D)";CD$
1100 IF CD$="D" THEN 1140
1110 IF CD$<>"C" THEN 1090
1120 OPEN 2,1,2:REM OPEN TAPE FOR OUTPUT
1130 GOTO 1160
1140 INPUT "FILE NAME";D$
1150 OPEN 2,8,2,+D$+",S,W"
1160 FOR I=1 TO CTR
1170 PRINT# 2,X$(I)
1180 NEXT I
1190 PRINT# 2,"END"
1200 CLOSE 2
1210 GOTO 210
1220 IF PX$="3" THEN 1240
1230 CLOSE PR
1240 END
```

UNSORTED DATA AS READ FROM FILE

ACCT	NAME(LAST FIRST)	TELEPHONE	BAL DUE
0001	Jones Robert	588-9912	00080000
0003	Edwards Barnaby	466-2314	00004556
0002	Kramer James	233-1254	00000000
0210	White Mike	555-1234	00009803
0032	Hanferd Hank	324-9983	00000300
0021	Smith Sam	432-1256	00021025

DATA SORTED BY ACCOUNT NUMBER (ASCENDING)

0001	Jones Robert	588-9912	00080000
0002	Kramer James	233-1254	00000000
0003	Edwards Barnaby	466-2314	00004556
0021	Smith Sam	432-1256	00021025
0032	Hanferd Hank	324-9983	00000300
0210	White Mike	555-1234	00009803

DATA SORTED BY BAL DUE BY ACCT# (DESCENDING)

0001	Jones Robert	588-9912	00080000
0021	Smith Sam	432-1256	00021025
0210	White Mike	555-1234	00009803
0003	Edwards Barnaby	466-2314	00004556
0032	Hanferd Hank	324-9983	00000300
0002	Kramer James	233-1254	00000000

DATA SORTED BY ACCOUNT NUMBER (DESCENDING)

0210	White Mike	555-1234	00009803
0032	Hanferd Hank	324-9983	00000300
0021	Smith Sam	432-1256	00021025
0003	Edwards Barnaby	466-2314	00004556
0002	Kramer James	233-1254	00000000
0001	Jones Robert	588-9912	00080000

DATA SORTED BY LAST NAME BY ACCT#

0003	Edwards Barnaby	466-2314	00004556
0032	Hanferd Hank	324-9983	00000300
0001	Jones Robert	588-9912	00080000
0002	Kramer James	233-1254	00000000
0021	Smith Sam	432-1256	00021025
0210	White Mike	555-1234	00009803

```
DATA SORTED BY TELEPHONE#

0002        Kramer James        233-1254        00000000
0032        Hanferd Hank        324-9983        00000300
0021        Smith Sam           432-1256        00021025
0003        Edwards Barnaby     466-2314        00004556
0210        White Mike          555-1234        00009803
0001        Jones Robert        588-9912        00080000
```

TAG

```
10 REM *************************
20 REM *          TAG          *
30 REM *                       *
40 REM *     COPYRIGHT 1983    *
50 REM *   DONALD C. KREUTNER  *
60 REM *************************
70 PRINT CHR$(147):POKE 53280,14:
   POKE 53281,6:PRINT CHR$(5)
190 INPUT "MAX MOVES";MAX
200 ADD1$=" "
210 DOT$="C"
260 FLAG$=" "
270 REM FLAG$ CONTAINS ONE SPACE
300 SA=0
310 SB=0
320 GOSUB 940
330 COUNT=0
340 RA=3
350 CA=20
360 R2A=RA
370 C2A=CA
380 RB=21
390 CB=20
400 R3B=RB
410 C3B=CB
420 GOSUB 1000
430 GOSUB 1200
440 GOSUB 1400
450 IF ADD1$="A" THEN 1530
460 IF COUNT>=MAX THEN 1530
480 GET N$:IF N$="" THEN 480
490 IF N$="1" THEN 1710
500 IF N$="A" THEN 680
510 IF N$="S" THEN 710
520 IF N$="W" THEN 740
530 IF N$="Z" THEN 770
```

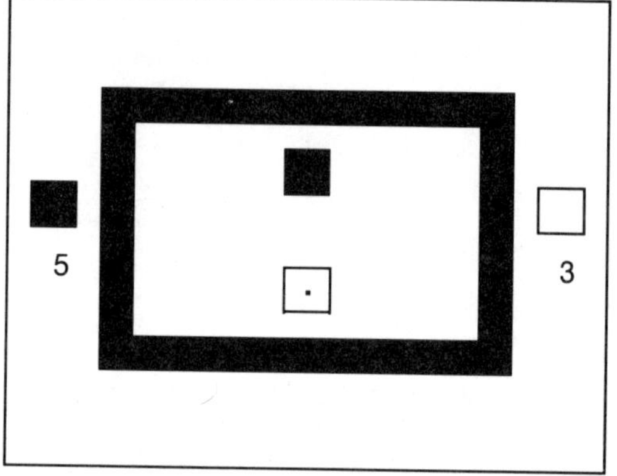

TAG, as the name implies, is a game in which two players try to catch one another, each taking turns at being "it." At the beginning of the program, you can specify the number of moves (line 190) in which the player who is "it" must try to catch the other player. One player is a solid dark square, while the other is a light square with a border around it. The scores of the two players are constantly visible to the left and right of the "playing field"—a large rectangle surrounded by dark borders through which a player cannot pass.

One player moves up, down, left, or right, using the arrow keys (**W**, **Z**, **A**, and **S**), while the other player uses the **@**, **/**, **:**, and **;** ("at" sign, slash, colon, and semicolon).

You can tell who is "it" by seeing which player has a reversed video character. Both players begin chasing or running until the one being chased gets caught (by occupy-

```
540 IF N$=":" THEN 800
550 IF N$=";" THEN 830
560 IF N$="@" THEN 860
570 IF N$="/" THEN 890
580 GOTO 480
680 REM
685 CA=CA-1
690 GOSUB 1000
700 GOTO 450
710 REM
715 CA=CA+1
720 GOSUB 1000
730 GOTO 450
740 REM
745 RA=RA-1
750 GOSUB 1000
760 GOTO 450
770 REM
775 RA=RA+1
780 GOSUB 1000
790 GOTO 450
800 REM
805 CB=CB-1
810 GOSUB 1200
820 GOTO 450
830 REM
835 CB=CB+1
840 GOSUB 1200
850 GOTO 450
860 REM
865 RB=RB-1
870 GOSUB 1200
880 GOTO 450
890 REM
895 RB=RB+1
900 GOSUB 1200
910 GOTO 450
940 PRINT CHR$(147)
950 FOR CL=5 TO 34
954 ROW=1:POKE 1024+CL+40*ROW,160
```

ing the same location as the player who is "it"), or until the maximum number of moves is reached. Then the appropriate player gets a point (for eluding or catching), the roles are switched, and the other player is "it."

The characters **POKE**d to the screen for player 1 are ASCII 87 (a graphic circle) and 215 (a reverse video, or "filled in" circle). Player 2 is represented by ASCII 91 (a crossbar) and 219 (a reversed crossbar). When a player is "it," the reverse video character is displayed. To **POKE** any character in reverse video mode, you just add 128 to the ASCII value of the character. (See lines 1130, 1180, 1330, and 1380.) The row and column position of each player is kept track of in RA, CA, RB, and CB. Lines 480-580 check for one of the appropriate keys to be pressed, indicating in which direction a player's figure is to be moved. These movements are effected in lines 680-900 and by the subroutines starting in line 1000 for one player and in line 1200 for the other. After each move, the positions are checked for boundaries that cannot be passed, for the figures occupying the same location, and for the maximum number of moves being reached.

Obviously, TAG is not the most advanced of arcade games, but it does show, in a fairly straightforward manner, how players can maneuver around a "board" and chase or run from an opponent.

```
956 POKE 55296+CL+40*ROW,1
958 NEXT CL
960 FOR CL=5 TO 34
964 ROW=23:POKE 1024+CL+40*ROW,160
966 POKE 55296+CL+40*ROW,1
968 NEXT CL
970 FOR ROW=2 TO 23
974 CL=5:POKE 1024+CL+40*ROW,160
976 POKE 55296+CL+40*ROW,1
978 NEXT ROW
980 FOR ROW=2 TO 23
984 CL=34:POKE 1024+CL+40*ROW,160
986 POKE 55296+CL+40*ROW,1
988 NEXT ROW
990 RETURN
1000 IF RA<2 THEN 1110
1010 IF RA>22 THEN 1110
1020 IF CA<6 THEN 1110
1030 IF CA>33 THEN 1110
1040 POKE 1024+C2A+40*R2A,32:
     POKE 55296+C2A+40*R2A,1
1050 R2A=RA
1060 C2A=CA
1080 IF DOT$="C" THEN 1100
1090 COUNT=COUNT+1
1100 GOTO 1130
1110 RA=R2A
1120 CA=C2A
1130 POKE 1024+CA+40*RA,87:
     POKE 55296+CA+40*RA,1
1140 IF RA<>RB THEN 1170
1150 IF CA<>CB THEN 1170
1160 ADD1$="A"
1170 IF DOT$="C" THEN 1190
1180 POKE 1024+CA+40*RA,215:
     POKE 55296+CA+40*RA,1
1190 RETURN
1200 IF RB<2 THEN 1310
1210 IF RB>22 THEN 1310
1220 IF CB<6 THEN 1310
1230 IF CB>33 THEN 1310
1240 POKE 1024+C3B+40*R3B,32:
     POKE 55296+C3B+40*R3B,1
1250 R3B=RB
1260 C3B=CB
1280 IF DOT$="S" THEN 1300
1290 COUNT=COUNT+1
1300 GOTO 1330
1310 RB=R3B
1320 CB=C3B
1330 POKE 1024+CB+40*RB,91:
     POKE 55296+CB+40*RB,1
1340 IF RA<>RB THEN 1370
1350 IF CA<>CB THEN 1370
1360 ADD1$="A"
1370 IF DOT$="S" THEN 1390
1380 POKE 1024+CB+40*RB,219:
     POKE 55296+CB+40*RB,1
1390 RETURN
1400 ROW=12:CL=2
1402 POKE 1024+CL+40*ROW,87:
     POKE 55296+CL+40*ROW,1
1403 ROW=12:CL=36
1404 POKE 1024+CL+40*ROW,91:
     POKE 55296+CL+40*ROW,1
1420 SA$=STR$(SA)
1430 SB$=STR$(SB)
1440 ROW=14:CL=2:
     POKE 1024+CL+40*ROW,ASC(MID$(SA$,2,1)):
     POKE 55296+CL+40*ROW,1
1450 IF SA<10 THEN 1470
1460 ROW=14:CL=3:
     POKE 1024+CL+40*ROW,ASC(MID$(SA$,3,1)):
     POKE 55296+CL+40*ROW,1
1470 ROW=14:CL=36:
     POKE 1024+CL+40*ROW,ASC(MID$(SB$,2,1)):
     POKE 55296+CL+40*ROW,1
1480 IF SB<10 THEN 1500
```

```
1490 ROW=14:CL=37:
     POKE 1024+CL+40*ROW,ASC(MID$(SB$,3,1)):
     POKE 55296+CL+40*ROW,1
1500 RETURN
1530 IF DOT$="C" THEN 1600
1540 IF COUNT>=MAX THEN 1610
1550 SA=SA+1
1560 GOSUB 1400
1570 IF COUNT>=MAX THEN 1640
1580 DOT$="C"
1590 GOTO 1650
1600 IF COUNT>=MAX THEN 1550
1610 SB=SB+1
1620 GOSUB 1400
1630 IF COUNT>=MAX THEN 1580
1640 DOT$="S"
1650 ADD1$=" "
1655 REM ADD1$ HAS ONE SPACE
1660 GOTO 320
1710 PRINT CHR$(147)
1720 END
```

TICHUMAN

```
10 REM *************************
20 REM *        TICHUMAN       *
30 REM *                       *
40 REM *     COPYRIGHT 1983    *
50 REM *    DONNA S. PADGETT   *
60 REM *************************
70 PRINT CHR$(147):POKE 53280,14:
   POKE 53281,6:PRINT CHR$(5)
75 DIM P1(10),P2(10),PICK(17),
   PX(11),R3(24),TRY(9),MOVE$(9)
80 FOR I=1 TO 10:READ P1(I):NEXT I
85 FOR I=1 TO 10:READ P2(I):NEXT I
90 FOR I=1 TO 17:READ PICK(I):NEXT I
95 FOR I=1 TO 11:READ PX(I):NEXT I
100 FOR I=1 TO 24:READ R3(I):NEXT I
110 FOR I=1 TO 9:READ TRY(I):NEXT I
115 DATA 80,76,65,89,69,82,32,49,44,32
120 DATA 80,76,65,89,69,82,32,50,44,32
125 DATA 80,73,67,75,32,89,79,85,82,32,83,81,85,
    65,82,69,58
130 DATA 80,76,65,89,69,82,32,49,32,61,32
140 DATA 1,2,3,4,5,6,7,8,9,1,4,7,2,5,8,3,6,9,1,
    5,9,3,5,7
150 DATA 84,82,89,32,65,71,65,73,78
160 PRINT CHR$(147)
170 W1=O
180 W2=0
190 NOWIN=0
200 M1$="H E L L O"
210 M2$="W E L C O M E"
220 M3$="T O"
230 4$="T I C H U M A N"
240 PRINT TAB(11);M1$
250 PRINT:PRINT:PRINT
260 PRINT TAB(9);M2$
270 PRINT:PRINT
```

TICHUMAN is a version of TICTACTO, the program described following this one. Unlike TICTACTO, TICHUMAN allows two people to play one another in tick-tack-toe without using any paper or bothering to keep score. In TICTACTO, however, you play against the Commodore 64—which is pretty tough to beat!

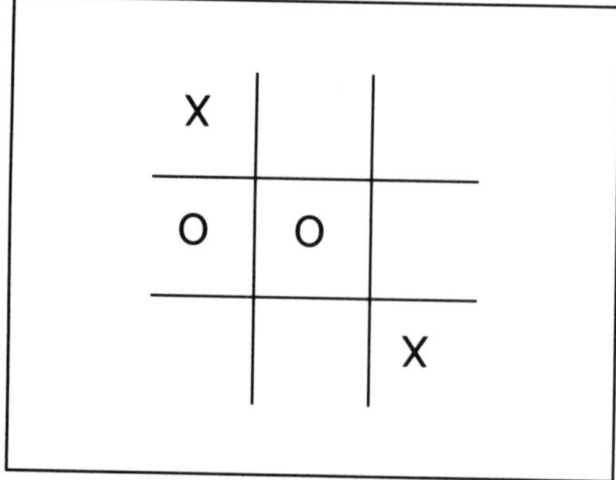

Lines 170-190 set up the win counters to zero for both players, as well as the counter for ties. Then lines 200-350 print a welcome message to the screen and ask player 1, "Are you X or O?"

Since X always goes first, the program knows whose turn it is at any time. Lines 490-630 "paint" the tick-tack-toe grid on the screen.

Lines 690-740 clear the nine-element array MOVE$, which keeps track of the moves that have been made to the nine possible locations on the grid. Lines 760-830 then

```
280 PRINT TAB(14);M3$
290 PRINT:PRINT
300 PRINT TAB(8);M4$
310 PRINT:PRINT
320 PRINT "X MAKES THE FIRST MOVE"
330 INPUT "PLAYER 1, ARE YOU X OR O";P1$
340 IF P1$="X" THEN 380
350 IF P1$="O" THEN 400
360 PRINT "PLEASE RESPOND WITH AN X OR O"
370 GOTO 160
380 P2$="O"
390 GOTO 410
400 P2$="X"
410 PRINT:PRINT
420 PRINT "ALRIGHT, PLAYERS, GOOD LUCK!"
430 IF P1$="X" THEN 460
440 PRINT "PLAYER 2 GOES FIRST"
450 GOTO 470
460 PRINT "PLAYER 1 GOES FIRST"
470 PRINT:PRINT
480 INPUT "PRESS RETURN TO BEGIN";BEG$
490 REM *PUTS GRID ON SCREEN*
500 PRINT CHR$(147)
510 RX=9
512 FOR CX=7 TO 24
514 POKE 1024+CX+40*RX,42
515 POKE 55296+CX+40*RX,1
516 NEXT CX
520 RX=14
522 FOR CX=7 TO 24
524 POKE 1024+CX+40*RX,42
525 POKE 55296+CX+40*RX,1
526 NEXT CX
530 CX=13
532 FOR RX=5 TO 18
534 POKE 1024+CX+40*RX,42
535 POKE 55296+CX+40*RX,1
536 NEXT RX
540 CX=18
542 FOR RX=5 TO 18
```

remind you whether player 1 is X or O; with two players you might forget which you were and make a bad move.

Lines 850-1125 then determine whose move it is, spell out "Player ... Pick your Square," and wait for a number to be keyed. By keying a number between 1 and 9 in line 1130, the player attempts an appropriate move; if unsuccessful, the player must key a new try. The KEY statements of lines 1190-1290 analyze what number the player keyed, and lines 1300-1470 send the program to the correct square to record the move. If there is already an X or an O in that square, the player must key a move again (lines 1590-1600).

The X or O is moved to the appropriate position, and the board is checked for a win or a tie (lines 2240-2550). The turn is then given in lines 2560-2600 to the next player. If there is a win or a tie, the score is displayed, and another game can be played (lines 2610-2790).

```
544 POKE 1024+CX+40*RX,42
545 POKE 55296+CX+40*RX,1
546 NEXT RX
550 RX=5:CX=9:VX=49:
    POKE 1024+CX+40*RX,VX:
    POKE 55296+CX+40*RX,1
560 RX=5:CX=14:VX=50:
    POKE 1024+CX+40*RX,VX:
    POKE 55296+CX+40*RX,1
570 RX=5:CX=19:VX=51:
    POKE 1024+CX+40*RX,VX:
    POKE 55296+CX+40*RX,1
580 RX=10:CX=9:VX=52:
    POKE 1024+CX+40*RX,VX:
    POKE 55296+CX+40*RX,1
590 RX=10:CX=14:VX=53:
    POKE 1024+CX+40*RX,VX:
    POKE 55296+CX+40*RX,1
600 RX=10:CX=19:VX=54:
    POKE 1024+CX+40*RX,VX:
    POKE 55296+CX+40*RX,1
610 RX=15:CX=9:VX=55:
    POKE 1024+CX+40*RX,VX:
    POKE 55296+CX+40*RX,1
620 RX=15:CX=14:VX=56:
    POKE 1024+CX+40*RX,VX:
    POKE 55296+CX+40*RX,1
630 RX=15:CX=19:VX=57:
    POKE 1024+CX+40*RX,VX:
    POKE 55296+CX+40*RX,1
690 REM *MOVE$ HOLDS MOVES MADE*
710 REM *S MEANS SPACE - NO VALUE*
720 FOR I=1 TO 9
730 MOVE$(I)="S"
740 NEXT I
750 X=0
760 FOR I=3 TO 13
770 X=X+1
775 A=PX(X):IF A>63 THEN A=A-64
780 RX=21:CX=I:POKE 1024+CX+40*RX,A:
    POKE 55296+CX+40*RX,1
790 NEXT I
830 RX=21:CX=14:VX=ASC(P1$)-64:
    POKE 1024+CX+40*RX,VX:
    POKE 55296+CX+40*RX,1
840 REM *TURN$/P1=PLAYER1/P2=PLAYER2
850 IF P1$="X" THEN 880
860 TURN$="P2"
870 GOTO 890
880 TURN$="P1"
890 REM *NEXT LINES ASK PERSON
    FOR INPUT*
900 X=0
910 FOR I=3 TO 12
915 X=X+1
920 IF TURN$="P1" THEN A=P1(X)
930 IF TURN$="P2" THEN A=P2(X)
950 IF A>63 THEN A=A-64
960 RX=23:CX=I:POKE 1024+CX+40*RX,A:
    POKE 55296+CX+40*RX,1
970 NEXT I
1090 REM *ASCII CODES FOR PICK
     YOUR SQUARE*
1100 X=0
1110 FOR I=13 TO 29
1115 X=X+1:A=PICK(X):IF A>63 THEN A=A-64
1120 RX=23:CX=I:POKE 1024+CX+40*RX,A:
     POKE 55296+CX+40*RX,1
1125 NEXT I
1130 GET KEY$:IF KEY$="" THEN 1130
1140 KEY=ASC(KEY$)
1145 FOR CX=3 TO 29
1150 RX=23:POKE 1024+CX+40*RX,32:
     POKE 55296+CX+40*RX,1
1155 NEXT CX
1160 REM *ABOVE LOOP ERASES PICK
     YOUR SQUARE"
1165 FOR CX=7 TO 16
```

```
1170 RX=24:POKE 1024+CX+40*RX,32:
     POKE 55296+CX+40*RX,1
1175 NEXT CX
1180 REM *ABOVE LOOP ERASES TRY AGAIN*
1190 IF KEY<49 THEN 1500
1200 IF KEY>57 THEN 1500
1210 IF KEY=49 THEN 1300
1220 IF KEY=50 THEN 1320
1230 IF KEY=51 THEN 1340
1240 IF KEY=52 THEN 1360
1250 IF KEY=53 THEN 1380
1260 IF KEY=54 THEN 1400
1270 IF KEY=55 THEN 1420
1280 IF KEY=56 THEN 1440
1290 IF KEY=57 THEN 1460
1300 J=1
1310 GOTO 1590
1320 J=2
1330 GOTO 1590
1340 J=3
1350 GOTO 1590
1360 J=4
1370 GOTO 1590
1380 J=5
1390 GOTO 1590
1400 J=6
1410 GOTO 1590
1420 J=7
1430 GOTO 1590
1440 J=8
1450 GOTO 1590
1460 J=9
1470 GOTO 1590
1480 REM *BAD INPUT MSG HERE*
1490 REM *TRY AGAIN*
1500 X=0
1510 FOR CX=7 TO 15
1520 X=X+1:A=TRY(X):IF A>63 THEN A=A-64
1530 RX=24:POKE 1024+CX+40*RX,A:
     POKE 55296+CX+40*RX,1
1540 NEXT CX
1580 GOTO 1130
1590 IF MOVE$(J)="X" THEN 1500
1600 IF MOVE$(J)="O" THEN 1500
1610 IF TURN$="P2" THEN 1640
1620 MOVE$(J)=P1$
1630 GOTO 1660
1640 MOVE$(J)=P2$
1660 REM *NEXT LINES MOVE IN APPROPRIATE
     X OR O*
1670 ON J GOTO 1780,1810,1840,1870,1900,1930,
     1960,1990,2020
1760 GOTO 2820
1770 REM *MOVE IN X'S HERE*
1780 IF MOVE$(J)="O" THEN 2060
1790 RX=7:CX=11:VX=24:
     POKE 1024+CX+40*RX,VX:
     POKE 55296+CX+40*RX,1
1800 GOTO 2240
1810 IF MOVE$(J)="O" THEN 2080
1820 RX=7:CX=16:VX=24:
     POKE 1024+CX+40*RX,VX:
     POKE 55296+CX+40*RX,1
1830 GOTO 2240
1840 IF MOVE$(J)="O" THEN 2100
1850 RX=7:CX=21:VX=24:
     POKE 1024+CX+40*RX,VX:
     POKE 55296+CX+40*RX,1
1860 GOTO 2240
1870 IF MOVE$(J)="O" THEN 2120
1880 RX=12:CX=11:VX=24:
     POKE 1024+CX+40*RX,VX:
     POKE 55296+CX+40*RX,1
1890 GOTO 2240
1900 IF MOVE$(J)="O" THEN 2140
1910 RX=12:CX=16:VX=24:
     POKE 1024+CX+40*RX,VX:
     POKE 55296+CX+40*RX,1
1920 GOTO 2240
1930 IF MOVE$(J)="O" THEN 2160
```

```
1940 RX=12:CX=21:VX=24:
     POKE 1024+CX+40*RX,VX:
     POKE 55296+CX+40*RX,1
1950 GOTO 2240
1960 IF MOVE$(J)="O" THEN 2180
1970 RX=17:CX=11:VX=24:
     POKE 1024+CX+40*RX,VX:
     POKE 55296+CX+40*RX,1
1980 GOTO 2240
1990 IF MOVE$(J)="O" THEN 2200
2000 RX=17:CX=16:VX=24:
     POKE 1024+CX+40*RX,VX:
     POKE 55296+CX+40*RX,1
2010 GOTO 2240
2020 IF MOVE$(J)="O" THEN 2220
2030 RX=17:CX=21:VX=24:
     POKE 1024+CX+40*RX,VX:
     POKE 55296+CX+40*RX,1
2040 GOTO 2240
2050 REM *MOVE IN O'S HERE*
2060 RX=07:CX=11:VX=15:
     POKE 1024+CX+40*RX,VX:
     POKE 55296+CX+40*RX,1
2070 GOTO 2240
2080 RX=07:CX=16:VX=15:
     POKE 1024+CX+40*RX,VX:
     POKE 55296+CX+40*RX,1
2090 GOTO 2240
2100 RX=07:CX=21:VX=15:
     POKE 1024+CX+40*RX,VX:
     POKE 55296+CX+40*RX,1
2110 GOTO 2240
2120 RX=12:CX=11:VX=15:
     POKE 1024+CX+40*RX,VX:
     POKE 55296+CX+40*RX,1
2130 GOTO 2240
2140 RX=12:CX=16:VX=15:
     POKE 1024+CX+40*RX,VX:
     POKE 55296+CX+40*RX,1
2150 GOTO 2240
2160 RX=12:CX=21:VX=15:
     POKE 1024+CX+40*RX,VX:
     POKE 55296+CX+40*RX,1
2170 GOTO 2240
2180 RX=17:CX=11:VX=15:
     POKE 1024+CX+40*RX,VX:
     POKE 55296+CX+40*RX,1
2190 GOTO 2240
2200 RX=17:CX=16:VX=15:
     POKE 1024+CX+40*RX,VX:
     POKE 55296+CX+40*RX,1
2210 GOTO 2240
2220 RX=17:CX=21:VX=15:
     POKE 1024+CX+40*RX,VX:
     POKE 55296+CX+40*RX,1
2230 GOTO 2240
2240 REM *CHECKS FOR 3/ROW*
2250 ROW3$="N"
2260 X=0
2350 FOR I=1 TO 8
2360 IF ROW3$="Y" THEN 2450
2370 X=X+1:K1=R3(X):X=X+1:
     K2=R3(X):X=X+1:K3=R3(X)
2380 IF MOVE$(K1)="S" THEN 2440
2390 IF MOVE$(K1)=MOVE$(K2) THEN 2410
2400 GOTO 2440
2410 IF MOVE$(K2)=MOVE$(K3) THEN 2430
2420 GOTO 2440
2430 ROW3$="Y"
2440 NEXT I
2450 REM *IF ROW3$="Y" - 3 IN A ROW!*
2460 IF ROW3$="Y" THEN 2610
2470 REM *CHECK FOR NO WIN (TIE)*
2480 SPACE$="N"
2490 FOR I=1 TO 9
2500 IF SPACE$="Y" THEN 2550
2510 IF MOVE$(I)="X" THEN 2540
2520 IF MOVE$(I)="O" THEN 2540
2530 SPACE$="Y"
2540 NEXT I
```

```
2550 IF SPACE$="N" THEN 2690
2560 IF TURN$="P1" THEN 2590
2570 TURN$="P1"
2580 GOTO 890
2590 TURN$="P2"
2600 GOTO 890
2610 REM * IF HERE, 3/ROW*
2620 IF TURN$="P1" THEN 2660
2630 W2=W2+1
2635 PRINT CHR$(147)
2640 PRINT "CONGRATULATIONS, PLAYER 2!!!"
2650 GOTO 2720
2660 W1=W1+1
2665 PRINT CHR$(147)
2670 PRINT "CONGRATULATIONS, PLAYER 1!!!"
2680 GOTO 2720
2690 REM *IF HERE, CAT WON!*
2700 NOWIN=NOWIN+1
2705 PRINT CHR$(147)
2710 PRINT "IT'S A DRAW!!!"
2720 PRINT:PRINT
2730 PRINT "THE SCORE IS: "
2740 PRINT "PLAYER 1: ";W1
2750 PRINT "PLAYER 2: ";W2
2760 PRINT "TIES: ";NOWIN
2770 PRINT:PRINT
2780 INPUT "DO YOU WANT TO PLAY AGAIN
     (Y/N)";YN$
2790 IF YN$="Y" THEN 320
2800 PRINT:PRINT
2810 PRINT "ALRIGHT, 'TIL NEXT TIME..."
2820 END
```

TICTACTO

```
10 REM ***************************
20 REM *          TICTACTO        *
30 REM *                          *
40 REM *       COPYRIGHT 1983     *
50 REM *     DONNA S. PADGETT     *
60 REM ***************************
70 PRINT CHR$(147):POKE 53280,14:
   POKE 53281,6:PRINT CHR$(5)
75 DIM P1(10),BL(12),PICK(17),CO(12),R3(24),
   TRY(9),MOVE$(9),OC(12)
80 FOR I=1 TO 10:READ P1(I):NEXT I
85 FOR I=1 TO 12:READ BL(I):NEXT I
90 FOR I=1 TO 17:READ PICK(I):NEXT I
95 FOR I=1 TO 12:READ CO(I):NEXT I
100 FOR I=1 TO 24:READ R3(I):NEXT I
105 FOR I=1 TO 12:READ OC(I):NEXT I
110 FOR I=1 TO 9:READ TRY(I):NEXT I
115 DATA 80,76,65,89,69,82,32,49,44,32
120 DATA 2,4,1,2,6,3,6,8,9,4,8,7
125 DATA 80,73,67,75,32,89,79,85,82,32,83,81,85,
   65,82,69,58
130 DATA 1,3,9,1,7,9,3,7,9,1,3,7
140 DATA 1,2,3,4,5,6,7,8,9,1,4,7,2,5,8,3,6,9,1,5,9,3,5,7
145 DATA 1,3,9,1,7,9,3,7,9,3,1,7
150 DATA 84,82,89,32,65,71,65,73,78
160 PRINT CHR$(147)
170 W1=O
180 W2=0
190 NOWIN=0
200 M1$="H E L L O"
210 M2$="W E L C O M E"
220 M3$="T O"
230 M4$="T I C T A C T O"
240 PRINT TAB(11);M1$
250 PRINT:PRINT:PRINT
260 PRINT TAB(9);M2$
```

TICTACTO, as mentioned earlier, is a game between a human and a computer, whereas TICHUMAN serves as an electronic blackboard and scoring machine for two people wanting to play tick-tack-toe.

TICTACTO has logic that is similar to that of TICHUMAN, but TICTACTO differs substantially. This program has sections in which the Commodore 64 has to figure out the best possible move in order to avoid getting caught in a no-win situation.

Lines 3410-5110 contain the logic that is significantly different. Lines 3420-3670 look for a win situation. (Why should the computer waste time looking for blocks or other moves if it can win right away?) Lines 3680-3920 look for situations in which the "human zapper" (the computer) must block in order to survive. Then lines 3930-4050 block the human player's corner between two sides to avoid a "double threat." Lines 4100-4140 will take the middle square if no better move is available. Finally, lines 4150-5110 look for progressively lower choice moves, always looking for corner moves since they offer good winning alternatives.

When a win or tie is reached, you are asked if you want to play again, and the score to that point is given.

Good luck!

```
270 PRINT:PRINT
280 PRINT TAB(14);M3$
290 PRINT:PRINT
300 PRINT TAB(8);M4$
310 PRINT:PRINT
320 PRINT "X MAKES THE FIRST MOVE"
330 INPUT "DO YOU WANT TO BE X OR O";XO$
340 IF XO$="X" THEN 410
350 IF XO$="O" THEN 410
360 PRINT "PLEASE RESPOND WITH AN X OR O"
370 GOTO 160
410 PRINT:PRINT
420 PRINT "ALRIGHT, ";XO$;", GOOD LUCK!"
430 IF XO$="X" THEN 460
440 PRINT "I GO FIRST"
450 GOTO 470
460 PRINT "YOU GO FIRST"
470 PRINT:PRINT
480 INPUT "PRESS RETURN TO BEGIN";BEG$
490 REM *PUTS GRID ON SCREEN*
500 PRINT CHR$(147)
510 RX=9
512 FOR CX=7 TO 24
514 POKE 1024+CX+40*RX,42
515 POKE 55296+CX+40*RX,1
516 NEXT CX
520 RX=14
522 FOR CX=7 TO 24
524 POKE 1024+CX+40*RX,42
525 POKE 55296+CX+40*RX,1
526 NEXT CX
530 CX=13
532 FOR RX=5 TO 18
534 POKE 1024+CX+40*RX,42
535 POKE 55296+CX+40*RX,1
536 NEXT RX
540 CX=18
542 FOR RX=5 TO 18
544 POKE 1024+CX+40*RX,42
545 POKE 55296+CX+40*RX,1
546 NEXT RX
550 RX=5:CX=9:VX=49:POKE 1024+CX+40*RX,VX:
    POKE 55296+CX+40*RX,1
560 RX=5:CX=14:VX=50:
    POKE 1024+CX+40*RX,VX:
    POKE 55296+CX+40*RX,1
570 RX=5:CX=19:VX=51:
    POKE 1024+CX+40*RX,VX:
    POKE 55296+CX+40*RX,1
580 RX=10:CX=9:VX=52:
    POKE 1024+CX+40*RX,VX:
    POKE 55296+CX+40*RX,1
590 RX=10:CX=14:VX=53:
    POKE 1024+CX+40*RX,VX:
    POKE 55296+CX+40*RX,1
600 RX=10:CX=19:VX=54:
    POKE 1024+CX+40*RX,VX:
    POKE 55296+CX+40*RX,1
610 RX=15:CX=9:VX=55:
    POKE 1024+CX+40*RX,VX:
    POKE 55296+CX+40*RX,1
620 RX=15:CX=14:VX=56:
    POKE 1024+CX+40*RX,VX:
    POKE 55296+CX+40*RX,1
630 RX=15:CX=19:VX=57:
    POKE 1024+CX+40*RX,VX:
    POKE 55296+CX+40*RX,1
690 REM *MOVE$ HOLDS MOVES MADE*
710 REM *S MEANS SPACE - NO VALUE*
720 FOR I=1 TO 9
730 MOVE$(I)="S"
740 NEXT I
840 REM *TURN$/P=PERSON/C=COMPUTER*
850 IF XO$="X" THEN 880
860 TURN$="C"
865 COMP$="X"
870 GOTO 890
880 TURN$="P"
885 COMP$="O"
```

```
890 REM *NEXT LINES ASK PERSON
    FOR INPUT*
895 IF TURN$="C" THEN 3410
900 X=0
910 FOR I=3 TO 12
915 X=X+1
920 A=P1(X)
950 IF A>63 THEN A=A-64
960 RX=23:CX=I:POKE 1024+CX+40*RX,A:
    POKE 55296+CX+40*RX,1
970 NEXT I
1090 REM *ASCII CODES FOR PICK
     YOUR SQUARE*
1100 X=0
1110 FOR I=13 TO 29
1115 X=X+1:A=PICK(X):IF A>63 THEN A=A-64
1120 RX=23:CX=I:POKE 1024+CX+40*RX,A:
     POKE 55296+CX+40*RX,1
1125 NEXT I
1130 GET KEY$:IF KEY$=" " THEN 1130
1140 KEY=ASC(KEY$)
1145 FOR CX=3 TO 29
1150 RX=23:POKE 1024+CX+40*RX,32:
     POKE 55296+CX+40*RX,1
1155 NEXT CX
1160 REM *ABOVE LOOP ERASES PICK
     YOUR SQUARE"
1165 FOR CX=7 TO 16
1170 RX=24:POKE 1024+CX+40*RX,32:
     POKE 55296+CX+40*RX,1
1175 NEXT CX
1180 REM *ABOVE LOOP ERASES TRY AGAIN*
1190 IF KEY<49 THEN 1500
1200 IF KEY>57 THEN 1500
1210 IF KEY=49 THEN 1300
1220 IF KEY=50 THEN 1320
1230 IF KEY=51 THEN 1340
1240 IF KEY=52 THEN 1360
1250 IF KEY=53 THEN 1380
1260 IF KEY=54 THEN 1400
1270 IF KEY=55 THEN 1420
1280 IF KEY=56 THEN 1440
1290 IF KEY=57 THEN 1460
1300 J=1
1310 GOTO 1590
1320 J=2
1330 GOTO 1590
1340 J=3
1350 GOTO 1590
1360 J=4
1370 GOTO 1590
1380 J=5
1390 GOTO 1590
1400 J=6
1410 GOTO 1590
1420 J=7
1430 GOTO 1590
1440 J=8
1450 GOTO 1590
1460 J=9
1470 GOTO 1590
1480 REM *BAD INPUT MSG HERE*
1490 REM *TRY AGAIN*
1500 X=0
1510 FOR CX=7 TO 15
1520 X=X+1:A=TRY(X):IF A>63 THEN A=A-64
1530 RX=24:POKE 1024+CX+40*RX,A:
     POKE 55296+C+40*RX,1
1540 NEXT CX
1580 GOTO 1130
1590 IF MOVE$(J)="X" THEN 1500
1600 IF MOVE$(J)="0" THEN 1500
1620 MOVE$(J)=XO$
1660 REM *NEXT LINES MOVE IN APPOPRIATE
     X OR O*
1670 ON J GOTO 1780,1810,1840,1870,1900,1930,
     1960,1990,2020
1760 GOTO 2800
1770 REM *MOVE IN X'S HERE*
1780 IF MOVE$(J)="O" THEN 2060
```

```
1790 RX=7:CX=11:VX=24:
     POKE 1024+CX+40*RX,VX:
     POKE 55296+CX+40*RX,1
1800 GOTO 2240
1810 IF MOVE$(J)="O" THEN 2080
1820 RX=7:CX=16:VX=24:
     POKE 1024+CX+40*RX,VX:
     POKE 55296+CX+40*RX,1
1830 GOTO 2240
1840 IF MOVE$(J)="O" THEN 2100
1850 RX=7:CX=21:VX=24:
     POKE 1024+CX+40*RX,VX:
     POKE 55296+CX+40*RX,1
1860 GOTO 2240
1870 IF MOVE$(J)="O" THEN 2120
1880 RX=12:CX=11:VX=24:
     POKE 1024+CX+40*RX,VX:
     POKE 55296+CX+40*RX,1
1890 GOTO 2240
1900 IF MOVE$(J)="O" THEN 2140
1910 RX=12:CX=16:VX=24:
     POKE 1024+CX+40*RX,VX:
     POKE 55296+CX+40*RX,1
1920 GOTO 2240
1930 IF MOVE$(J)="O" THEN 2160
1940 RX=12:CX=21:VX=24:
     POKE 1024+CX+40*RX,VX:
     POKE 55 96+CX+40*RX,1
1950 GOTO 2240
1960 IF MOVE$(J)="O" THEN 2180
1970 RX=17:CX=11:VX=24:
     POKE 1024+CX+40*RX,VX:
     POKE 55296+CX+40*RX,1
1980 GOTO 2240
1990 IF MOVE$(J)="O" THEN 2200
2000 RX=17:CX=16:VX=24:
     POKE 1024+CX+40*RX,VX:
     POKE 55296+CX+40*RX,1
2010 GOTO 2240
2020 IF MOVE$(J)="O" THEN 2220
2030 RX=17:CX=21:VX=24:
     POKE 1024+CX+40*RX,VX:
     POKE 55296+CX+40*RX,1
2040 GOTO 2240
2050 REM *MOVE IN O'S HERE*
2060 RX=07:CX=11:VX=15:
     POKE 1024+CX+40*RX,VX:
     POKE 55296+CX+40*RX,1
2070 GOTO 2240
2080 RX=07:CX=16:VX=15:
     POKE 1024+CX+40*RX,VX:
     POKE 55296+CX+40*RX,1
2090 GOTO 2240
2100 RX=07:CX=21:VX=15:
     POKE 1024+CX+40*RX,VX:
     POKE 55296+CX+40*RX,1
2110 GOTO 2240
2120 RX=12:CX=11:VX=15:
     POKE 1024+CX+40*RX,VX:
     POKE 55296+CX+40*RX,1
2130 GOTO 2240
2140 RX=12:CX=16:VX=15:
     POKE 1024+CX+40*RX,VX:
     POKE 55296+CX+40*RX,1
2150 GOTO 2240
2160 RX=12:CX=21:VX=15:
     POKE 1024+CX+40*RX,VX:
     POKE 55296+CX+40*RX,1
2170 GOTO 2240
2180 RX=17:CX=11:VX=15:
     POKE 1024+CX+40*RX,VX:
     POKE 55296+CX+40*RX,1
2190 GOTO 2240
2200 RX=17:CX=16:VX=15:
     POKE 1024+CX+40*RX,VX:
     POKE 55296+CX+40*RX,1
2210 GOTO 2240
2220 RX=17:CX=21:VX=15:
     POKE 1024+CX+40*RX,VX:
     POKE 55296+CX+40*RX,1
```

```
2230 GOTO 2240
2240 REM *CHECKS FOR 3/ROW*
2250 ROW3$="N"
2260 X=0
2350 FOR I=1 TO 8
2360 IF ROW3$="Y" THEN 2450
2370 X=X+1:K1=R3(X):X=X+1:
     K2=R3(X):X=X+1:K3=R3(X)
2380 IF MOVE$(K1)="S" THEN 2440
2390 IF MOVE$(K1)=MOVE$(K2) THEN 2410
2400 GOTO 2440
2410 IF MOVE$(K2)=MOVE$(K3) THEN 2430
2420 GOTO 2440
2430 ROW3$="Y"
2440 NEXT I
2450 REM *IF ROW3$="Y" - 3 IN A ROW!*
2460 IF ROW3$="Y" THEN 2610
2470 REM *CHECK FOR NO WIN (TIE)*
2480 SPACE$="N"
2490 FOR I=1 TO 9
2500 IF SPACE$="Y" THEN 2550
2510 IF MOVE$(I)="X" THEN 2540
2520 IF MOVE$(I)="O" THEN 2540
2530 SPACE$="Y"
2540 NEXT I
2550 IF SPACE$="N" THEN 2690
2560 IF TURN$="P" THEN 2590
2570 TURN$="P"
2580 GOTO 890
2590 TURN$="C"
2600 GOTO 890
2610 REM * IF HERE, 3/ROW*
2620 IF TURN$="P" THEN 2660
2630 W2=W2+1
2635 PRINT CHR$(147)
2640 PRINT "SORRY, BUT YOU LOSE!"
2650 GOTO 2720
2660 W1=W1+1
2665 PRINT CHR$(147)
2670 PRINT "CONGRATULATIONS, YOU WIN!!!"
2680 GOTO 2720
2690 REM *IF HERE CAT WON*
2700 NOWIN=NOWIN+1
2705 PRINT CHR$(147)
2710 PRINT "IT'S A DRAW!!!"
2720 PRINT:PRINT
2730 PRINT "THE SCORE IS: "
2740 PRINT "COMPUTER: ";W1
2750 PRINT "PLAYER 2: ";W2
2760 PRINT "TIES: ";NOWIN
2770 PRINT:PRINT
2780 INPUT "DO YOU WANT TO PLAY AGAIN
     (Y/N)";YN$
2790 IF YN$="Y" THEN 320
2800 PRINT:PRINT
2810 PRINT "ALRIGHT, 'TIL NEXT TIME..."
2820 GOTO 5120
3410 REM *NEXT LINES FIGURE
     COMPUTER'S MOVE*
3420 REM *FIRST LOOK FOR WIN*
3430 CMOVE=0
3440 X=0
3442 FOR I=1 TO 8
3444 IF CMOVE>0 THEN 5100
3450 X=X+1:K1=R3(X):X=X+1:K2=R3(X):
     X=X+1:K3=R3(X)
3480 IF MOVE$(K1)=MOVE$(K2) THEN 3520
3490 IF MOVE$(K1)=MOVE$(K3) THEN 3540
3500 IF MOVE$(K2)=MOVE$(K3) THEN 3560
3510 GOTO 3660
3520 IF MOVE$(K1)=COMP$ THEN 3580
3530 GOTO 3660
3540 IF MOVE$(K1)=COMP$ THEN 3610
3550 GOTO 3660
3560 IF MOVE$(K2)=COMP$ THEN 3640
3570 GOTO 3660
3580 IF MOVE$(K3)=XO$ THEN 3660
3590 CMOVE=K3
3600 GOTO 3660
3610 IF MOVE$(K2)=XO$ THEN 3660
```

```
3620 CMOVE=K2
3630 GOTO 3660
3640 IF MOVE$(K1)=XO$ THEN 3660
3650 CMOVE=K1
3660 NEXT I
3670 IF CMOVE>0 THEN 5100
3680 REM *2ND LOOK FOR BLOCK*
3690 X=0
3700 FOR I=1 TO 8
3705 IF CMOVE>0 THEN 5100
3710 X=X+1:K1=R3(X):X=X+1:K2=R3(X):
     X=X+1:K3=R3(X)
3730 IF MOVE$(K1)=MOVE$(K2) THEN 3770
3740 IF MOVE$(K1)=MOVE$(K3) THEN 3790
3750 IF MOVE$(K2)=MOVE$(K3) THEN 3810
3760 GOTO 3910
3770 IF MOVE$(K1)=XO$ THEN 3830
3780 GOTO 3910
3790 IF MOVE$(K1)=XO$ THEN 3860
3800 GOTO 3910
3810 IF MOVE$(K2)=XO$ THEN 3890
3820 GOTO 3910
3830 IF MOVE$(K3)=COMP$ THEN 3910
3840 CMOVE=K3
3850 GOTO 3910
3860 IF MOVE$(K2)=COMP$ THEN 3910
3870 CMOVE=K2
3880 GOTO 3910
3890 IF MOVE$(K1)=COMP$ THEN 3910
3900 CMOVE=K1
3910 NEXT I
3920 IF CMOVE>0 THEN 5100
3930 REM *3RD BLOCK PERSONS CORNER
     BETWEEN TWO SIDES*
3940 X=0
3950 FOR I=1 TO 4
3960 IF CMOVE>0 THEN 5100
3970 X=X+1:K1=BL(X):X=X+1:K2=BL(X):
     X=X+1:K3=BL(X)
3980 IF MOVE$(K1)=XO$ THEN 4000
3990 GOTO 4050
4000 IF MOVE$(K2)=XO$ THEN 4020
4010 GOTO 4050
4020 IF MOVE$(K3)="S" THEN 4040
4030 GOTO 4050
4040 CMOVE=K3
4050 NEXT I
4100 REM *4TH TAKE MIDDLE SQUARE*
4110 IF MOVE$(5)="X" THEN 4140
4120 IF MOVE$(5)="O" THEN 4140
4130 CMOVE=5
4140 IF CMOVE>0 THEN 5100
4150 REM *5TH TRY FOR 3RD CORNER*
4160 X=0
4170 FOR I=1 TO 4
4180 IF CMOVE>0 THEN 5100
4190 X=X+1:K1=CO(X):X=X+1:K2=CO(X):
     X=X+1:K3=CO(X)
4200 IF MOVE$(K1)=MOVE$(K2) THEN 4240
4210 IF MOVE$(K1)=MOVE$(K3) THEN 4290
4220 IF MOVE$(K2)=MOVE$(K3) THEN 4340
4230 GOTO 4390
4240 IF MOVE$(K1)=XO$ THEN 4390
4250 IF MOVE$(K3)=XO$ THEN 4390
4260 IF MOVE$(K3)=COMP$ THEN 4390
4270 CMOVE=K3
4280 GOTO 4390
4290 IF MOVE$(K1)=XO$ THEN 4390
4300 IF MOVE$(K2)=XO$ THEN 4390
4310 IF MOVE$(K2)=COMP$ THEN 4390
4320 CMOVE=K2
4330 GOTO 4390
4340 IF MOVE$(K2)=XO$ THEN 4390
4350 IF MOVE$(K1)=XO$ THEN 4390
4360 IF MOVE$(K1)=COMP$ THEN 4390
4370 CMOVE=K1
4380 GOTO 4390
4390 NEXT I
4440 IF CMOVE>0 THEN 5100
4450 REM *6TH TRY FOR OPPOSITE CORNER*
```

```
4460 X=0
4510 FOR I=1 TO 4
4520 IF CMOVE>0 THEN 5100
4530 X=X+1:K1=OC(X):X=X+1:K2=OC(X):
     X=X+1:K3=OC(X)
4540 IF MOVE$(K1)=XO$ THEN 4650
4550 IF MOVE$(K2)=XO$ THEN 4650
4560 IF MOVE$(K3)=XO$ THEN 4650
4570 IF MOVE$(K1)=COMP$ THEN 4600
4580 IF MOVE$(K3)=COMP$ THEN 4630
4590 GOTO 4650
4600 IF MOVE$(K3)=COMP$ THEN 4650
4610 CMOVE=K3
4620 GOTO 4650
4630 IF MOVE$(K1)=COMP$ THEN 4650
4640 CMOVE=K1
4650 NEXT I
4660 IF CMOVE>0 THEN 5100
4670 REM *7TH BLOCK TRY FOR 3RD CORNER
4680 X=0
4690 FOR I=1 TO 4
4700 IF CMOVE>0 THEN 5100
4710 X=X+1:K1=OC(X):X=X+1:K2=OC(X):
     X=X+1:K3=OC(X)
4720 IF MOVE$(K1)=XO$ THEN 4740
4730 GOTO 4880
4740 IF MOVE$(K3)=XO$ THEN 4760
4750 GOTO 4880
4760 FOR N=1 TO 2
4765 ON N GOTO 4770,4775
4766 GOTO 4870
4770 K4=2:K5=8
4772 GOTO 4780
4775 K4=4:K5=6
4780 IF MOVE$(K4)=XO$ THEN 4860
4800 IF MOVE$(K5)=XO$ THEN 4860
4810 IF MOVE$(K4)=COMP$ THEN 4840
4820 CMOVE=K4
4830 GOTO 4880
4840 IF MOVE$(K5)=COMP$ THEN 4860
4850 CMOVE=K5
4860 GOTO 4880
4870 NEXT N
4880 NEXT I
4910 IF CMOVE>0 THEN 5100
4920 FOR I=1 TO 4
4930 IF CMOVE>0 THEN 5100
4940 ON I GOTO 4945,4950,4960,4965
4942 GOTO 5010
4945 K1=1:GOTO 4980
4950 K1=3:GOTO 4980
4960 K1=7:GOTO 4980
4965 K1=9:GOTO 4980
4980 IF MOVE$(K1)=XO$ THEN 5010
4990 IF MOVE$(K1)=COMP$ THEN 5010
5000 CMOVE=K1
5010 NEXT I
5020 IF CMOVE>0 THEN 5100
5030 REM *9TH TAKE ANY AVAILABLE MOVE*
5040 FOR I=1 TO 9
5050 IF CMOVE>0 THEN 5100
5060 IF MOVE$(I)=XO$ THEN 5090
5070 IF MOVE$(I)=COMP$ THEN 5090
5080 CMOVE=I
5090 NEXT I
5100 J=CMOVE
5110 MOVE$(J)=COMP$
5115 GOTO 1660
5120 END
```

3

Business and Educational Programs

CKBOOK

```
10 REM **************************
20 REM *          CKBOOK          *
30 REM *                          *
40 REM *      COPYRIGHT 1983      *
50 REM *    DONALD C. KREUTNER    *
60 REM **************************
70 PRINT CHR$(147):POKE 53280,14:
   POKE 53281,6:PRINT CHR$(5)
75 INPUT "1525 PRTR(1), RS232(2),
   NONE(3)";PX$
80 IF PX$="3" THEN 120
85 IF PX$="1" THEN 100
90 IF PX$="2" THEN 100
95 GOTO 75
100 PR=126
105 IF PX$="1" THEN 115
110 PR=PR+2:OPEN PR,2,0,CHR$(8):
    PR=128:PX$="2":GOTO 120
115 PR=PR+1:OPEN PR,4
120 PRINT CHR$(147):REM CLR SCREEN
170 DIM N2(100),A2(100),O2(100),N6(100),A6(100),
    O6(100),Q$(100)
180 REM READS IN A LIST OF CANCELLED
```

CKBOOK is a program that reads in a list of canceled checks and a list of issued checks, matches the two groups, and produces the following:

1. A list of returned checks, noting any discrepancies in amounts issued and paid
2. A message telling you whenever a check is paid that you failed to record as issued
3. A report of checks that are still outstanding and their amounts

The input for CKBOOK comes from the **DATA** statements in lines 210-80. Notice that these **DATA** statements are divided into two groups, one for returned checks and one for issued checks. In lines 210 to 250, input for returned checks includes the check number, a comma, the payee in quotes, a comma, and the check amount.

```
190 REM CHECKS AND CHECKS ISSUED AND
200 REM PRINTS A LIST OF CHECKS
210 DATA 110,PUBLIC SERVICE INDIANA,24.82
220 DATA 118,JOHNSON HARDWARE,20.00
230 DATA 200,BAD CK NOT RECORDED,35.09
240 DATA 115,COMPUTER MGT,35.73
250 DATA -9999,END OF RETURNED
    CHECKS,999
260 DATA 110,24.83,111,25.00,113,17.82
270 DATA 115,35.73,117,16.57,118,20
280 DATA -999,999
290 FOR I=1 TO 100
300 READ N1,P$,A1
310 IF N1=-9999 THEN 390
320 N2(I)=N1
330 Q$(I)=P$
340 A2(I)=A1
350 C2=I
360 O2(I)=I
370 NEXT I
380 LCTR=0
390 REM SORT THE RETURNED CHECKS
400 REM ************************
410 INPUT "PRINT (Y/N)";PYN$
420 IF PX$="3" THEN PYN$="N"
430 IF PYN$<>"Y" THEN 460
440 PRINT# PR,"CK#";SPC(7);"PAYEE";SPC(26);
    "AMT RETURNED";SPC(3);"AMT ISSUED"
450 PRINT# PR
460 PRINT CHR$(147)
470 S=0
480 FOR I=1 TO C2-1
490 IF N2(I)>N2(I+1) THEN 510
500 GOTO 580
510 T=O2(I)
520 T1=N2(I)
530 O2(I)=O2(I+1)
540 N2(I)=N2(I+1)
550 O2(I+1)=T
560 N2(I+1)=T1
```

The returned checks are terminated by a -9999 for the check number. (See line 250.)

Input for the issued checks includes check number, a comma, the amount of the check, a comma, the next check number, a comma, the amount for that check, etc. The end of the issued checks is designated by a -999 check number. (See line 280.) You can add to, alter, and delete these **DATA** statements to balance your own checkbook.

Lines 290-370 read the returned checks into several arrays (N2 for the check number, Q$ for the payee, and A2 for the amount). When the -9999 check number is encountered in line 310, a sort of the data for the returned checks begins in line 470 and continues to line 590. In line 410 you are asked if you want a printout.

Then, the data for the issued checks is read in and sorted, in similar fashion, in lines 600-820.

The returned check list is printed in lines 850-1220. The check numbers of checks returned are compared, one at a time, to check numbers of the checks issued, in order to find a match (lines 960-1050). If a match is found, the amounts of those two checks are compared. If they are not equal, the discrepancy is clearly noted on the listing, and the totals of issued and returned checks will be different.

Then in lines 1280-1520, an outstanding check list is given, telling you which checks have not been returned, their amounts, and the total amount still outstanding. Lines 1530-1720 and lines 1730-1820 contain subroutines used to print details in portions

```
570 S=1
580 NEXT I
590 IF S=1 THEN 470
600 REM READ IN ISSUED CHECKS
610 REM *********************
620 FOR I=1 TO 100
630 READ N5,A5
640 IF N5=-999 THEN 700
650 N6(I)=N5
660 A6(I)=A5
670 C6=I
680 O6(I)=I
690 NEXT I
700 S=0
710 FOR I=1 TO C6-1
720 IF N6(I)>N6(I+1) THEN 740
730 GOTO 810
740 T=O6(I)
750 T1=N6(I)
760 O6(I)=O6(I+1)
770 N6(I)=N6(I+1)
780 O6(I+1)=T
790 N6(I+1)=T1
800 S=1
810 NEXT I
820 IF S=1 THEN 700
830 A7=0
840 A8=0
850 REM PRINT THE RETURNED CHECKS
860 REM *************************
870 PRINT "RETURNED CHECK LIST"
880 PRINT "——————————-"
890 IF PYN$<>"Y" THEN 940
900 PRINT# PR,"**************************
    ***********************************"
910 PRINT# PR,"*CHECKS RETURNED*"
920 PRINT# PR,"**************************
    ***********************************"
930 PRINT# PR
940 LCTR=LCTR+1
```

of the program that deal with returned and outstanding checks.

```
950 FOR I=1 TO C2
960 FOR J=1 TO C6
970 IF N2(I)=N6(J) THEN 1070
980 NEXT J
990 GOSUB 1530
1000 PRINT
1010 PRINT "NO MATCH FOR: ";N2(I)
1020 IF PYN$<>"Y" THEN 1050
1030 PRINT# PR,"*NO MATCH FOR CK#:
     ";N2(I);"*"
1040 PRINT# PR
1050 LCTR=LCTR+2
1060 GOTO 1090
1070 GOSUB 1530
1080 A8=A8+A6(J)
1090 NEXT I
1100 REM A7=TOT RETURNED
1110 REM A8=TOT ISSUED
1120 FOR I=1 TO C2
1130 A7=A7+A2(I)
1140 NEXT I
1150 REM PRINT THE OUTSTANDING CHECKS
1160 REM ****************************
1170 PRINT
1180 PRINT "*************************
     *******"
1190 PRINT "TOTAL ISSUED: ";A8
1200 PRINT "TOTAL RETURNED: ";A7
1210 IF PYN$<>"Y" THEN 1230
1220 PRINT# PR,"*TOTALS*";SPC(32);A7;
     SPC(15-LEN(STR$(A7)));A8
```

```
1230 LCTR=LCTR+4
1240 IF LCTR<20 THEN 1270
1250 PRINT "RETURN TO CONTINUE"
1260 GET CO$:IF CO$="" THEN 1260
1270 A7=0
1280 REM A7 NOW = TOT OUTSTANDING
     CHECKS
1290 REM *************************
1300 PRINT
1310 PRINT "OUTSTANDING CHECK LIST"
1320 PRINT "————————————————"
1330 LCTR=LCTR+3
1340 IF PYN$<>"Y" THEN 1390
1350 PRINT# PR
1360 PRINT# PR,"**************************
     *******************************"
1370 PRINT# PR,"*OUTSTANDING CHECKS*"
1380 PRINT# PR,"**************************
     *******************************"
1390 FOR I=1 TO C6
1400 FOR J=1 TO C2
1410 IF N6(I)=N2(J) THEN 1450
1420 NEXT J
1430 A7=A7+A6(O6(I))
1440 GOSUB 1730
1450 NEXT I
1460 PRINT
1470 PRINT "TOTAL OUTSTANDING: ";A7
1480 IF PYN$<>"Y" THEN 1510
1490 PRINT# PR
1500 PRINT# PR,"*TOTAL OUTSTANDING*";
     SPC(36);A7
1510 LCTR=LCTR+2
1520 GOTO 1830
1530 PRINT
1540 PRINT "CK# ";N6(J);" FOR ";A6(O6(J))
1550 PRINT "RETURNED FROM ";
     Q$(O2(I));A2(O2(I))
1560 IF PYN$<>"Y" THEN 1580
1570 PRINT# PR,N6(J);SPC(10-LEN(STR$(N6(J))));
     Q$(O2(I));
1575 PRINT# PR,SPC(30-LEN(Q$(O2(I))));A2(O2(I));
1577 PRINT# PR,SPC(15-LEN(STR$(A2(O2(I)))));
     A6(O6(J))
1580 LCTR=LCTR+4
1590 IF LCTR<20 THEN 1620
1600 PRINT "RETURN TO CONTINUE"
1605 GET CO$:IF CO$="" THEN 1605
1610 LCTR=0
1620 IF A2(O2(I))=A6(O6(J)) THEN 1720
1630 PRINT "***RETURNED AMT NOT =
     REGISTER AMT***"
1640 IF PYN$<>"Y" THEN 1680
1650 PRINT# PR
1660 PRINT# PR,"*RETURNED AMT NOT =
     REGISTER AMT*"
1670 PRINT# PR
1680 LCTR=LCTR+2
1690 IF LCTR<20 THEN 1720
1700 PRINT "RETURN TO CONTINUE"
1705 GET CO$:IF CO$="" THEN 1705
1710 LCTR=0
1720 RETURN
1730 PRINT
1740 PRINT "CK# ";N6(I);" FOR ";A6(O6(I))
1750 PRINT "STILL OUTSTANDING"
1760 IF PYN$<>"Y" THEN 1780
1770 PRINT# PR,N6(I);SPC(55-LEN(STR$(N6(I))));
     A6(O6(I))
1780 LCTR=LCTR+3
1790 IF LCTR<20 THEN 1820
1800 PRINT "RETURN TO CONTINUE"
1805 GET CO$:IF CO$="" THEN 1805
1810 LCTR=0
1820 RETURN
1830 IF PX$="3" THEN 1850
1835 INPUT "RETURN TO CONTINUE";X$
1840 CLOSE PR
1850 END
```

```
CK#      PAYEE                               AMT RETURNED   AMT ISSUED

******************************************************************
  *CHECKS RETURNED*
******************************************************************

110      PUBLIC SERVICE INDIANA              24.82          24.83

  *RETURNED AMT NOT = REGISTER AMT*

115      COMPUTER MGT                        35.73          35.73
118      JOHNSON HARDWARE                    20             20
0        BAD CK NOT RECORDED                 35.09          0

  *RETURNED AMT NOT = REGISTER AMT*

  * NO MATCH FOR CK#: 200 *

  *TOTALS*                                   115.64         80.56

******************************************************************
  *OUTSTANDING CHECKS*
******************************************************************
111                                                         25
113                                                         17.82
117                                                         16.57

  *TOTAL OUTSTANDING*                                       59.39
```

EXPENSE

```
10 REM ***************************
20 REM *          EXPENSE          *
30 REM *                           *
40 REM *      COPYRIGHT 1983       *
50 REM *    DONALD C. KREUTNER     *
60 REM ***************************
70 PRINT CHR$(147):POKE 53280,14:
   POKE 53281,6:PRINT CHR$(5)
75 INPUT "1525 PRTR(1), RS232(2),
   NONE(3)";PX$
80 IF PX$="3" THEN 120
85 IF PX$="1" THEN 100
90 IF PX$="2" THEN 100
95 GOTO 75
100 PR=126
105 IF PX$="1" THEN 115
110 PR=PR+2:OPEN PR,2,0,CHR$(8):PR=128:
    PX$="2":120
115 PR=PR+1:OPEN PR,4
120 REM *************************
190 DIM E$(200)
200 DIM N$(12)
210 REM MM/DD/YY ####### DESCRIPTION
220 PRINT CHR$(147)
230 PRINT TAB(5);"***EXPENSE REPORT***"
240 PRINT
250 INPUT "CASSETTE OR DISK (C/D)";CD$
260 IF CD$="C" THEN 300
270 INPUT "FILE NAME";D$
280 OPEN 2,8,2,"0:"+D$+",S,R"
290 GOTO 310
300 OPEN 2,2,0:REM OPEN CASSETTE
    FOR INPUT
310 FOR I=1 TO 200
320 INPUT# 2,E$(I)
330 IF E$(I)="END" THEN 360
```

EXPENSE is designed to provide you with a list of expense items and a total of their amounts. This program is ideal for month-end expense summaries for salesmen and others who need to keep track of business expenses.

Once again, the input for the program is created by one of the two EDIT programs, EDIT1 or EDIT2. EDIT2 is perhaps the most flexible, since it allows you to resequence your data and insert records where you want them, keeping them properly sequenced by month, day, and year.

The data you key must be in the following format:

Pos. 1-8	Date, by month/day/year (MM/DD/YY)
Pos. 10-16	Amount of the expense, with numbers of exactly seven digits Example: $45.00 is keyed as 0004500
Pos. 18 to end of record	Description of the expense

Following are examples of input data:

```
09/01/83 0004500 AUTO
09/05/83 0025000 RENT EXP
09/10/83 0000100 PARKING
09/13/83 0050000 SALARIES
09/14/83 0002000 DUES
```

Notice that all the date fields and the amount fields must be of the same length,

```
340 PRINT I
350 NEXT I
360 CN=I-1
370 CLOSE 2
380 REM *************************
390 PRINT CHR$(147)
400 PRINT "P";TAB(10);"PRINTER"
410 PRINT "L";TAB(10);"LIST TO SCREEN"
420 PRINT "E";TAB(10);"END PROGRAM"
430 PRINT
440 INPUT "SELECTION";S$
450 PRINT CHR$(147)
460 TTL=0
470 IF S$="E" THEN 1110
480 IF S$="L" THEN 570
490 IF S$<>"P" THEN 390
500 REM *************************
520 INPUT "ENTER MM/DD/YY";DATE$
530 PRINT# PR,SPC(20);"EXPENSE REPORT -
    ";DATE$
540 PRINT# PR
550 PRINT# PR,"DATE";SPC(16);
    "DESCRIPTION";TAB(26);"AMOUNT"
560 PRINT# PR
570 FOR J=1 TO CN
580 IF E$(J)="END" THEN 750
590 DT$=MID$(E$(J),1,8)
600 AMT$=MID$(E$(J),10,7)
610 DESC$=MID$(E$(J),18,LEN(E$(J))-17)
620 AMT=VAL(AMT$)
630 TTL=TTL+AMT
640 NUM1=AMT
650 GOSUB 870
660 PRINT
670 PRINT DT$;TAB(15);N2$
680 PRINT DESC$
690 PRINT "*****************************"
700 IF S$="P" THEN 730
715 GET X$:IF X$="" THEN 715
720 IF S$<>"P" THEN 740
```

since the program "expects" to find those fields in those exact locations. However, the description fields above vary from four to eight characters in length. They could be much longer (for example, 30 to 40 characters, or even more).

Line 250 asks you whether the data file to be used for input is on tape or disk. After the file is loaded into memory by lines 310-370, you are given the option of listing the report to the screen (**L**) or to the printer (**P**), or of ending the program (**E**) in lines 390-440.

If you choose to list the report to the printer, line 520 first asks for the date you want on the heading of the printout. As described earlier, three main details are given on the report: the date, the amount, and the description.

The amount is edited from the raw input data, using the subroutine in lines 860-1100. For instance, 0002000 is changed to 20.00. You may notice that this routine differs from other similar routines that are in the book. This difference simply illustrates that in programming, there are a multitude of alternatives. Even though a particular programmer designs a program one way, the design may not be perfect or even the best. It may not even be good. If you let your imagination flow while writing programs, you will frequently find better alternatives to those you've used before.

In this subroutine, NUM1$ contains the number to be edited. The 12 parts of the array N$ are set to space in lines 890-910. Then the number is examined, right to left, and a decimal point is inserted in the tenth position (lines 920 and 980-990). Finally,

```
730 PRINT# PR,DT$;SPC(12);DESC$;
    SPC(30-LEN(DESC$));N2$
740 NEXT J
750 PRINT
760 NUM1=TTL
770 GOSUB 870
780 PRINT "**TOTAL EXPENSES**";N2$
790 IF S$="P" THEN 820
800 PRINT "RETURN TO CONTINUE"
805 GET X$:IF X$="" THEN 805
810 IF S$<>"P" THEN 390
820 PRINT# PR
830 PRINT# PR,"**TOTAL EXPENSES**";
    SPC(32);N2$
840 GOTO 390
860 REM **************************
870 NUM1$=STR$(NUM1)
880 LN=LEN(NUM1$)
890 FOR I=1 TO 12
900 N$(I)=" ":REM ONE SPACE HERE
910 NEXT I
920 N$(10)="."
930 CTR=13
940 FOR I=LN TO 1 STEP -1
950 CTR=CTR-1
960 IF CTR<1 THEN 1020
970 PS$=MID$(NUM1$,I,1)
980 IF CTR<>10 THEN 1000
990 CTR=CTR-1
1000 N$(CTR)=PS$
1010 NEXT I
1020 IF N$(11)<>" " THEN 1040
```

N2$ (the edited result) is created by concatenating (joining) the 12 parts of N$ in lines 1070-1090.

```
1025 REM ONE SPACE IN 1020, 1040, 1060
1030 N$(11)="0"
1040 IF N$(12)<>" " THEN 1060
1050 N$(12)="0"
1060 N2$=" "
1070 FOR I=1 TO 12
1080 N2$=N2$+N$(I)
1090 NEXT I
1100 RETURN
1110 END
```

EXPENSE REPORT - 09/30/83

DATE	DESCRIPTION	AMOUNT
09/01/83	TRIP EXPENSE	40.50
09/02/83	MISCELLANEOUS	50.00
09/02/83	PARKING	1.50
09/02/83	SUPPLIES	500.98
09/05/83	MISC EXPENSES	35.00
09/10/83	OFFICE SALARY	200.00
09/15/83	CHAIR	100.00
09/20/83	MILEAGE EXPENSE	198.75
09/23/83	PAPER	3.00
09/25/83	MILEAGE EXPENSE	232.43
09/30/83	ENTERTAINMENT	54.30
TOTAL EXPENSES		1416.46

FLASHCARD

```
10 REM **************************
20 REM *        FLASHCARD       *
30 REM *                        *
40 REM *      COPYRIGHT 1983    *
50 REM *    DONALD C. KREUTNER  *
60 REM **************************
70 PRINT CHR$(147):POKE 53280,14:
   POKE 53281,6:PRINT CHR$(5)
180 DIM Q$(200)
190 DIM A$(200)
200 E=0
210 C=0
220 LAST1=0
240 PRINT CHR$(147)
250 PRINT TAB(7);"FLASHCARD"
260 PRINT
270 PRINT "C    CLEAR PREVIOUS QUIZ"
280 PRINT "R    READ QUIZ FROM FILE"
290 PRINT "Q    QUIZ WITH QUESTIONS"
300 PRINT "A    QUIZ WITH ANSWERS"
310 PRINT "E    END PROGRAM"
320 PRINT
330 INPUT "SELECTION";S$
340 IF S$="C" THEN 380
350 IF S$="R" THEN 410
360 IF S$="Q" THEN 630
370 IF S$="A" THEN 630
380 IF S$="E" THEN 1000
390 LAST1=0
400 GOTO 240
410 INPUT "CASSETTE OR DISK (C/D)";CD$
420 IF CD$="C" THEN 470
430 IF CD$<>"D" THEN 410
440 INPUT "FILE NAME";D$
450 OPEN 2,8,2,"0:"+D$+",S,R"
460 GOTO 480
```

FLASHCARD is a program that can be of immense benefit to any student.

Many programs may be purchased to help you learn about different subjects. With most of these programs, however, you are forced to use the data that comes with the programs. Usually, you are not able to influence the selection of questions and answers on which you want to be drilled.

But with FLASHCARD you can key in all the new Spanish words, for example, as you encounter them, chapter by chapter. Thus, you can tailor data files for your own personal use, rather than review information you may not even need in the actual course work you are taking.

You can also save practically unlimited amounts of information on cassette or disk files for use at any time. Thus, you can effectively collect, add to, and review all the educational data you need.

What a tool this program can be for any subject! Students can drill on their special problem areas at their own pace and receive individual, "computerized" attention with the benefits of immediate feedback.

The beauty of this simple program is that you can ask any kind of question on any subject. The input files for FLASHCARD, as for many other programs in this book, can be created and modified easily by using EDIT1 or EDIT2. The first record the pro-

```
470 OPEN 2,1,0:REM OPEN TAPE FOR INPUT
480 IF LAST1<200 THEN 510
490 PRINT "200 MAXIMUM QUESTIONS"
500 GOTO 240
510 FOR I=LAST1+1 TO 200
520 INPUT# 2,X$
530 IF X$="END" THEN 610
540 PRINT I
550 Q$(I)=X$
560 INPUT# 2,X$
570 A$(I)=X$
580 IF X$="END" THEN 610
590 LAST1=I
600 NEXT I
610 CLOSE 2
620 GOTO 240
630 PRINT CHR$(147)
640 INPUT "SEQUENTIAL OR RANDOM
    (S/R)";SR$
650 R=0
660 IF SR$="R" THEN 710
670 R=R+1
680 IF R<=LAST1 THEN 720
690 R=1
700 GOTO 720
710 R=INT(LAST1*RND(1))+1
720 IF S$="A" THEN 750
730 PRINT Q$(R)
740 GOTO 760
750 PRINT A$(R)
760 INPUT A1$
770 IF A1$="END" THEN 240
780 IF LEN(A1$)<1 THEN 240
790 IF A1$="STOP" THEN 240
800 IF S$="Q" THEN 830
810 IF A1$=Q$(R) THEN 940
820 GOTO 840
830 IF A1$=A$(R) THEN 940
840 PRINT "*****"
850 PRINT "WRONG"
```

gram reads will be considered the "question" and the next record the "answer"; the third record will be another question followed by another answer; and so on, until the end of the file. Up to 200 questions and answers can be read in by FLASHCARD for use at one time. But the length of the questions and answers can limit how many items can be maintained in memory.

The arrays of Q$ and A$ hold the questions and answers (lines 180-190). C and E keep track of how many correct and incorrect answers the person who is answering has obtained since the beginning of the program. And LAST1 (line 220) "remembers" where the last question/answer is located within the Q$ and A$ arrays.

You can clear the memory of a quiz that you've read in, or you can accumulate one or more files by not clearing memory (using the command **C**). You can read in a file (**R**), and you are allowed two modes of quizzes. **Q** means you want the standard question-and-answer quiz, whereas **A** means you want to be "asked" the answers and respond with the questions.

A good way to use this last feature (in Spanish, for example) would be to give either the English answers or the Spanish answers simply by asking for the questions or answers (**Q** or **A**). If you consider home computer prices, this program alone makes the computer a worthwhile investment for not only a school but also a family.

In FLASHCARD, when you ask for a quiz, you can specify whether you want the questions to be asked randomly or whether you want to go through the questions one at

```
860 PRINT
870 PRINT Q$(R)
880 PRINT A$(R)
890 PRINT "*****"
900 E=E+1
910 PRINT
920 PRINT "ERRORS=";E;" CORRECT=";C
930 GOTO 660
940 PRINT
945 PRINT Q$(R)
950 PRINT A$(R)
960 C=C+1
970 PRINT "ERRORS=";E;" CORRECT=";C
980 PRINT
990 GOTO 660
1000 PRINT CHR$(147)
1010 PRINT "CORRECT: ";C
1020 PRINT "ERRORS: ";E
1030 IF E+C<1 THEN 1050
1040 PRINT INT((100*C)/(E+C));"%"
1050 END
```

a time, repetitively. The random approach helps you to master the material so that you are not dependent on the order of the questions. At times, especially when you are reviewing information, you may prefer to go through the list of questions (or answers) quickly, over and over again. As one professor used to say, "Repetition and review, repetition and review." The key to learning is proper training.

At the end of the program, the number correct and the number of errors are displayed, along with the percentage of correct answers.

The following two programs, GENLED1 and GENLED2, are to be used together. GENLED1 is used to key financial data, whereas GENLED2 reads that data and produces a formatted report with totals. They accumulate income and/or expense data in a disk or cassette file and produce reports summarizing the monthly and year-to-date totals of all transactions by account number and date. Together, these programs can be a most versatile tool for a small business in maintaining documents like general ledgers or for home use in tracking income and expense information. You are free to set up your own "chart of accounts," and all the data files created by GENLED1 can be added to or changed as new transactions become available. Note that in the following descriptions of each program, frequent reference is made to the other program.

```
LA PLUMA
THE PEN
LA MUJER
THE WOMAN
EL HOMBRE
THE MAN
EL MUCHACHO
THE BOY
EL HERMANO
THE BROTHER
LA MUCHACHA
THE GIRL
LA HERMANA
THE SISTER
YO
I
DAR
TO GIVE
EL COLOR
THE COLOR
EL TREN
THE TRAIN
EL AVION
THE AIRPLANE
LA MANANA
THE MORNING
LA TARDE
THE AFTERNOON
BUENAS NOCHES
GOOD EVENING
LA NOCHE
THE NIGHT
USTED
YOU
ELLA
SHE
EL
HE
HABLAR
TO SPEAK
INGLES
ENGLISH
ESPANOL
SPANISH
QUIEN
WHO
EL DINERO
THE MONEY
EL DIA
THE DAY
LUNES
MONDAY
MARTES
TUESDAY
MIERCOLES
WEDNESDAY
JUEVES
THURSDAY
VIERNES
FRIDAY
SABADO
SATURDAY
DOMINGO
SUNDAY
```

GENLED1

```
10 REM **************************
20 REM *          GENLED1              *
30 REM *                                     *
40 REM *       COPYRIGHT 1983        *
50 REM *    DONALD C. KREUTNER     *
60 REM **************************
70 PRINT CHR$(147):POKE 53280,14:
   POKE 53281,6:PRINT CHR$(5)
75 INPUT "1525 PRTR(1), RS232(2),
   NONE(3)";PX$
80 IF PX$="3" THEN 120
85 IF PX$="1" THEN 100
90 IF PX$="2" THEN 100
95 GOTO 75
100 PR=126
105 IF PX$="1" THEN 115
110 PR=PR+2:OPEN PR,2,0,CHR$(8):
    PR=128:PX$="2":GOTO 120
115 PR=PR+1:OPEN PR,4
120 PRINT CHR$(147)
180 DIM A$(500)
190 DIM A2$(500)
200 FOR I= 1 TO 500
210 A$(I)="@"
220 NEXT I
230 LAST1=1
235 GOTO 390
240 REM *****COMMANDS*****
250 INPUT B$
260 IF B$="HELP" THEN 390
270 IF B$="C" THEN 200
280 IF B$="A" THEN 530
290 IF B$="D" THEN 780
300 IF B$="T" THEN 890
310 IF B$="L" THEN 1080
320 IF B$="K" THEN 1150
```

GENLED1 is actually a modified version of EDIT2. In fact, youcan use either EDIT1 or EDIT2 to key the data for GENLED2. However, the advantage to a program like GENLED1 is that some editing of the fields is done as they are entered. For example, the date is checked for slashes in the 3rd and 6th positions of the 8-character date field (lines 610-620). The source code (check number or any other identifying information for each transaction) must be exactly four characters long (lines 635-695). The account number and payee number must each be exactly three characters long (lines 590 and 630). These data checks greatly reduce the possibility of keying errors.

GENLED1 can be modified to create data for other programs by altering the lines that do the actual keying and editing (lines 520-760). You can key any fields and join them together into a record, as in line 710.

All data to be used by GENLED2 is contained in one string of character data; that is, there are no integers or real numbers in the file itself. The first three characters represent the account number of the transaction. Positions 4-11 contain the eight-digit transaction date separated by two slashes. Note that each digit must be keyed. (For example, January 1, 1983, is keyed as **01/01/83.**) Positions 12-14 contain the three-digit payee number. (You must decide what numbers you want to assign to each payee, just as you must create your

```
330 IF B$="LU" THEN 1300
340 IF B$="R" THEN 1370
350 IF B$="P" THEN 1550
360 IF B$="PU" THEN 1650
370 IF B$="E" THEN 1730
380 REM *****HELP SCREEN*****
390 PRINT TAB(5);"*GENLED1*"
395 PRINT "HELPPRINT THESE INSTRUCTIONS"
400 PRINT "A     ADD LINES"
410 PRINT "C     CLEAR WORKFILE"
420 PRINT "D     DELETE LINES"
430 PRINT "T     TEXT IN A FILE"
440 PRINT "L     LIST WORKFILE"
450 PRINT "K     KEEP A FILE"
460 PRINT "LU    LIST WORKFILE
                 UNNUMBERED"
470 PRINT "R     RENUMBER WORKFILE"
480 PRINT "P     PRINT WORKFILE"
490 PRINT "PU    PRINT WORKFILE
                 UNNUMBERED"
500 PRINT "E     END PROGRAM"
510 GOTO 250
512 REM GENLED1 IS A MODIFIED VERSION
514 REM OF EDIT2 THAT ALLOWS YOU TO
516 REM KEY FIELD BY FIELD THE INPUT
517 REM DATA FOR GENLED2 TO AVOID
518 REM DATA ENTRY ERRORS
520 REM *****ADD LINES*****
530 INPUT "LINE #";A
540 INPUT "STEP #";S1
550 IF S1<>0 THEN 570
560 S1=5
570 IF A$(A)<>"@" THEN 740
575 PRINT "REC# ";A
580 INPUT "ACCT# (OR END)";ACCT$
585 IF A<LAST1 THEN 605
590 IF LEN(ACCT$)<>3 THEN 580
595 IF A<LAST1 THEN 605
600 LAST1=A
605 IF ACCT$="END" THEN 760
```

own account number descriptions in the DATA statements of GENLED2.)

Notice that if an account is an income account, the "payee" can be used to classify different categories of the same account number and to keep appropriate subtotal information. The source field in positions 15-18 is used to record the check number or other appropriate identifying information for the transaction. For example, check #101 could have 101 or 0101 in the position 4 source field. The amount of the transaction is encoded starting in position 19. Leading zeros are suppressed from the amount field. The number of account numbers and payee numbers allowed is set at 100 each by SIZEA.

These limits can be changed by modifying the statements in lines 210-240 of GENLED2, but raising them too high can cause the report program to run out of memory. For most applications fewer than 100 of each should be quite satisfactory. Obviously, this tool is not designed for a very large business (although appropriate summary financial information can be provided).

The **DATA** statements in lines 330-680 in GENLED2 provide the account names and payee information for the desired numbers. As mentioned earlier, these lines can be changed for your own personal use. Lines 780-880 read in the account and payee data and provide a printout, if one is desired. Lines 910-1000 cause a data file to be read in from cassette or diskette, and subsequently a report is printed (to the screen only or to a printer) as the file is read.

```
610 INPUT "DATE (MM/DD/YY)";DATE$
615 IF MID$(DATE$,3,1)<>"/" THEN 610
620 IF MID$(DATE$,6,1)<>"/" THEN 610
625 INPUT "PAYEE#";PAY$
630 IF LEN(PAY$)<>3 THEN 625
635 INPUT "SOURCE";SRC$
640 IF LEN(SRC$)=4 THEN 700
645 IF LEN(SRC$)>4 THEN 635
650 IF LEN(SRC$)<>3 THEN 665
655 SRC$=SRC$+" ":REM ONE SPACE HERE
660 GOTO 700
665 IF LEN(SRC$)<>2 THEN 680
670 SRC$=SRC$+"  ":REM 2 SPACES HERE
675 GOTO 700
680 IF LEN(SRC$)<>1 THEN 695
685 SRC$=SRC$+"   ":REM 3 SPACES HERE
690 GOTO 700
695 SRC$="    ";REM 4 SPACES HERE
700 INPUT "AMOUNT";AMT
705 AMT$=STR$(AMT)
710 A$(A)=ACCT$+DATE$+PAY$+SRC$+AMT$
715 A=A+S1
730 GOTO 570
740 PRINT "THIS LINE ALREADY EXISTS"
750 PRINT A$(A)
760 GOTO 250
770 REM *****DELETE LINES*****
780 INPUT "BEG LINE #";B
790 INPUT "END LINE #";E
791 IF E<LAST1 THEN 800
792 LAST1=B
793 A$(B)="END"
800 IF E>500 THEN 790
810 FOR I=B TO E
820 IF A$(I)="@" THEN 860
830 REM ***SAME AS ABOVE LINES***
840 PRINT " ";A$(I)
850 A$(I)="@"
860 NEXT I
870 GOTO 250
```

Because the report appears simultaneously with the file that is read, you must maintain the records in the proper order; that is, all of the records for account number 001 should be first, in the order of date sequence. With this method, month-to-date and year-to-date totals can be obtained from the file for any month.

The data entry portion of GENLED1 has several interesting features to ensure that only "clean" data is entered. Of course, more edits can be added for any other errors you may want to check.

If you are starting a new data file, you can begin with record number 1 after responding **A** to the beginning menu screen. You are required to give the starting record number (1 for a new file) and the desired increment. An increment of 1 means the records added will be numbered 1, 2, 3, etc., whereas an increment of 5 causes numbering of 1, 6, 11, etc.

When adding new records, you can insert them where desired by renumbering the file and by leaving empty record number gaps. You can then request to add record number 2 after renumbering by a step of 5.

To stop entering records, just key **END**, to terminate the entry and return you to the menu screen (which is just like the EDIT2 menu). To save the data you have entered, key **K** to keep the file. If saving to disk, you will be prompted for the name of the file whose data you want to save. (You might select a name like GL83.) If you are writing the data to tape, the screen will prompt you to rewind the tape, press record, etc.

```
880 REM *****TEXT IN FILE*****
890 INPUT "CASSETTE OR DISK (C/D)";CD$
900 IF CD$="D" THEN 940
910 IF CD$<>"C" THEN 890
915 OPEN 2,1,0:REM OPEN TAPE FOR INPUT
920 GOTO 960
940 INPUT "FILE NAME";F$
950 OPEN 2,8,2,"0:"+F$+",S,R"
960 INPUT "STEP #";S1
970 IF S1<>0 THEN 990
980 S1=5
990 FOR I=LAST1 TO 500 STEP S1
1000 INPUT# 2,X$
1005 A$(I)=X$
1010 IF A$(I)="END" THEN 1040
1020 LAST1=I
1030 NEXT I
1040 CLOSE 2
1045 IF I>500 THEN I=500
1050 A$(I)="@"
1060 GOTO 250
1070 REM *****LIST WORKFILE*****
1080 FOR I=1 TO 500
1090 IF I>LAST1 THEN 1130
1100 IF A$(I)="@" THEN 1120
1110 PRINT I;A$(I)
1120 NEXT I
1130 GOTO 250
1140 REM *****KEEP AS A FILE*****
1150 INPUT "CASSETTE OR DISK (C/D)";CD$
1160 IF CD$="D" THEN 1190
1170 OPEN 2,1,2:REM OPEN TAPE FOR OUTPUT
1180 GOTO 1210
1190 INPUT "OUTPUT FILE NAME";F$
1200 OPEN 2,8,2,"@0:"+F$+",S,W"
1210 FOR I=1 TO 500
1220 IF I>LAST1 THEN 1260
1230 IF A$(I)="@" THEN 1250
1240 PRINT# 2,A$(I)
1250 NEXT I
```

You can also print out the data you have keyed by using the **P** or **PU** command. Then you can see what you have keyed, and you can correct any errors or make additions to the file.

To delete a detail record, you need only key **D** to the menu prompts, followed by the record number range that you want to delete. If you want to change a record, you first need to delete it and then add it back by using the **A** command mentioned earlier.

```
1260 PRINT# 2,"END"
1270 CLOSE 2
1280 GOTO 250
1290 REM *****LIST WORKFILE
     UNNUMBERED*****
1300 FOR I=1 TO 500
1310 IF I>LAST1 THEN 1350
1320 IF A$(I)="@" THEN 1340
1330 PRINT A$(I)
1340 NEXT I
1350 GOTO 250
1360 REM *****RENUMBER WORKFILE*****
1370 INPUT "STEP #";S1
1380 J=0
1390 IF STP1<>0 THEN 1410
1400 S1=5
1410 FOR I=1 TO 500
1420 A2$(I)="@"
1430 NEXT I
1440 FOR I=1 TO 500
```

```
1450 IF I>LAST1 THEN 1500
1460 IF A$(I)="@" THEN 1490
1470 J=J+S1
1480 A2$(J)=A$(I)
1490 NEXT I
1500 FOR I=1 TO 500
1510 A$(I)=A2$(I)
1515 IF A$(I)="@" THEN 1520
1516 LAST1=I
1520 NEXT I
1530 GOTO 250
1540 REM *****PRINT WORKFILE*****
1550 FOR I=1 TO 500
1570 IF I>LAST1 THEN 1620
1580 IF A$(I)="@" THEN 1610
1590 REM *****VARIOUS LINES FOR
     LENGTH OF A*****
1600 PRINT# PR,I;TAB(5);A$(I)
1610 NEXT I
1620 GOTO 250
1640 REM *****PRINT WORKFILE
     UNNUMBERED*****
1650 FOR I=1 TO 500
1660 IF I>LAST1 THEN 1710
1680 IF A$(I)="@" THEN 1700
1690 PRINT# PR,A$(I)
1700 NEXT I
1710 GOTO 250
1730 IF PX$="3" THEN 1750
1740 CLOSE PR
1750 END
```

GENLED2

```
10 REM ***************************
20 REM *          GENLED2         *
30 REM *                          *
40 REM *       COPYRIGHT 1983     *
50 REM *     DONALD C. KREUTNER   *
60 REM ***************************
70 PRINT CHR$(147):POKE 53280,14:
   POKE 53281,6:PRINT CHR$(5)
75 INPUT "1525 PRTR(1), RS232(2),
   NONE(3)";PX$
80 IF PX$="3" THEN 120
85 IF PX$="1" THEN 100
90 IF PX$="2" THEN 100
95 GOTO 75
100 PR=126
105 IF PX$="1" THEN 115
110 PR=PR+2:OPEN PR,2,0,CHR$(8):
    PR=128:PX$="2":GOTO 120
115 PR=PR+1:OPEN PR,4
120 REM *************************
170 REM DETAIL$ LAYOUT
180 REM AC# DATE PYE SRC AMT
190 REM ###XX/XX/XX###XXXX#####...
200 SIZEA=100
210 DIM ACCT$(100)
220 DIM PAY$(100)
230 DIM PM(100)
240 DIM PY(100)
250 REM BELOW 3 DIGIT ACCT #
260 REM FOLLOWED BY A + OR -
270 REM FOLLOWED BY ACCT DESC
280 FOR I=1 TO SIZEA
290 PM(I)=0
300 PY(I)=0
310 NEXT I
320 REM *************************
```

GENLED2 reads the data keyed from GENLED1 and produces reports from that data. As discussed in the previous program, GENLED1 keys the detail records and updates already existing files as new data becomes available. Be sure to key the data in the proper order. For instance, you will want to maintain your input in account number by date order. If, by chance, your file size gets too large for GENLED1 to handle easily, you can summarize the year-to-date activity for each account number/payee with one transaction in a new file, preceding the new details.

Now let's go through the following example.

1. To start a new file, run the GENLED1 program.
2. Type **A** after the **/** to add new records when the menu screen appears (described below).

```
          *GENLED1*

A         ADD LINES
C         CLEAR WORKFILE
D         DELETE LINES
T         TEXT IN A FILE
L         LIST WORKFILE
K         KEEP A FILE
LU        LIST UNNUMBERED
R         RENUMBER WORKFILE
P         PRINT WORKFILE
PU        PRINT UNNUMBERED
E         END PROGRAM
```

```
330 DATA "001-ACCOUNTING, LEGAL"
340 DATA "002-ADVERTISING"
350 DATA "005-AUTO EXPENSE"
360 DATA "010-BAD DEBTS"
370 DATA "012-DEPRECIATION"
380 DATA "015-DONATIONS"
390 DATA "020-EMPLOYEE RETIREMENT"
400 DATA "021-EMPLOYEE BENEFITS"
410 DATA "022-EMPLOYEE SALARIES"
420 DATA "025-INSURANCE"
430 DATA "030-INTEREST PAID"
440 DATA "035-LICENSE"
450 DATA "040-OFFICE/POSTAGE"
460 DATA "042-RENT"
470 DATA "044-REPAIRS/MAINTENANCE"
480 DATA "046-SELLING EXPENSE"
490 DATA "047-TELEPHONE"
500 DATA "048-TRAVEL/ENTERTAINMENT"
510 DATA "049-WARRANTIES"
520 DATA "070-FED INCOME CORP"
530 DATA "071-FED FICA CORP"
540 DATA "073-FED UNEMPLOYMENT"
550 DATA "080-INDIANA INCOME CORP"
560 DATA "082-INDIANA UNEMPLOYMENT"
570 DATA "083-INDIANA SALES TAX"
580 DATA "084-INDIANA REAL PROPERTY"
590 DATA "085-INDIANA MISC"
600 DATA "087-KY MISC"
610 DATA "088-KY SALES TAX"
620 DATA "100+INCOME"
625 DATA "999-NO DESCRIPTION"
630 REM ************************
640 REM FOLLOWING ARE PAYEES
650 DATA "001-PAYEE # 1"
660 DATA "002-PAYEE # 2"
670 DATA "003-PAYEE # 3"
680 DATA "999-NO DESCRIPTION"
690 REM ************************
700 REM ACCT$=ACCT # INFO
710 REM PAY$=PAYEE INFO
```

3. Key **1** to the "LINE#:" prompt; key **1** to the "STEP#:" prompt.
4. Start entering data by hitting **ENTER** after each field is keyed.

ACCT# (or END):	001
DATE (MM/DD/YY):	01/01/83
PAYEE#:	001
SOURCE:	101
AMOUNT:	5500

After you key the amount (remember that 5500 means fifty-five dollars, since two decimal positions are implied), you will be prompted for the account number of "REC# 2."

Continue in the same manner until you have entered all the records desired. As you finish each record, the data is stored in the A$ array of GENLED1 in the following format:

```
ACCT DATE PYE SRC AMOUNT
###01/01/83###XXXX......
```

Notice that each field immediately follows the previous one, with no spaces in between. However, for maximum readability, the data that follows, from records 1 to 17, has one space between each field:

```
001 01/01/83 001 101 5500
001 01/15/83 002 105 4000
001 02/10/83 001 115 5098
001 02/20/83 001 120 5500
001 03/08/83 002 130 4650
001 03/25/83 001 138 5400
002 01/01/83 003 102 2500
002 01/24/83 003 107 2000
002 02/25/83 003 122 2325
002 03/17/83 003 135 2575
```

```
720 REM DETAIL$=DETAIL INFO
730 REM A2$=DETAIL ACCT #
740 REM MY$=DETAIL MO/DAY/YR
750 REM PN$=DETAIL PAYEE #
760 REM AMT$=DETAIL AMT
770 REM ************************
780 FOR I=1 TO SIZEA
790 READ X$
795 PRINT X$
800 ACCT$(I)=X$
810 IF MID$(X$,1,3)="999" THEN 830
820 NEXT I
830 REM *END OF ACCT # READ*
840 FOR I=1 TO SIZEA
850 READ X$
855 PRINT X$
860 PAY$(I)=X$
870 IF MID$(X$,1,3)="999" THEN 890
880 NEXT I
890 REM *END OF PAYEE READ*
900 REM ************************
910 INPUT "CASSETTE OR DISK (C/D)";RE$
920 IF RE$="D" THEN 960
930 OPEN 2,1,0:REM OPEN TAPE FOR INPUT
940 GOTO 990
950 REM ************************
960 INPUT "FILE NAME";F$
970 OPEN 2,8,2,"0:"+F$+",S,R"
980 REM ************************
990 PRINT CHR$(147)
1000 A$="A"
1010 INPUT "MM/YY DESIRED";MMYY$
1020 YYMM$=MID$(MMYY$,4,2)+MID$(MMYY$,1,2)
1030 INPUT "LIST DETAILS";DYN$
1040 INPUT "PRINTER (Y/N)";PYN$
1045 IF PX$="3" THEN PYN$="N"
1050 IF PYN$<>"Y" THEN 1240
1070 GOSUB 1090
1080 GOTO 1240
1090 REM ********************
```

```
002 03/19/83 003 136 2480
002 03/28/83 003 140 2900
005 01/01/83 999 103 5500
005 01/11/83 002 104 5350
005 02/05/83 999 113 7500
005 03/09/83 002 131 45040
005 03/25/83 999 139 5000
END
```

After keying **END** for the ACCT# following the last transaction, you key **K** after the **/** to keep the file on cassette or disk. Key **C** or **D** to the "CASSETTE or DISK (C/D):" prompt. If you are keeping to disk, you will be asked for the output file name, to which you key whatever name you choose, for example, **GL83**. To keep the file to tape, key **C** and respond to the prompts of "REWIND CASSETTE...," "PRESS RECORD...," etc.

When you use GENLED1, you can also list the file you have stored in memory by keying either **LU** to list unnumbered records or **L** to reveal the record numbers. The commands **PU** and **P** will do the same thing to the printer.

At this time you could print your report using GENLED2, but let's say that you left out a record, included one you shouldn't have, and made an error on a third. Either you can make those changes right now, or days later you can text in the same file from tape or disk by using the **T** command of GENLED1.

To text in a file, key **T** and answer **C** or **D** again (for cassette or disk). Then tell the program the disk file name (**GL83**, for example) or respond to the prompts of "PRESS PLAY...," etc., for a tape file. You will next be asked for the "STEP#:"—to

```
1100 IF A$="A" THEN 1150
1110 PRINT# PR,SPC(30);"SUMMARY BY PAYEE"
1120 PRINT# PR
1130 PRINT# PR,"PAYEE";SPC(15);"SRC";SPC(3);
     "ACCOUNT";SPC(33);MMYY$;SPC(1);
1135 PRINT# PR,"YTD"
1140 GOTO 1180
1150 PRINT# PR,SPC(30);"SUMMARY BY
     ACCOUNT #"
1160 PRINT# PR
1170 PRINT# PR,"ACCOUNT";SPC(13);"SRC";
     SPC(2);"PAYEE";SPC(33);MMYY$;SPC(8);
1175 PRINT# PR,"YTD"
1180 FOR I=1 TO 79
1190 PRINT# PR,"-";
1200 NEXT I
1210 PRINT# PR
1220 LINECTR=4
1230 RETURN
1240 LTTL3=0
1250 DETAILCTR=0
1260 YMLTTL=0
1270 GL3TTL=0
1280 LGTTLYM=0
1290 L3$="999"
1300 LYYMM$="9999"
1310 FOR I=1 TO 500
1320 INPUT# 2,DETAIL$
1325 IF DETAIL$<>"END" THEN 1340
1326 GOSUB 2290
1330 IF DETAIL$="END" THEN 1930
1340 IF MID$(DETAIL$,1,3)="000" THEN 1920
1350 TYYMM$=MID$(DETAIL$,10,2)+MID$
     (DETAIL$,4,2)
1360 T3$=MID$(DETAIL$,1,3)
1370 LD=LEN(DETAIL$)
1380 L2D=LD-18
1390 AMT1$=MID$(DETAIL$,19)
1400 AMT1=VAL(AMT1$)
1410 SRC$=MID$(DETAIL$,15,4)
```

which you might answer **3** or **5** if you want to be able to insert a few records into their proper order. (Let's key **3** here.) This method will renumber the records as they are read in, but the same thing can be done again and again by using the **R** (RENUMBER) command.

Now let's add a record before the second record (001 01/15/83 002 1054000) with the information that follows:

001 01/16/83 001 106 2500

You can first list the resequenced data by keying **L** or **P**, which shows the gaps that have been left. Then you key **A** followed by the "new" line number to be added (**2**) and a step of **1**. You enter the ACCT#, DATE, PAYEE#, SOURCE, and AMOUNT fields, just as before. An **L** command will then show the new data in proper sequence.

To delete record number 4 (originally the third record as resequenced), key **D** to the **/**, followed by **4** for the "BEG LINE#:" and **4** for the "END LINE#:". Notice that when you delete a record, the record after the one deleted is displayed to the screen. Now an **L** command shows that record 4 is gone.

To correct a record—for instance, the last record (now renumbered to 49)—first delete it (**D** and **49** for the beginning and ending numbers) and then add it back correctly using the **A** command. Now reenter it as

005 03/26/83 999 139 5000

by keying **A**, then **49** for the "LINE#:" and **1** for the "STEP#:" followed by the new data and **END**.

```
1420 REM IF T3$="999" THEN 1450
1430 IF L3$=T3$ THEN 1460
1440 IF L3$="999" THEN 1460
1450 GOSUB 2290
1460 L3$=T3$
1470 LYYMM$=TYYMM$
1480 PX$=MID$(DETAIL$,12,3)
1490 FOR K=1 TO SIZEA
1500 P3$=MID$(PAY$(K),1,3)
1510 IF P3$>=PX$ THEN 1530
1520 NEXT K
1530 FOR L=1 TO SIZEA
1540 A3$=MID$(ACCT$(L),1,3)
1550 IF A3$>=MID$(DETAIL$,1,3) THEN 1570
1560 NEXT L
1570 LP=LEN(PAY$(K))
1580 LA=LEN(ACCT$(L))
1590 IF MID$(ACCT$(L),4,1)<>"-" THEN 1610
1600 AMT1=AMT1*(-1)
1610 IF T3$="999" THEN 1930
1620 LSTACCT$=ACCT$(L)
1630 LPAY$=PAY$(K)
1640 IF TYYMM$>YYMM$ THEN 1680
1650 LTTL3=LTTL3+AMT1
1660 GL3TTL=GL3TTL+AMT1
1670 PY(K)=PY(K)+AMT1
1680 IF TYYMM$<>YYMM$ THEN 1920
1690 YMLTTL=YMLTTL+AMT1
1700 LGTTLYM=LGTTLYM+AMT1
1710 PM(K)=PM(K)+AMT1
1720 IF DYN$<>"Y" THEN 1920
1730 NUMED=AMT1
1740 MASK$="XXX,XXX.XX-"
1750 GOSUB 2570
1760 IF MID$(DETAIL$,12,3)=MID$(PAY$(K),1,3)
     THEN 1790
1770 STR1$=MID$(DETAIL$,12,3)+"-NO
     DESCRIPTION"
1780 GOTO 1800
```

Again, you *must* keep the file to cassette or disk (the same file name unless you purposely don't want to overlay the original file). As with all files, you should keep a backup copy of any file worth saving. Now that you have the proper input data, you are ready to run the report using GENLED2. First, of course, you must end GENLED1 by keying **E** after the **/**. (Be sure you have "kept" your file first.)

Running GENLED2 is fairly easy. Once you get familiar with entering and changing files using GENLED1, both programs should be quite simple to use. You may need to step through these detailed instructions to become thoroughly at ease with the file creation. In running GENLED2, you are first asked if the input file is on "CASSETTE or DISK:". As usual, key **C** or **D** and, if on disk, the filename, such as **GL83**.

Next are requested the months and year you want on the report ("MM/YY DESIRED:"), to which you key, for example, **03/83**. Then "LIST DETAILS? (Y/N):" asks whether you want to have only ACCT# totals or all the details for the month requested. Answer **Y** for the details or **N** for totals only.

"PRINTER (Y/N):" allows you to print the report either on the screen only or to a printer. Now, as the file is read, the report is displayed either on the screen, or on both the screen and your printer. On the screen each transaction is displayed with the date and source code, followed by the payee number and description, and the amount. The next records are displayed in the same

```
1790 STR1$=MID$(DETAIL$,12,3)+"-"+MID$
     (PAY$(K),5)
1800 IF LINECTR<50 THEN 1820
1810 GOSUB 1090
1820 DETAILCTR=DETAILCTR+1
1830 IF PYN$<>"Y" THEN 1890
1840 IF DETAILCTR>1 THEN 1870
1850 PRINT# PR
1860 LINECTR=LINECTR+1
1870 PRINT# PR,SPC(10);MID$(DETAIL$,4,8);
     SPC(2);MID$(DETAIL$,15,4);SPC(1);
1875 PRINT# PR,STR1$;
     SPC(24-LEN(STR1$));MASK$
1880 LINECTR=LINECTR+1
1890 PRINT MID$(DETAIL$,4,8);
     SPC(1);MID$(DETAIL$,15,4)
1900 PRINT STR1$
1910 PRINT MASK$
1920 NEXT I
1930 LTTL3=GL3TTL
1940 YMLTTL=LGTTLYM
1942 PMTTL=0
1944 PYTTL=0
1950 CLOSE 2
1960 GOSUB 2480
1970 IF PYN$<>"Y" THEN 2000
1980 PRINT# PR
1990 PRINT# PR,"*TOTAL*";SPC(51);YMLTTL$;
     SPC(11-LEN(YMLTTL$));L3TTL$
2000 PRINT "*TOT*";YMLTTL$;SPC(1);L3TTL$
2010 IF PYN$<>"Y" THEN 2090
2020 PRINT# PR,CHR$(12)
2030 PRINT# PR,"PAYEE SUMMARY FOR -
     ";MMYY$;SPC(35);"CURRENT";SPC(8);"YTD
2040 FOR I=1 TO 79
2050 PRINT# PR,"-";
2060 NEXT I
2070 PRINT# PR
2080 PRINT# PR
2090 FOR I=1 TO SIZEA
```

fashion. When the account number changes, a total for the account is given. And at the end of the report, totals are given for the month and year-to-date, as well as totals for each payee number.

One final feature of GENLED2 is important to mention. A minus sign (-) between the account number and the description in the **DATA** statements will cause values to be kept as negative totals for that account, but a plus sign (+) will cause positive totals. This can be shown by adding the following final record to the file above:

```
100 03/30/83 999 SALE 150000
```

Now see the final report at the end of the program.

```
2100 IF PM(I)<>0 THEN 2120
2110 IF PY(I)=0 THEN 2250
2120 NUMED=PY(I)
2130 MASK$="XXX,XXX.XX-"
2140 GOSUB 2570
2150 L3TTL$=MASK$
2160 NUMED=PM(I)
2170 MASK$="XXX,XXX.XX-"
2180 GOSUB 2570
2190 YMLTTL$=MASK$
2192 PMTTL=PMTTL+PM(I)
2194 PYTTL=PYTTL+PY(I)
2200 IF PYN$<>"Y" THEN 2220
```

```
2210 PRINT# PR,"PAYEE# ";PAY$(I);
     SPC(50-LEN(PAY$(I)));YMLTTL$;
     SPC(1);L3TTL$
2220 PRINT "PAYEE# ";PAY$(I)
2230 PRINT MMYY$;SPC(1);YMLTTL$
2240 PRINT "YTD ";L3TTL$
2250 NEXT I
2261 NUMED=PMTTL
2262 MASK$="XXX,XXX.XX-"
2263 GOSUB 2570
2264 PM$=MASK$
2265 NUMED=PYTTL
2266 MASK$="XXX,XXX.XX-"
2267 GOSUB 2570
2268 P9Y$=MASK$
2269 IF PYN$<>"Y" THEN 2275
2270 PRINT# PR
2271 PRINT# PR,SPC(58);PM$;
     SPC(11-LEN(PM$));P9Y$
2275 PRINT "PAYEE MO TOT: ";PM$
2276 PRINT "PAYEE YR TOT: ";P9Y$
2280 GOTO 2920
2290 REM **********************
2300 IF L3$=MID$(LSTACCT$,1,3) THEN 2330
2310 ADESC$=L3$+"-NO DESCRIPTION"
2320 GOTO 2340
2330 ADESC$=L3$+"-"+MID$(LSTACCT$,5)
2340 GOSUB 2480
2350 IF PYN$<>"Y" THEN 2390
2360 IF LINECTR<50 THEN 2380
2370 GOSUB 1090
2380 PRINT# PR,ADESC$;SPC(58-LEN(ADESC:
     YMLTTL$;SPC(11-LEN(YMLTTL$));L3TTL$
2390 PRINT ADESC$
2400 PRINT YMLTTL$;SPC(1);L3TTL$
2410 PRINT "*********************"
2420 LINECTR=LINECTR+1
2430 LTTL3=0
2440 YMLTTL=0
2450 DETAILCTR=0
2460 PRT$="Y"
2470 RETURN
2480 NUMED=YMLTTL
2490 MASK$="XXX,XXX.XX-"
2500 GOSUB 2570
2510 YMLTTL$=MASK$
2520 NUMED=LTTL3
2530 MASK$="XXX,XXX.XX-"
2540 GOSUB 2570
2550 L3TTL$=MASK$
2560 RETURN
2570 REM ***EDIT1***
2580 REM ***EDITING SUBROUTINE***
2590 REM ***MASK$=MASK FOR EDITED
     RESULT
2600 REM ***EXAMPLE: XXX,XXX.XX-
2610 REM ***NUMED=NUMBER TO EDIT
     (INTEGER FORM)
2620 IF NUMED<>0 THEN 2650
2630 MASK$=" "
2640 GOTO 2910
2650 N2ED=NUMED
2660 NUMED=ABS(NUMED)
2670 LMASK=LEN(MASK$)
2680 NUMED$=STR$(NUMED)
2690 LNUMED=LEN(NUMED$)
2700 CN=LNUMED+1
2710 FOR CM=LMASK TO 1 STEP -1
2720 CN=CN-1
2730 IF CN<2 THEN 2890
2740 IF MID$(MASK$,CM,1)<>"-" THEN 2820
2750 IF N2ED>0 THEN 2790
2760 MASK$=MID$(MASK$,1,CM-1)+"-"
2770 CN=CN+1
2780 GOTO 2810
2790 MASK$=MID$(MASK$,1,CM-1)+" "
2800 CN=CN+1
2810 GOTO 2900
2820 IF MID$(MASK$,CM,1)="," THEN 2850
2830 IF MID$(MASK$,CM,1)="." THEN 2850
```

```
2840 GOTO 2870
2850 CN=CN+1
2860 GOTO 2900
2870 M2$=MID$(MASK$,1,CM-1)+MID$
     (NUMED$,CN,1)
2875 MASK$=M2$+MID$
     (MASK$,CM+1,(LMASK-(CM-1)-1))
2880 GOTO 2900
2890 MASK$=MID$(MASK$,1,CM-1)+" "+MID$
     (MASK$,CM+1,(LMASK-(CM-1)-1))
2900 NEXT CM
2910 RETURN
2920 IF PX$="3" THEN 2940
2925 FOR I=1 TO 2000:NEXT I
2930 PRINT# PR:CLOSE PR
2940 END
```

```
                                  SUMMARY BY ACCOUNT #
ACCOUNT                SRC  PAYEE                                      03/83          YTD

         03/08/83  130  002-PAYEE # 2                  46.50-
         03/25/83  138  001-PAYEE # 1                  54.00-
001-ACCOUNTING, LEGAL                                              100.50-      286.48-

         03/17/83  135  003-PAYEE # 3                  25.75-
         03/19/83  136  003-PAYEE # 3                  24.80-
         03/28/83  140  003-PAYEE # 3                  29.00-
002-ADVERTISING                                                     79.55-      147.80-

         03/09/83  131  002-PAYEE # 2                 450.40-
         03/26/83  139  999-NO DESCRIPTION             50.00-
005-AUTO EXPENSE                                                   500.40-      683.90-

         03/30/83  SALE 999-NO DESCRIPTION          1,500.00
100-INCOME                                                       1,500.00     1,500.00

*TOTAL*                                                            819.55       381.82


PAYEE SUMMARY FOR - 03/83                                          CURRENT         YTD

PAYEE# 001-PAYEE # 1                                                54.00-      239.98-
PAYEE# 002-PAYEE # 2                                               496.90-      550.40-
PAYEE# 003-PAYEE # 3                                                79.55-      147.80-
PAYEE# 999-NO DESCRIPTION                                         1,450.00     1,320.00

                                                                   819.55       381.82
00101/01/83001101 5500
00101/16/83001106 2500
00102/10/83001115 5098
00102/20/83001120 5500
00103/08/83002130 4650
00103/25/83001138 5400
00201/01/83003102 2500
00201/24/83003107 2000
00202/25/83003122 2325
00203/17/83003135 2575
00203/19/83003136 2480
00203/28/83003140 2900
00501/01/83999103 5500
00501/01/83002104 5350
00502/05/83999113 7500
00503/09/83002131 45040
00503/26/83999139 5000
10003/30/83999SALE150000
```

GRADES

```
10 REM ************************
20 REM *          GRADES          *
30 REM *                          *
40 REM *      COPYRIGHT 1983      *
50 REM *    DONALD C. KREUTNER    *
60 REM ************************
70 PRINT CHR$(147):POKE 53280,14:POKE
   53281,6:PRINT CHR$(5)
75 INPUT "1525 PRTR(1), RS232(2),
   NONE(3)";PX$
80 IF PX$="3" THEN 120
85 IF PX$="1" THEN 100
90 IF PX$="2" THEN 100
95 GOTO 75
100 PR=126
105 IF PX$="1" THEN 115
110 PR=PR+2:OPEN
   PR,2,0,CHR$(8):PR=128:PX$="2":GO TO 120
115 PR=PR+1:OPEN PR,4
120 PRINT CHR$(147):REM CLR SCREEN
180 DIM N$(40)
190 DIM S$(40,20)
200 DIM N(40)
210 DIM T(40)
220 REM ***********************
230 PRINT CHR$(147)
240 PRINT "CLEARING MEMORY"
250 FOR I=1 TO 40
260 N(I)=I
270 T(I)=0
280 FOR J=1 TO 20
290 S$(I,J)="@"
300 NEXT J
310 NEXT I
320 REM ***********************
330 PRINT CHR$(147)
```

GRADES is a program that will keep total grade scores for a class of up to 40 students. The file that keeps the data can be kept on tape or disk and altered as new data becomes available.

The input file is created using EDIT1 or EDIT2. Sample data is as follows:

```
*PERFECT SCORE
100
100
150
150
DOE JOHN
99
97
134
145
DOE JANE
100
98
125
149
END
```

After data has been entered, GRADES can then process it. Each name record is followed by the scores for test (or quiz) number 1, 2, 3, etc. The first record "*PERFECT SCORE" is recognized as the master score record because of the asterisk in the first position. Any record that starts with an asterisk (*) or an alphabetical letter causes a new accumulation of the records that follow that name record (lines 470-500). Any other record that does not begin with a

```
340 PRINT "NAME/SCORE FILE INPUT"
350 INPUT "CASSETTE OR DISK (C/D)";CD$
360 IF CD$="C" THEN 410
370 IF CD$<>"D" THEN 330
380 INPUT "FILE NAME";D$
390 OPEN 2,8,2,"O:"+D$+",S,R"
400 GOTO 420
410 OPEN 2,1,0:REM OPEN TAPE FOR INPUT
420 CN=0
430 CD=0
440 INPUT# 2,X$
450 IF X$="END" THEN 600
460 X1$=MID$(X$,1,1)
470 IF X1$<"A" THEN 500
480 IF X1$>"Z" THEN 440
490 GOTO 560
500 IF X1$="*" THEN 560
510 IF X1$<"0" THEN 440
520 IF X1$>"9" THEN 440
530 CD=CD+1
540 S$(CN,CD)=X$
550 GOTO 440
560 CN=CN+1
570 CD=0
580 N$(CN)=X$
590 GOTO 440
600 PRINT CHR$(147)
610 CLOSE 2
620 PRINT "SORTING BY NAME..."
630 PASS=0
640 FL$="N"
650 PASS=PASS+1
660 PRINT "SORT PASS";PASS
670 FOR I=1 TO CN-1
680 IF N$(I)<=N$(I+1) THEN 760
690 NX$=N$(I)
700 N$(I)=N$(I+1)
710 N$(I+1)=NX$
720 NX=N(I)
730 N(I)=N(I+1)
```

number is rejected (lines 510-520), and the next record is read.

As in other programs, the input file can be from tape or disk (lines 350-430). After all the data is read in and the END record is encountered, a sort of the name records takes place. The score details are kept in the array S$, whereas the array N keeps track of that part of the array where the scores for the sorted names are located after the sort (lines 620-780).

When the sort is ended, you are then asked if you want a pause, which causes the display to delay until you hit **RETURN** after each student's scores. You can also direct the report to a printer or to the screen only (lines 800-860).

The scores are printed left to right to save space on the screen and on the printer. And in order to change or add to the data, you can modify the input file by using one of the edit programs.

One last alternative is to save the sorted data to a new file. Then you can add new students at the end of your data and save the sorted file without having to insert many new records in the middle of the file.

```
740 N(I+1)=NX
750 FL$="Y"
760 NEXT I
770 IF FL$="Y" THEN 640
780 PRINT "SORT COMPLETE..."
790 PRINT CHR$(147)
800 INPUT "PAUSE (Y/N)";PAYN$
810 INPUT "PRINTER (Y/N)";PYN$
820 IF PX$="3" THEN PYN$="N"
830 IF PYN$<>"Y" THEN 870
840 INPUT "TITLE";T$
850 PRINT# PR,SPC(5);T$
860 PRINT# PR
870 FOR I=1 TO CN
880 TTLI=0
890 I$=STR$(I)
900 PRINT I$;".";TAB(6);N$(I)
910 IF PYN$<>"Y" THEN 930
920 PRINT# PR,I$;".";SPC(7-LEN(I$));N$(I)
930 FOR J=1 TO 20
940 IF S$(N(I),J)="@" THEN 1010
950 PRINT S$(N(I),J);SPC(1);
960 IF PYN$<>"Y" THEN 980
970 PRINT# PR,S$(N(I),J);SPC(1);
980 SC1=VAL(S$(N(I),J))
990 TTLI=TTLI+SC1
1000 NEXT J
1010 PRINT
1020 T(I)=TTLI
1030 PRINT "*TOTAL*";TTLI
1040 PRINT
1050 IF PYN$<>"Y" THEN 1090
1060 PRINT# PR
1070 PRINT# PR,"*TOTAL*";TTLI
1080 PRINT# PR
1090 IF PAYN$<>"Y" THEN 1110
1100 GET CO$:IF CO$="" THEN 1100
1110 NEXT I
1120 IF PYN$<>"Y" THEN 1140
1130 CLOSE 2
1140 INPUT "REPEAT (Y/N)";YN$
1150 IF YN$="Y" THEN 790
1160 PRINT CHR$(147)
1170 INPUT "SAVE NEW FILE (Y/N)";FYN$
1180 IF FYN$<>"Y" THEN 1340
1190 INPUT "CASSETTE OR DISK (C/D)";CD$
1200 IF CD$="C" THEN 1250
1210 IF CD$<>"D" THEN 1160
1220 INPUT "FILE NAME";F$
1230 OPEN 2,8,2,"@0:"+F$+",S,W"
1240 GOTO 1260
1250 OPEN 2,1,2:REM OPEN TAPE FOR OUTPUT
1260 FOR I=1 TO CN
1270 PRINT# 2,N$(I)
1280 PRINT I;N$(I)
1290 PRINT# 2,MID$(STR$(T(I)),2)
1300 PRINT MID$(STR$(T(I)),2)
1310 NEXT I
1320 PRINT# 2,"END"
1330 CLOSE 2
1340 END
```

```
*PERFECT SCORE          MILLER CHARLES
100                     90
150                     143
100                     96
50                      46
200                     185
DOE JANE                NEILS ROBERT
90                      87
130                     146
99                      97
45                      45
187                     186
DOE JOHN                PATTERSON KEVIN
89                      80
135                     145
95                      95
47                      40
180                     180
LARSON JIM              PAYTON RUSSELL
88                      90
140                     140
100                     99
50                      44
190                     184
```

```
    TOTAL SCORES (09/83)

1.  *PERFECT SCORE
100 150 100 50 200
*TOTAL* 600

2.  DOE JANE
90 130 99 45 187
*TOTAL* 551

3.  DOE JOHN
89 135 95 47 180
*TOTAL* 546

4.  LARSON JIM
88 140 100 50 190
*TOTAL* 568

5.  MILLER CHARLES
90 143 96 46 185
*TOTAL* 560

6.  NEILS ROBERT
87 146 97 45 186
*TOTAL* 561

7.  PATTERSON KEVIN
80 145 95 40 180
*TOTAL* 540

8.  PAYTON RUSSELL
90 140 99 44 184
*TOTAL* 557
```

MEMO

```
10 REM  *************************
20 REM  *          MEMO         *
30 REM  *                       *
40 REM  *     COPYRIGHT 1983    *
50 REM  *   DONALD C. KREUTNER  *
60 REM  *************************
70 PRINT CHR$(147):POKE 53280,14:
   POKE 53281,6:PRINT CHR$(5)
75 INPUT "1525 PRTR(1), RS232(2), NONE(3)";PX$
80 IF PX$="3" THEN 120
85 IF PX$="1" THEN 100
90 IF PX$="2" THEN 100
95 GOTO 75
100 PR=126
105 IF PX$="1" THEN 115
110 PR=PR+2:OPEN PR,2,0,CHR$(8):
    PR=128:PX$="2":GOTO 120
115 PR=PR+1:OPEN PR,4
120 REM ************************
130 QUOT$=CHR$(34)
190 DIM A$(300)
200 REM INPUT DATA FOR MEMO IS KEYED
210 REM BY EDIT1 OR EDIT2 PROGRAM
220 REM RECORD LAYOUT:
230 REM MM/DD/YY HH:MM AM
    (ANY MEMO INFO)
240 PRINT CHR$(147)
250 PRINT SPC(8);"***MEMO***"
260 PRINT
270 INPUT "CASSETTE OR DISK (C/D)";CD$
280 IF CD$="C" THEN 330
290 IF CD$<>"D" THEN 240
300 INPUT "FILE NAME";D$
310 OPEN 2,8,2,"0:"+D$+",S,R"
320 GOTO 340
330 OPEN 2,1,0:REM OPEN TAPE FOR INPUT
```

MEMO is designed to serve as a personal calendar or note pad to remind you of important events and appointments.

The input file is keyed by EDIT1 or EDIT2, programs discussed in Chapter 2. The records you key require the following format:

Pos. 1-8	Date of the memo, by month, day, and year (MM/DD/YY) Example: 01/01/83
Pos. 10-17	Time of the appointment or event (hour:minute followed by AM, PM, or blank) Example: 10:30 AM
Pos. 19 to the end	The appointment, person, or event to be remembered

When you key in these memos, you will most likely add them in chronological order. Remember that if you want to add new records later by using EDIT2, you can insert, delete, and alter records, thus keeping them in proper sequence. You can have many different "memo" files that keep track of different categories. The input data that follows is for the report example below:

```
09/10/83 10:30 AM MEETING AT L.R.D.
09/10/83 12:30 AM LUNCH WITH DAVE
09/10/83  2:30 PM REPORT DUE
09/11/83  9:30 AM CHECK FILES
```

```
340 FOR I=1 TO 300
350 INPUT# 2,A$(I)
360 IF A$(I)="END" THEN 380
370 NEXT I
380 CLOSE 2
390 PASS=0
400 CN=I-1
410 PRINT CHR$(147)
420 SW$="N"
430 PASS=PASS+1
440 PRINT "SORT PASS ";PASS
450 FOR I=1 TO CN-1
460 S1$=MID$(A$(I),7,2)+MID$
    (A$(I),1,6)+MID$(A$(I),16,1)+MID$(A$(I),10,10)
470 S2$=MID$(A$(I+1),7,2)+MID$
    (A$(I+1),1,6)+MID$(A$(I+1),16,1)
475 S2$=S2$+MID$(A$(I+1),10,10)
480 IF S1$<=S2$ THEN 530
490 AX$=A$(I)
500 A$(I)=A$(I+1)
510 A$(I+1)=AX$
520 SW$="Y"
530 NEXT I
540 IF SW$="Y" THEN 420
550 PRINT "SORT COMPLETE"
560 PRINT CHR$(147)
570 INPUT "PRINTER (Y/N)";PYN$
580 INPUT "PAUSE (Y/N)";PAUS$
590 IF PX$="3" THEN PYN$="N"
600 IF PYN$<>"Y" THEN 630
610 PRINT# PR,SPC(2);"DATE";SPC(7);
    "TIME";SPC(8);"MEMORANDUM"
620 PRINT# PR
630 FOR I=1 TO CN
640 DT$=MID$(A$(I),1,8)
650 TM$=MID$(A$(I),10,8)
660 ME$=MID$(A$(I),19)
670 PRINT DT$;SPC(2);TM$
680 PRINT ME$
690 PRINT "****************************"
```

```
09/11/83 11:00 AM MEET WITH NEW
CLIENT
09/11/83  1:30 PM BOARD MEETING
09/11/83  7:00 PM ENTERTAIN GUESTS
```

Notice that in keying the time, you must skip two spaces after the date ending in position 8 (or key a zero) in front of a single-hour digit (1:30 PM). So that events are sorted correctly, the AM or PM designation is necessary. Obviously, these fields must be in exactly the same locations, or the sort in lines 410-550 is completely ineffective.

The file that you read in from cassette or disk in lines 270-380 can be in order, in fairly good order, or even in very bad order. The program will sort the memos by date and time if you have keyed in the times in the correct positions. But how long the sort will take, of course, depends on how the data is and on how many memos you have read in. The data is placed in the array A$ (lines 190 and 350).

You are then asked in lines 570 and 580 whether you want a printout or whether you want the program to pause so that you can key **RETURN**, preventing the memos from rolling off the screen.

After the report is completed, you can repeat the report, or before the program ends, you can rewrite the data in sorted order to a new data file, which you can then manipulate with the edit programs.

```
700 IF PAUS$<>"Y" THEN 720
710 GET X$:IF X$="" THEN 710
720 IF PYN$<>"Y" THEN 740
730 PRINT# PR,DT$;SPC(3);TM$;SPC(6);ME$
740 NEXT I
750 PRINT
780 INPUT "REPEAT (Y/N)";RYN$
790 IF RYN$="Y" THEN 560
800 INPUT "REWRITE SORTED FILE (Y/N)";WYN$
810 IF WYN$<>"Y" THEN 950
820 INPUT "CASSETTE OR DISK (C/D)";CD$
830 IF CD$="C" THEN 880
840 IF CD$<>"D" THEN 820
850 INPUT "FILE NAME";D$
860 OPEN 2,8,2,"@0:"+D$+",S,W"
870 GOTO 890
880 OPEN 2,1,2:REM OPEN TAPE FOR OUTPUT
890 FOR I=1 TO CN
900 PRINT# 2,QUOT$+A$(I)+QUOT$
910 PRINT I;A$(I)
920 NEXT I
930 PRINT# 2,"END"
940 CLOSE 2
950 IF PX$="3" THEN 970
960 CLOSE PR
970 END
```

```
  DATE        TIME         MEMORANDUM

09/10/83   10:30 AM     MEETING AT L.R.D.
09/10/83   12:30 PM     LUNCH WITH DAVE
09/10/83    2:30 PM     REPORT DUE
09/11/83    9:30 AM     CHECK FILES
09/11/83   11:00 AM     MEET WITH NEW CLIENT
09/11/83    1:30 PM     BOARD MEETING
09/11/83    7:00 PM     ENTERTAIN GUESTS
```

PHONEADD

```
10 REM **************************
20 REM *         PHONEADD        *
30 REM *                         *
40 REM *      COPYRIGHT 1983     *
50 REM *    DONALD C. KREUTNER   *
60 REM **************************
70 PRINT CHR$(147):POKE 53280,14:POKE
   53281,6:PRINT CHR$(5)
170 DATA 812-999-1234 BIRK WILLIAM/3299
   SECOND STREET/KANSAS CITY
180 DATA 812-111-4321 BROWN RALPH
190 DATA 812-222-1111 CRAWFORD MAURICE
195 DATA 812-777-1456 DAUDT JACK
200 DATA 812-123-2134 GERDES JESSE/4960
   WESTMINSTER/LONDON ENGLAND
210 DATA 812-333-2233 HATFIELD DAVID
220 DATA 812-233-2266 HUBLAR AL
230 DATA 987-127-7654 JENSEN MARY
240 DATA 900-435-2222 KOCH WILLIAM
250 DATA 807-213-5555 LANG NEIL
260 DATA 812-333-4441 MANOR JANE
265 DATA 812-222-9963 MARRA ANNA
270 DATA 900-111-3544 MCALLISTER SCOTT
280 DATA 888-222-2133 MEADOR STEVE
290 DATA 344-123-2186 MILLER RONALD
300 DATA 412-210-2211 MILLSPAUGH RICHARD
310 DATA 322-133-4455 SCOTT DAVID
320 DATA 277-900-0001 STEWART CHARLES
330 DATA 244-122-4321 STEWART GARY
340 DATA 345-222-8888 STOKES ROBERT
350 DATA 367-323-4466 TRNKA JOHN
360 DATA 999-233-7777 VAN BRUSSELL
   CORNELIA
370 DATA 888-223-2211 WALTERS DARYLL
380 DATA 723-299-8867 YATES WILLIAM
390 DATA END
```

PHONEADD is a phone/name/address directory program. It is capable of looking up (by last name) an individual's phone number and address, if desired.

In this program the input data can come from three sources (lines 470-490): cassette, disk, or program data (C/D/P). You can, therefore, use many different files to obtain telephone numbers and addresses of various categories of people. And you can put the most frequently used list into the program's **DATA** statements. (See lines 170-390.) Furthermore, if you arrange these **DATA** statements in alphabetical order (as well as the files you create when using EDIT1 or EDIT2), you can obtain a very rapid data "load," since the alphabetical sort in lines 900-1010 will be required to make only one pass through the data to verify that it is in order.

Line 460 allows you to by-pass the phone number sort, again saving valuable time in preparing the program's data for use. This by-pass is very reasonable since in most cases you will want to look up by last name rather than telephone number. If, however, you also want to search by telephone number, the sort in lines 700-850 will accomplish just that.

The actual lookup takes place in lines 1030-1520. If you select the phone number key also, the number or name you

```
410 DIM PH$(200)
420 DIM NM$(200)
430 PRINT CHR$(147)
440 PRINT SPC(6);"***PHONEADD***"
450 PRINT
460 INPUT "ALPHABETIC ONLY (Y/N)";AYN$
470 PRINT "CASSETTE OR DISK"
480 PRINT "OR PROGRAM DATA (C/D/P):"
490 INPUT CD$
500 IF CD$="P" THEN 570
510 IF CD$="C" THEN 560
520 IF CD$<>"D" THEN 430
530 INPUT "FILE NAME";D$
540 OPEN 2,8,2,"0:"+D$+",S,R"
550 GOTO 570
560 OPEN 2,1,0:REM OPEN TAPE FOR INPUT
570 FOR I=1 TO 200
580 IF CD$<>"P" THEN 610
590 READ X$
600 GOTO 620
610 INPUT# 2,X$
620 IF X$="END" THEN 670
630 IF AYN$="Y" THEN 650
640 PH$(I)=X$
650 NM$(I)=X$
660 NEXT I
670 CN=I-1
680 IF CD$="P" THEN 700
690 CLOSE 2
700 PASS=0
710 IF AYN$="Y" THEN 860
720 SW$="N"
730 PASS=PASS+1
740 PRINT "PHONE# SORT PASS ";PASS
750 FOR I=1 TO CN-1
760 P1$=MID$(PH$(I),1,12)
770 P2$=MID$(PH$(I+1),1,12)
780 IF P1$<=P2$ THEN 830
790 SW$="Y"
800 PX$=PH$(I)
```

key in line 1080 is analyzed so that the program "knows" whether you are looking up by number or name. But if you decline the phone number search in line 460, you may look up by name only (line 1040, instead of line 1060).

PHONEADD will display one entry after another as long as you keep hitting **RETURN**, but you may look up any other name or number by keying that name or number.

As mentioned earlier, an entry may or may not contain the address associated with the name. If you want to have the addresses on all or some entries, as in this program, simply key the addresses, where desired, following the name (perhaps separated by slashes).

Records you key in a file are similar to the **DATA** statements in the program:

Pos. 1-12	The telephone number preceded by area code and separated by hyphens (999-999-9999)
Pos. 14 to the end of record	The name and, if desired, an abbreviated address (as short as possible for memory conservation)

Following is an example of an entry for PHONEADD:

999-999-9999 WHITE
MAX/9999 WHITESIDE
DRIVE/ANYTOWN USA

(All data appears on one line.)

```
810 PH$(I)=PH$(I+1)
820 PH$(I+1)=PX$
830 NEXT I
840 IF SW$="Y" THEN 720
850 PRINT "PHONE# SORT COMPLETE"
860 PASS=0
870 SW$="N"
880 PASS=PASS+1
890 REM ********************
900 PRINT "NAME SORT PASS ";PASS
910 FOR I=1 TO CN-1
920 N1$=MID$(NM$(I),14)
930 N2$=MID$(NM$(I+1),14)
940 IF N1$<=N2$ THEN 990
950 SW$="Y"
960 NX$=NM$(I)
970 NM$(I)=NM$(I+1)
980 NM$(I+1)=NX$
990 NEXT I
1000 IF SW$="Y" THEN 870
1010 PRINT "NAME SORT COMPLETE"
1020 PRINT CHR$(147)
1030 IF AYN$<>"Y" THEN 1060
1040 PRINT "PARTIAL/COMPLETE NAME"
1050 GOTO 1070
1060 PRINT "PARTIAL/COMPLETE #/NAME"
1070 PRINT "(OR END TO END PROGRAM)"
1080 INPUT K$
1090 IF K$="END" THEN 1540
1100 LK=LEN(K$)
1110 IF AYN$<>"Y" THEN 1150
1120 IF LEFT$(K$,1)<"A" THEN 1020
1130 IF LEFT$(K$,1)>"Z" THEN 1020
1140 GOTO 1360
1150 IF LEFT$(K$,1)>="A" THEN 1360
1160 IF LEFT$(K$,1)=" " THEN 1190
1170 IF LEFT$(K$,1)<"0" THEN 1020
1180 IF LEFT$(K$,1)>"9" THEN 1020
1190 FOR I=1 TO CN
1200 LP=LEN(PH$(I))
1210 IF LP>LK THEN 1230
1220 LK=LP
1230 IF MID$(PH$(I),1,LK)>=K$ THEN 1280
1240 NEXT I
1250 PRINT "NO RECORD >=";K$
1260 GET X$:IF X$="" THEN 1260
1270 GOTO 1020
1280 FOR J=1 TO CN
1290 PRINT MID$(PH$(J),1,13)
1300 PRINT MID$(PH$(J),14)
1310 PRINT "**************************"
1320 GET X$:IF X$="" THEN 1320
1330 IF X$<>CHR$(13) THEN 1350
1340 NEXT J
1350 GOTO 1020
1360 IF LEFT$(K$,1)>"Z" THEN 1020
1370 FOR I=1 TO CN
1380 LE=LEN(NM$(I))
1390 IF LE>LK THEN 1410
1400 LK=LE
1410 IF MID$(NM$(I),14,LK)>=K$ THEN 1460
1420 NEXT I
1430 PRINT "NO RECORD >= ";K$
1440 GET X$:IF X$="" THEN 1430
1450 GOTO 1020
1460 FOR J=I TO CN
1470 PRINT MID$(NM$(J),1,13)
1480 PRINT MID$(NM$(J),14)
1490 PRINT "**************************"
1500 GET X$:IF X$="" THEN 1500
1510 IF X$<>CHR$(13) THEN 1530
1520 NEXT J
1530 GOTO 1020
1540 END
```

PRICELIST

```
10 REM *************************
20 REM *        PRICELIST       *
30 REM *                        *
40 REM *     COPYRIGHT 1983     *
50 REM *   DONALD C. KREUTNER   *
60 REM *************************
70 PRINT CHR$(147):POKE 53280,14:
   POKE 53281,6:PRINT CHR$(5)
75 INPUT "1525 PRTR(1), RS232(2),
   NONE(3)";PX$
80 IF PX$="3" THEN 120
85 IF PX$="1" THEN 100
90 IF PX$="2" THEN 100
95 GOTO 75
100 PR=126
105 IF PX$="1" THEN 115
110 PR=PR+2:OPEN PR,2,0,CHR$(8):
    PR=128:PX$="2":GOTO 120
115 PR=PR+1:OPEN PR,4
120 REM ************************
170 REM THIS PROGRAM USES AN EDIT
180 REM FILE THAT IS READ IN OR
190 REM DATA STATEMENTS CAN BE
200 REM USED WITHIN THE PROGRAM.
201 REM PRICE IS IN POS. 1-8
202 REM COST IS IN 10-17
203 REM DESCRIPTION IS IN 19-END
204 REM THE DESCRIPTION'S 1ST
205 REM CHARACTERS ARE THE ITEM #
210 DATA 00005000 00003000 0101 ITEM X
215 DATA 00010000 00005000 0150 ITEM Y
220 DATA 00020000 00010000 0250 ITEM Z
225 DATA 00030000 00015000 0350 ITEM XYZ
230 DATA END
270 DIM P$(250)
280 DIM ITEM$(50)
```

PRICELIST is a versatile program that can provide you with an estimate of prices for a client or costs for the production of an item, based on costs and prices for components or parts that you have given in a file. Or the program can simply give to a customer the total price for a group of items.

The input for the master price list can be program **DATA** statements, or a tape or disk file created by EDIT1 or EDIT2. (See the menu screen in lines 340-400.) The file record layout is as follows:

Pos. 1-8	The price (needs leading zeros) Example: $45.75 is 00004575
Pos. 10-17	The cost (needs leading zeros)
Pos. 19 to end of record	Item number and description

PRICELIST does not require you to have a certain kind of item number (specified as so many characters long, composed of leading alphabetical characters, etc.). Instead, the item number can simply be the leading characters of the description. Then, when you later key an item number to be priced, the number keyed is searched for in the ITEM$ array, by the length of the number you enter. If there is no match for the item number keyed, you are asked to rekey it for a correct match (at the time you key the item

```
290 DIM ITEMNO(50)
300 DIM Q(50)
310 P$(1)="END"
320 ITEM$(1)="END"
330 PRINT CHR$(147)
340 PRINT "R     READ PRICE FILE"
350 PRINT "D     READ PROGRAM DATA"
360 PRINT "W     WRITE PRICE FILE"
370 PRINT "S     SELECT PRICE ITEMS"
380 PRINT "L     LIST PRICE ITEMS"
390 PRINT "E     END PROGRAM"
400 PRINT
410 INPUT "SELECTION";S$
420 IF S$="R" THEN 500
430 IF S$="D" THEN 590
440 IF S$="W" THEN 880
450 IF S$="S" THEN 1010
460 IF S$="L" THEN 1210
470 IF S$="E" THEN 2240
480 GOTO 410
490 REM **********************
500 INPUT "CASSETTE OR DISK (C/D)";CD$
510 IF CD$="C" THEN 560
520 IF CD$<>"D" THEN 500
530 INPUT "FILE NAME";D$
540 OPEN 2,8,2,"0:"+D$+",S,R"
550 GOTO 600
560 OPEN 2,1,0:REM OPEN TAPE FOR INPUT
570 IF S$<>"D" THEN 600
580 REM **********************
590 RESTORE
600 FOR I=1 TO 250
610 IF S$<>"D" THEN 640
620 READ P$(I)
630 GOTO 650
640 INPUT# 2,P$(I)
650 IF P$(I)="END" THEN 670
660 NEXT I
670 CP=I-1
680 IF S$="D" THEN 700
```

number, not when you have finished and requested a report).

In PRICELIST you simply key each item number and quantity in lines 1020-1170 until you are finished. Then you key **END** for the item number and return to the menu screen. At that time you can request a printout or screen listing of the prices you have just keyed.

Lines 1210-2010 produce the price list of selected parts. You can select price or cost, or both (line 1220). In line 1300 you can supply a customer name or any other suitable description.

A pause is built in to line 1760 (which you can remove if you want only to print these lists to the printer).

Again, the program will run more smoothly if you input a price file that is sorted by item number, although the program will sort the data (lines 720-860) if the items are out of sequence. Also, if you use the same price list again and again, you should use **DATA** statements to replace those now in the program. Just be sure to end them with an END record. Following is an example of a price list file:

```
00040000 00027500 A001
CEDAR BOX

00000995 00000545 A002
HAMMER

00039795 00022000 B010
COLOR TELEVISION

00001095 00000650 C0098
SHIN GUARDS

END
```

```
690 CLOSE 2
700 IF CP>0 THEN 720
710 CP=1
720 PASS=0
730 FL$="N"
740 PASS=PASS+1
750 PRINT CHR$(147)
760 PRINT "SORT PASS ";PASS
770 FOR I=1 TO CP
780 IF MID$(P$(I),19)<=MID$(P$(I+1),19) THEN 830
790 FL$="Y"
800 P2$=P$(I)
810 P$(I)=P$(I+1)
820 P$(I+1)=P2$
830 NEXT I
840 IF FL$="Y" THEN 730
850 PRINT "SORT COMPLETE"
860 GOTO 330
870 REM ************************
880 INPUT "CASSETTE OR DISK (C/D)";CD$
890 IF CD$="C" THEN 940
900 IF CD$<>"D" THEN 880
910 INPUT "FILE NAME";D$
920 OPEN 2,8,2,"@0:"+D$+",S,W"
930 GOTO 950
940 OPEN 2,1,2:REM OPEN TAPE FOR OUTPUT
950 FOR I=1 TO CP+1
960 PRINT# 2,P$(I)
970 NEXT I
980 CLOSE 2
990 GOTO 330
1000 REM **********************
1010 PRINT CHR$(147)
1020 FOR I=1 TO 49
1030 PRINT I;SPC(6);"ITEM # (OR END)";
1040 INPUT ITEM$(I)
1050 ITEMNO(I)=0
1060 IF ITEM$(I)="END" THEN 330
1070 LI=LEN(ITEM$(I))
1080 FOR J=1 TO CP
```

Notice that the item number C0098 is longer than the others. This difference does not really matter. When you key **C0098**, the program will look for an item number of exactly that length. In fact, some item numbers could be one character long, whereas other numbers in the same file might consist of 20 or more characters, although this is unlikely.

You can also write out the sorted price file to a tape or disk file to speed up the sort process at program startup. Of course, if your items are already in ordered **DATA** statements, you will not need to do this step.

```
1090 IF MID$(P$(J),19,LI)<>ITEM$(I) THEN 1120
1100 ITEMNO(I)=J
1110 GOTO 1130
1120 NEXT J
1130 IF ITEMNO(I)>0 THEN 1160
1140 PRINT CHR$(7)
1150 GOTO 1030
1160 INPUT "QTY";Q(I)
1170 NEXT I
1180 ITEM$(I)="END"
1190 GOTO 330
1200 REM **********************
1210 PRINT CHR$(147)
1220 INPUT "PRICE/COST/BOTH (P/C/B)";PCB$
1230 IF PCB$="P" THEN 1260
1240 IF PCB$="C" THEN 1260
1250 IF PCB$<>"B" THEN 1210
```

```
1260 INPUT "PRINTER (Y/N)";PYN$
1265 IF PX$="3" THEN PYN$="N"
1270 TC=0
1280 TP=0
1290 IF PYN$<>"Y" THEN 1410
1300 INPUT "CUSTOMER NAME";CN$
1330 PRINT# PR,CN$
1340 PRINT# PR
1350 IF PCB$="C" THEN 1370
1360 PRINT# PR,SPC(5);"PRICE";
1370 IF PCB$="P" THEN PRINT# PR,SPC(14);
1372 IF PCB$="P" THEN 1390
1375 IF PCB$="C" THEN PRINT# PR,SPC(9);
1380 PRINT# PR,SPC(10);"COST";
1390 PRINT# PR,SPC(4);"QTY";SPC(5);
     "ITEM#/DESCRIPTION"
1400 PRINT# PR
1410 CS=0
1420 FOR I=1 TO 50
1430 IF ITEM$(I)="END" THEN 1790
1440 IDESC$=MID$(P$(ITEMNO(I)),19)
1450 PRINT I;TAB(5);IDESC$
1460 P1$=MID$(P$(ITEMNO(I)),1,8)
1470 P1=VAL(P1$)
1480 C1$=MID$(P$(ITEMNO(I)),10,8)
1490 C1=VAL(C1$)
1500 P1=Q(I)*P1
1510 C1=Q(I)*C1
1520 Q$=STR$(Q(I))
1530 PRINT Q$;SPC(6);
1540 IF PCB$="C" THEN 1590
1550 A1=P1
1560 GOSUB 2030
1570 P2$=A2$
1580 PRINT TAB(5);P2$;SPC(1);
1590 IF PCB$="P" THEN 1640
1600 A1=C1
1610 GOSUB 2030
1620 C2$=A2$
1630 PRINT TAB(20);C2$;"*";
1640 PRINT
1650 PRINT
1660 IF PYN$<>"Y" THEN 1720
1670 IF PCB$="C" THEN 1690
1680 PRINT# PR,P2$;
1690 IF PCB$="P" THEN PRINT# PR,SPC(15);
1692 IF PCB$="P" THEN 1710
1694 IF PCB$="C" THEN PRINT# PR,SPC(9);
1700 PRINT# PR,SPC(4);C2$;"*";
1710 PRINT# PR,SPC(2);Q$;
     SPC(9-LEN(Q$));IDESC$
1720 TC=TC+C1
1730 TP=TP+P1
1740 CS=CS+1
1750 IF CS<7 THEN 1780
1760 INPUT "ENTER TO CONTINUE";CON$
1770 CS=0
1780 NEXT I
1790 PRINT "***TOTALS***"
1810 IF PCB$="C" THEN 1870
1820 A1=TP
1830 GOSUB 2030
1840 TP$=A2$
1850 PRINT TAB(8);A2$;SPC(1);
1860 IF PCB$="P" THEN 1910
1870 A1=TC
1880 GOSUB 2030
1890 TC$=A2$
1900 PRINT TAB(20);A2$;"*";
1910 PRINT
1920 IF PYN$<>"Y" THEN 2010
1930 PRINT# PR,"************************"
1940 IF PCB$="C" THEN 1960
1950 PRINT# PR,TP$;
1960 IF PCB$="P" THEN 1980
1965 IF PCB$="C" THEN PRINT# PR,SPC(9);
1970 PRINT# PR,SPC(4);TC$;"*";
1980 PRINT# PR
1990 PRINT# PR,"***********************"
2010 INPUT "RETURN TO CONTINUE";CON$
```

```
2020 GOTO 330
2030 A1$=MID$(STR$(A1),2)
2040 LA=LEN(A1$)
2050 ON LA GOTO 2080,2100,2120,2140,2160,
     2180,2200,2220
2060 A2$="ERROR"
2070 RETURN
2080 A2$="       .0"+A1$
2085 REM 7 SPACES ABOVE
2090 RETURN
2100 A2$="       ."+A1$
2105 REM 7 SPACES ABOVE
2110 RETURN
2120 A2$="      "+ MID$(A1$,1,1)+"."+MID$(A1$,2,2)
2125 REM 6 SPACES ABOVE
2130 RETURN
2140 A2$="     "+MID$(A1$,1,2)+"."+MID$(A1$,3,2)
2145 REM 5 SPACES ABOVE
2150 RETURN
2160 A2$="    "+MID$(A1$,1,3)+"."+MID$(A1$,4,2)
2165 REM 4 SPACES ABOVE
2170 RETURN
2180 A2$="  "+MID$(A1$,1,1)+","+MID$
     (A1$,2,3)+"."+MID$(A1$,5,2)
2185 REM 2 SPACES ABOVE
2190 RETURN
2200 A2$=" "+MID$(A1$,1,2)+","+MID$
     (A1$,3,3)+"."+MID$(A1$,6,2)
2205 REM 1 SPACE ABOVE
2210 RETURN
2220 A2$=MID$(A1$,1,3)+","+MID$
     (A1$,4,3)+"."+MID$(A1$,7,2)
2230 RETURN
2240 IF PX$="3" THEN 2260
2250 CLOSE PR
2260 END
```

```
JEFF GORDON

      PRICE        COST QTY    ITEM#/DESCRIPTION

    500.00       300.00* 10    0101 ITEM X
    500.00       250.00* 5     0150 ITEM Y
  1,400.00       700.00* 7     0250 ITEM Z
  4,500.00     2,250.00* 15    0350 ITEM XYZ
     50.00        30.00* 1     0101 ITEM X
*********************
  6,950.00     3,530.00*
***TOTAL*************
```

```
JEFF GORDON

      PRICE             QTY    ITEM#/DESCRIPTION

    500.00              10     0101 ITEM X
    500.00              5      0150 ITEM Y
  1,400.00              7      0250 ITEM Z
  4,500.00              15     0350 ITEM XYZ
     50.00              1      0101 ITEM X
*********************
  6,950.00
***TOTAL*************
```

```
JEFF GORDON

                   COST QTY    ITEM#/DESCRIPTION

                 300.00* 10    0101 ITEM X
                 250.00* 5     0150 ITEM Y
                 700.00* 7     0250 ITEM Z
               2,250.00* 15    0350 ITEM XYZ
                  30.00* 1     0101 ITEM X
*********************
               3,530.00*
***TOTAL*************
```

RULE78

```
10 REM **************************
20 REM *          RULE78          *
30 REM *                          *
40 REM *      COPYRIGHT 1983      *
50 REM *    DONALD C. KREUTNER    *
60 REM **************************
70 PRINT CHR$(147):POKE 53280,14:
   POKE 53281,6:PRINT CHR$(5)
75 INPUT "1525 PRTR(1), RS232(2),
   NONE(3)";PX$
80 IF PX$="3" THEN 120
85 IF PX$="1" THEN 100
90 IF PX$="2" THEN 100
95 GOTO 75
100 PR=126
105 IF PX$="1" THEN 115
110 PR=PR+2:OPEN PR,2,0,CHR$(8):PR=128:
   PX$="2":GOTO 120
115 PR=PR+1:OPEN PR,4
120 REM ************************
160 PRINT CHR$(147)
170 GOTO 200
180 INPUT "ANOTHER (Y/N)";YN$
190 IF YN$="N" THEN 1080
200 INPUT "PRINTER (Y/N)";PYN$
205 IF PX$="3" THEN PYN$="N"
210 INPUT "PAUSE (Y/N)";PAYN$
240 INPUT "BORROWER";N$
250 INPUT "PRINCIPAL";P
260 INPUT "FINANCE AMT";F
270 INPUT "MONTHS OF PAYBACK";M
280 IF PYN$<>"Y" THEN 390
290 INPUT "COMPRESSED PRINT (Y/N)";CYN$
300 IF CYN$<>"Y" THEN 320
310 PRINT# PR,CHR$(29)
320 PRINT# PR,CHR$(12)
```

RULE78 should be a familiar title to the banking community. The basis of the program is this: on an installment loan, the finance amount that is assessed for the principal loaned is divided among the months over which the payments will be made by using the "rule of 78s" formula. The name comes from the sum of months 12, 11, 10, 9, and so on, down to 1. The sum of these digits over a one-year period is 78. And to split the interest over that year, the first month is 12/78ths of the total finance charge, the second is 11/78ths, etc., down to the 12th month, which gets 1/78th of the interest. With this formula you can determine the payoff balance of any loan, since you know how much interest has been earned as of any month.

Sound complicated? Well, there's more. Obviously, most loans are for more than 12 months. To calculate the sum of the months (for example, 12 down to 1, for a one-year loan), the program has only to multiply the number of months times the number of months plus 1, and divide by 2 (12 x 13 divided by 2 = 78).

That's the concept—but you say you couldn't care less? The beauty of RULE78 is that all you have to do is feed the computer these few numbers:

1. The number of months for the loan
2. The total finance charge
3. The original principal, or borrowed amount

```
330 PRINT# PR,"BORROWER: ";N$;SPC(2);
    "(RULE OF 78THS INTEREST)"
340 PRINT# PR,"ORIGINAL PRINCIPAL: ";P;
    SPC(6);"FINANCE AMT: ";F
350 PRINT# PR
360 PRINT# PR,"MO";SPC(4);"PRINCIPAL";
    SPC(9);"FIN AMT";SPC(6);"TOT FINAMT";
365 PRINT# PR,SPC(9);"PAYMENT"
370 PRINT# PR,"-----------------
    --------------------"
380 PRINT# PR
390 TF=0
400 PAY=(P+F)/M
410 AMT=PAY
420 GOSUB 790
430 PAY=AMT
440 FOR I=1 TO M
450 FM=(M+1-I)/((M*(M+1))/2)*F
460 AMT=FM
470 GOSUB 790
480 FM=AMT
490 PRINT "**********MONTH";I
500 IF I<>M THEN 560
510 FM=F-TF
515 FM=INT(FM*100)
516 FM=FM/100
520 PAY=P+FM
525 AMT=PAY:GOSUB 790
526 PAY=AMT
560 PRINT "FINANCE AMT",FM
570 P=P-PAY+FM
575 AMT=P
577 GOSUB 790
578 P=AMT
610 PRINT "PRINCIPAL     ",P
620 TF=TF+FM
630 AMT=TF:GOSUB 790
640 TF=AMT
660 PRINT "TOTAL FIN AMT",TF
700 PRINT "PAYMENT     ",PAY
```

From these inputs, the program will do all the number crunching and produce a nice schedule, showing the interest paid each month, the payment, the payoff balance, and the total finance amount.

As in several other programs, you can list the printout on the screen and/or to a printer. You can also choose to have a pause in the display to the screen (lines 200-210). Another interesting routine for editing numbers for dollars and cents takes place in the subroutine in lines 790-860, which rounds off the amount to the nearest whole cent.

```
710 IF PYN$<>"Y" THEN 730
720 PRINT# PR,I;SPC(5-LEN(STR$(I)));P;
    SPC(15-LEN(STR$(P)));FM;
722 PRINT# PR,SPC(15-LEN(STR$(FM)));TF;
725 PRINT# PR,SPC(15-LEN(STR$(TF)));PAY
730 IF PAYN$<>"Y" THEN 750
740 GET X$:IF X$="" THEN 740
750 NEXT I
760 GOTO 180
790 A2=AMT*100
800 A3=INT(A2)
810 A4=A3+.5
820 IF A4<=A2 THEN 850
830 AMT=A3/100
840 GOTO 860
850 AMT=(A3+1)/100
860 RETURN
1080 IF PX$="3" THEN 1100
1090 CLOSE PR
1100 END
```

BORROWER: JOHN JONES (Rule of 78s Interest)
ORIGINAL PRINCIPAL: 5000 FINANCE AMT: 1210.48

MO	PRINCIPAL	FIN AMT	TOT FINAMT	PAYMENT
1	4838.07	96.84	96.84	258.77
2	4672.1	92.8	189.64	258.77
3	4502.1	88.77	278.41	258.77
4	4328.06	84.73	363.14	258.77
5	4149.99	80.7	443.84	258.77
6	3967.88	76.66	520.5	258.77
7	3781.74	72.63	593.13	258.77
8	3591.56	68.59	661.72	258.77
9	3397.35	64.56	726.28	258.77
10	3199.1	60.52	786.8	258.77
11	2996.82	56.49	843.29	258.77
12	2790.5	52.45	895.74	258.77
13	2580.15	48.42	944.16	258.77
14	2365.76	44.38	988.54	258.77
15	2147.34	40.35	1028.89	258.77
16	1924.88	36.31	1065.2	258.77
17	1698.39	32.28	1097.48	258.77
18	1467.86	28.24	1125.72	258.77
19	1233.3	24.21	1149.93	258.77
20	994.7	20.17	1170.1	258.77
21	752.07	16.14	1186.24	258.77
22	505.4	12.1	1198.34	258.77
23	254.7	8.07	1206.41	258.77
24	0	4.07	1210.48	258.77

BORROWER: DON JENNINGS (Rule of 78s Interest)
ORIGINAL PRINCIPAL: 1000 FINANCE AMT: 120

MO	PRINCIPAL	FIN AMT	TOT FINAMT	PAYMENT
1	925.13	18.46	18.46	93.33
2	848.72	16.92	35.38	93.33
3	770.77	15.38	50.76	93.33
4	691.29	13.85	64.61	93.33
5	610.27	12.31	76.92	93.33
6	527.71	10.77	87.69	93.33
7	443.61	9.23	96.92	93.33
8	357.97	7.69	104.61	93.33
9	270.79	6.15	110.76	93.33
10	182.08	4.62	115.38	93.33
11	91.83	3.08	118.46	93.33
12	0	1.54	120	93.37

4

Commodore BASIC Commands, Statements, and Functions

Using Commodore 64 BASIC efficiently is important for successful operation of your computer. This chapter is designed to help you become more familiar with the commands, statements, and functions of Commodore BASIC. The *Commodore 64 User's Guide,* which you received with your system, will also be useful in reminding you of the appropriate commands for the programs you write.

Initially, the "trick" is in understanding the statements. Commodore also provides the *Commodore 64 Programmer's Guide.* If you are really serious about learning all you can, a thorough reading (and rereading) of both these books is suggested. The Commodore manuals provided with optional peripherals are also quite good in explaining how to access properly such devices as disk drives, printers, etc.

In the following discussion of commands, statements, and functions, each term is explained briefly, yet clearly.

Strings and Numeric Expressions

To understand any version of BASIC, a programmer needs to know the difference between strings and numeric variables.

Strings can have alphabetical, numerical, or other characters, as well as combinations of these. But a string expression (even one containing all numbers) cannot have arithmetic operations performed on it. For these operations, you first need to convert the string to a numeric variable (using the **VAL** function). You also can split strings or join them (using **MID$**, **LEFT$**, or **RIGHT$**; and the + in the **LET** statement). But to split or join numeric variables is difficult, if not impossible, without first converting them to strings. Strings can be thought of as expressions that can be contained within quotation marks (not to be added, subtracted, etc.).

Unlike strings, numeric variables are composed entirely of numbers. They can be positive or negative and can include decimal portions. Numeric variables should never be enclosed in quotation marks, and any arithmetic operations can be performed on these variables.

The names of string variables end with a $ (dollar sign), which you can pronounce "string." Thus, A$ is called "A STRING," whereas the numeric variable A is simply called A.

All variables (numeric and string) are recognized by Commodore BASIC by their first two characters. You can select longer variable names, but if any have the same first two characters (and both are strings or both are numeric), the names will use the same variable in the program. Also in Commodore BASIC a numeric variable followed by a percent sign (%) is an integer, whereas a variable without the % is a real number (capable of holding a decimal portion).

Following are some examples of string and numeric variable values.

Strings	Numeric Variables
1024 S. FIFTH	1024
"KEN RICHARDS"	-1.342
"1024"	0

Commands, Statements, and Functions

In the discussion of each BASIC command, statement, and function, you will notice that every entry is followed by a (C), (S), (0), or (F), to indicate whether the BASIC keyword is a command, a statement, an operator, or a function.

Commands	may be typed in and entered without a preceding line number. Commands are executed immediately, as they are entered.
Statements	are used within BASIC programs and follow a line number to cause program execution. Obviously, all programs must be composed of statements.
Operators	are used for arithmetic calculations (+, -, /, *, and ↑), for expressing inequalities and equalities (=, <, >, <=, >=, and <>), and as logical connectors (AND, OR, and NOT).
Functions	are certain special-purpose routines that have been built into BASIC. They enable the user to make certain calculations or string manipulations that would otherwise require writing more BASIC code.

Following are some examples of commands, statements, and functions.

Commands:

LIST	Causes a program to be displayed on the screen
LOAD	Causes a program to be retrieved from cassette tape

Statements:

10 PRINT "HELLO"	Displays HELLO on the screen when program line 10 is executed
20 PRINT CHR$(147)	Clears the screen when line 20 is executed

Functions:

PRINT ABS(-10)	Prints the positive value (absolute value) of -10
10 X=VAL(X$)	Returns the numeric value of the string contained in X$ (which should be a number)

After the discussion of each command, function, or statement, examples are given to enable you to understand better the use of the keyword.

Remember that the manual is always there when you need it!

A

ABS(<expression>)—returns the absolute value of a number, always producing a positive result.

```
10 A=-10
20 B=100
30 PRINT ABS(A)
40 PRINT ABS(B)
```

These lines result in printing 10 and 100. (F)

<expression> **AND** <expression>—joins **IF-THEN** statements. (O)

```
10 INPUT "X";X
20 INPUT "Y";Y
30 IF X > Y AND X > 0 THEN 6O
40 PRINT X
50 GOTO 70
60 PRINT "X IS POSITIVE AND > Y"
70 END
```

ASC(<string>)—gives the ASCII value of the first character in a string. If you want to display a string one character at a time to a certain place on the screen, you can use the **ASC** function in combination with **MID$** function to obtain the ASCII value of each character for the length of the string. (To determine its length, use the **LEN** function.) Then you can display a string on the screen using the **POKE** statements.

```
 5 PRINT CHR$(147)
10 A$="HELLO THERE"
20 LA=LEN(A$)
30 ROW=5
40 COL=5
50 FOR I=1 TO LA
60 COL=COL+1
70 SEGX$=MID$(A$,I,1)
80 A=ASC(SEGX$)
85 IF A>32 THEN A=A-64
90 POKE 1024+COL+40*R,A
100 POKE 55296+COL+40*R,1
110 NEXT I
```

In this example, line 20 gets the length of A$ in the numeric variable LA (which is 12, since A$ contains 11 characters and a leading space). Then both the row and column variables are set to 5 in lines 30 and 40. What we want to accomplish is done by a **FOR-NEXT** loop in lines 50-110, which increases the variable I from 1 to 12 (the value of LA) by 1, stepping through each statement between the **FOR** and **NEXT** statements 12 times. Each time through the loop, the variable COL is increased by 1 so that the letters of "HELLO THERE" are moved one at a time to the 6th column, the 7th, the 8th, and on up to the 18th column.

The character displayed each time is the one that corresponds to the ASCII value for the 1st character of A$, the 2nd, the 3rd, and so on, up to the 12th character. The **MID$** function returns the character starting in the 1st position for a length of one character, then the character in the 2nd position, and on through the character in the 12th position. The **ASC** function turns each character into an ASCII code so that the **POKE** statement can display the characters as they are encountered. (F)

ATN(<number>)—obtains the trigonometric arc tangent in radians. Along with certain other functions, **ATN** is useful to engineers and mathematicians.

```
10 A=ATN(.55)
```

This statement gives the angle in radians whose tangent is .55. (F)

C

CHR$(<number>)—returns the string character, when given an ASCII code, which that code represents.

```
10 PRINT CHR$(147):REM CLEARS SCREEN
20 INPUT "KEY AN ASCII CODE (33-126): ";C
30 IF C<33 THEN 20
40 IF C>126 THEN 20
50 PRINT "ASCII ";C; " IS: ";CHR$(C)
60 INPUT "MORE (Y/N): ";YN$
70 IF YN$="Y" THEN 10
80 END
```

The **CHR$** statement in line 50 obtains the string value for the ASCII code keyed, telling you what number the computer uses to keep track of different characters in its memory. (F)

CLOSE <file number>—closes, or disassociates from the program, a file that has been opened. After a file is closed, you can reuse its file number in opening another file. (See **OPEN**.)

```
10 OPEN 2,4
20 PRINT# 2,"HELLO"
30 CLOSE 2
40 OPEN 3,8,3,"@0:FILE1,S,W"
50 PRINT# 3,"HELLO"
60 CLOSE 3
```

The **CLOSE** statement in line 30 makes the printer file opened in line 10 no longer available to the program. Thus, if you add a line 40 (PRINT# 2,"GOODBYE"), the program will end in an error condition. (S)

CLR—erases the values of any variables in memory, but leaves the program as it is. When **RUN** is keyed in to execute a program, **CLR** is automatically performed to initialize variables.

```
10 A=5:B=6
20 PRINT A,B
30 CLR
40 PRINT A,B
```

Here A and B have their values erased by the **CLR** statement in line 30. (S)

CMD <file number> [,string]—transfers to the device specified the output normally sent to the screen. Thus **PRINT**s and **LIST**s can be redirected to a printer, a disk file, or a tape file. After

OPENing the device, **CMD** followed by the number of the file causes any **LIST**s or **PRINT**s to go to that device. The string can be used as a title.

```
OPEN 2,4        OPEN 8,8,8,"@0:LIST1,S,W"
CMD 2           CMD 8
LIST            LIST
PRINT# 2        PRINT# 8
CLOSE 2         CLOSE 8
```

The example on the left will list the program in memory to the 1525 printer, whereas the listing on the right goes to a disk file called "LIST1." Notice that after **LIST**ing, you must **PRINT** a blank record to the device and close that file. (S)

CONT—resumes the execution of a program after you have hit the **STOP** key, or after a **STOP** or **END** statement has been encountered by the program during execution. (C)

```
10 PRINT "LINE 10"
20 STOP
30 PRINT "LINE 30"

RUN
LINE 10
CONT
LINE 30
```

COS(<number>)—returns the trigonometric cosine of the number, an angle in radians. To get the cosine of an angle in degrees, you first need to multiply the angle in degrees by PI/180, which is .01745329251994, to get the radians for that angle. (F)

```
10 PRINT CHR$(147)
20 INPUT "COSINE OF DEGREES OR RADIANS (D/R): ";DR
30 INPUT "VALUE OF ANGLE: ":DR
40 IF DR$="R" THEN 60
50 DR=DR*.01745329251994
60 PRINT "COSINE OF ";DR;" IS ";COS(DR)
```

D

DATA <list of constants>—stores numeric or string data within a program's statements so that you can use the same data each time you run the program.

```
10 PRINT CHR$(147):REM CLEAR SCREEN
20 DATA 10,11,15,32,9,12,10,-99
```

```
30 READ A
40 IF A<0 THEN 70
50 PRINT A
60 GOTO 30
70 END
```

Line 20 provides the numeric program data to be read in by line 30. To end the program without an "out of data" message, line 40 will branch to the end of the program (line 70) if a negative number is read (-99). Line 50 prints the number read on the screen, and the program loops back to read the next data element from line 60. (S)

DEF FN <name>(<variable>)=<expression>—defines whatever functions you want in your own programs. You can substitute any number for the variable (see line 20) to calculate the value of the function. (See also **FN**xx(X).) (S)

```
10 DEF FNP(X)=X*1.7
20 INPUT "COST:";C
30 PRINT "PRICE:";FNP(C)
40 GOTO 20
```

DEF FN is not really necessary in a program like this since line 30 can just as easily state PRINT "PRICE: ";COST*1.7. (S)

DIM <variable> (<subscripts>) [,<variable> (<subscripts>) ...] —reserves space for arrays of 1 or more dimensions.

```
10 DIM A(100)
```

Here the statement reserves space for an array of 101 numbers (from 0 through 100).

```
10 DIM A$(50,50)
```

This statement dimensions a 2-dimensional array. Such an array can store the names of up to 50 family members for each of 50 families. For example, A$(1,1), A$(1,2), and A$(1,3) each would contain a different name for a member from family #1. (S)

E

END—terminates the execution of a program. The last statement is usually **END**, to which you branch to stop the program. However, **END** may be located elsewhere within the program, if desired. (S)

EXP(<number>)—provides the inverse value of the natural **LOG** function. The value returned represents e (that is, 2.718281828) to the power of the argument in parentheses. **EXP** is used in mathematical formulas and applications.

```
10 PRINT EXP(9)
```

This statement prints out the value of e to the 9th power. (F)

F

FN <name> (<number>)—returns the value from the user-defined function **DEF FN**xx(X). (F)

```
10 DEF FNA(X)=1.25*X/15.7
20 FOR I=1 TO 100
30 PRINT FNA(I)
40 NEXT I
```

FOR <variable>=<start> **TO** <limit> [**STEP** <increment>] —executes the statements that follow **FOR**, up to the **NEXT** control variable statement, which is located farther down in the program. This "loop" will be executed counting from the initial control variable until the limit is reached. Usually, the control variable is incremented by one, but this increment may vary by stating a **STEP** option. With **STEP** 5, for example, you can have the control variable incremented by 5 each time the loop is executed. After the limit has been reached, control passes to the statement after the **NEXT** statement. This statement is similar to the DO-LOOP of FORTRAN. (S)

```
10 PRINT CHR$(147):REM CLEAR SCREEN
20 INPUT "DISPLAY COUNT (Y/N): ";YN$
30 INPUT "HOW HIGH TO COUNT: ";L
40 INPUT "COUNT BY: ";S
50 INPUT "COUNT FROM: ";C
60 PRINT CHR$(147)
70 FOR I=C TO L STEP S
80 IF YN$<>"Y" THEN 100
90 PRINT I
100 NEXT I
110 INPUT "MORE (Y/N): ":YN$
120 IF YN$="Y" THEN 10
130 END
```

This program illustrates the versatility of the **FOR-NEXT** loop. With it, you can make the Commodore 64 display each number as it counts. You will be amazed at how much the speed of the computer is held back because it has to "show" you what it is doing as it does it. The speed of the computer is much more evident when you tell it not to display the count. You see, the baud rate (or speed at which the screen is filled with characters) is much slower than the speed at which the computer is capable of working. Obviously, one of the reasons for this discrepancy is that people must be able to read information as it is displayed on the screen. If material went by too fast, the machine would be of little use.

You can also key the limit to which you want the machine to count, as well as the number from which to start. For example, you can tell the computer to count from 1 to 1000. You can also give the computer a step of -1 and ask for a count to 1 from a starting number of 1000, causing a count backwards. Or you can request a count from 10 to 2000 by 10s, 20s, etc. (S)

FRE(<variable>)—gives the number of bytes (or characters) in memory that are free for use in the Commodore 64. If the number returned is negative, you will need to subtract 65,536 from it. (F)

```
PRINT FRE(0)
```

G

GET <variable list>—reads characters from the keyboard as you key them. The best way to use **GET** is to read the character into a string variable to avoid a "syntax" error. With the **GET** statement, the characters are not displayed on the screen as the information is keyed. Therefore, you can give the program a direction without disturbing the screen contents. (S)

```
5 DIM X$(40):PRINT CHR$(147)
10 PRINT "KEY NAME:"
20 FOR I=1 TO 40
30 GET X$:IF X$="" THEN 30
35 X$(I)=X$
40 IF X$=CHR$(13) THEN 60
50 NEXT I
60 PRINT CHR$(147)
65 FOR I=1 TO 40
70 IF X$(I)=CHR$(13) THEN 100
80 PRINT X$(I);
90 NEXT I
100 PRINT
```

This example keys a character at a time into the array X$ in the **FOR-NEXT** loop of lines 20-50 until a **RETURN** key is depressed—**CHR$(13)**. Then lines 60-100 print the name to the screen. **GET#** <file number>,<variable list>—reads data from a file one character at a time (including commas, **RETURN**s, and other data separators). (S)

```
10 OPEN 2,8,2,0:FILE1,S,R
20 GET# 2,X$
25 IF ST > 0 THEN 50
30 PRINT X$;
40 GOTO 20
50 CLOSE 2
```

GOSUB <line number>—enables you to "perform" (in COBOL terms) or "call" (in FORTRAN terms) a subroutine that can be done easily, over and over again, from different sections of a program. You can, for instance, load some numbers from one section of a program into certain variables, **GOSUB** to a certain line number, then return to the statement following the **GOSUB**. You can then use the variables, as they have been changed by the subroutine, in succeeding statements. Later, you can load any other numbers into the same variables, **GOSUB** to the same line number (from a completely different section of the program), and return, after encountering the **RETURN** statement, to the next statement after the **GOSUB**.

```
10 INPUT X
20 GOSUB 100
30 PRINT X
40 X=X*2
50 GOSUB 100
60 PRINT X
70 GOTO 10
100 X=X/2
110 RETURN
```

Here, when you key a number (X) in line 10, the **GOSUB** statement in line 20 transfers control to line 100, where X is divided by 2. When the **RETURN** statement is encountered in line 110, control passes back to line 30, where X is printed. (If you key 10 for X, the subroutine will print 5.) Line 40 then doubles X (back to its original value). But the **GOSUB** in line 50 again branches to line 110, where X is again divided by 2, and the value of X is once again printed in line 60. Then the **GOTO** in line 70 takes you back for another number to be input. Most subroutines have many more statements than the example above. (S)

GOTO <line number>—goes to the line number specified. Also called the unconditional branch, **GOTO** is one of the most frequently used BASIC statements. The **GOTO** (or **GO TO**) statement, in combination with the conditional branch **IF-THEN**, was used to develop the "stored program" concept in earlier generations of computers.

```
10 INPUT "Number 1: ";N1
20 INPUT "Number 2: ";N2
30 INPUT "Add or Subtract (A/S): ";AS$
40 IF AS$="A" THEN 70
50 PRINT N1-N2
60 GOTO 10
70 PRINT N1+N2
80 GOTO 10
```

The conditional branch in line 40 takes the program to line 70 if the user selected to add the two numbers. (Otherwise, the program goes to line 60 after printing the subtraction in line 50.) The **GOTO** statements of lines 60 and 80 both unconditionally branch to line 10. (S)

I

IF <expression> **THEN** <line number or statements>—executes the statement following **THEN** if the condition specified is true. If it is not true, control passes to the next statement. **THEN** can be replaced by **GOTO** if the statement is followed by a line number. **IF-THEN** is the conditional branch that helped make the computer one of the most important innovations of the 20th century.

```
10 INPUT N
20 IF N>0 THEN 60
30 IF N<0 THEN 80
40 PRINT "THE NUMBER WAS ZERO"
50 GOTO 100
60 PRINT N;"IS GREATER THAN ZERO"
70 GOTO 100
80 PRINT N;"IS LESS THAN ZERO"
100 INPUT "CONTINUE (Y/N): ";YN$
110 IF YN$<>"N" THEN 10
120 END
```

Here, after you key a number in line 10, line 20 passes control to line 60 if the number keyed is greater than 0; line 30 branches to line 80 if the number keyed is less than 0. Otherwise, the number has to be 0, and the program "falls through" to line 40, which is the next sequential statement. Another conditional branch evaluates the alphabetical string you answered in line 100. In line 110 the program causes any answer not equal to "N" to branch back to line 10. Otherwise, the program again "falls through" and ends at line 120. (S)

INPUT ["<input prompt>";] <variable list>—causes program execution to pause momentarily until you enter data from the keyboard and press the **RETURN** key. Along with the **GET** statement, **INPUT** is used to provide the program with responsive input from the keyboard. If more than one value is requested by a single **INPUT** statement, you can enter all of them separated by commas. Generally, it is better to ask for only one item of data (or field) at a time from any **INPUT** statement.

```
10 INPUT X
20 INPUT "NOW ENTER Y: ";Y
30 PRINT X,Y
```

It is also better to include an input prompt, as in line 20, to enable the person keying the data to know what needs to be keyed. In line 10 the only prompt to input data will be a question mark. (S)

INPUT# <file number>,<variable list>—inputs data elements (either numeric or string variables) from a file that has been opened for input. You can **INPUT** one or more variables at a time from a file, but usually you will **INPUT** back the same number of variables that you "wrote" to that file, using the **PRINT#** file number statement.

```
  5 INPUT "FILENAME: ";F$
 10 OPEN 2,8,2,"@0:"+F$+",S,W"
 20 INPUT A,B,C
 30 PRINT# 2,A,B,C
 40 IF A=-999 THEN 60
 50 GOTO 20
 60 CLOSE 2
 70 OPEN 2,8,2,"0:"+F$+",S,R"
 80 INPUT# 2,A,B,C
 90 PRINT A;B;C
100 IF A=-999 THEN 120
110 GOTO 80
120 CLOSE 2
130 END
```

These lines illustrate several important points to remember. First, notice that once a file number has been **CLOSE**d, it can be used again within the same program (line 70 reopens file #2 for input). However, using a different file # for the second input sequence of the program is also a possibility (and perhaps a better alternative for program readability). If you key **FILEX**, that disk file will be used.

Second, the -999 value for A causes the writing to the output file to stop (line 40). Reading that same value on input from the file also causes the input to stop (line 100).

Finally, notice that each input from file #2 in line 80 reads the same three variables from a record as those written out in the **PRINT** statement of line 30. (S)

INT <numeric>—gives the largest integer of the numeric expression in parentheses, without exceeding the number itself. In other words, **INT** will truncate any fractional or decimal portion of the number, leaving an integer.

```
10 A=10.43521
20 PRINT INT(A)
30 X=INT(A)
40 PRINT X
```

In this simple example, line 20 prints 10, the truncated integer of the variable A in line 10. Line 40 also prints 10, since the variable X has been set to the value of the integer of A in line 30. (F)

L

LEFT$(<string>,<integer>)—gives you a substring of the string specified in parentheses from position one (the leftmost character) for <integer> characters to the right.

```
10 X$="TELEVISION"
20 PRINT LEFT$(X$,4)
```

Line 20 will display "TELE," the first four characters of X$. See also **MID$** and **RIGHT$**. (F)

LEN(string expression)—determines quickly the length of any string that has been keyed in, read in from **DATA** statements, or input from a file.

```
10 INPUT X$
20 LX=LEN(X$)
30 IF LX>3 THEN 60
40 PRINT "ERROR... MUST BE AT LEAST 4 CHARACTERS, AND FIRST 3 CHARS MUST
   BE ACCT#"
50 GOTO 10
60 ACCT$=MID$(X$,1,3)
70 DESC$=MID$(X$,4)
80 PRINT ACCT$
90 PRINT DESC$
100 GOTO 10
```

In this miniprogram you must input a string of at least four characters in length in line 10. If you do not, you are told to redo it. The first three characters represent the account #. The description of the account is in the 4th position to the end of the string X$. Lines 60 and 70 use the **MID$** function to split the larger X$ into two segments. Notice that in line 70 the description begins in position 4 of X$ for the length of the string X$. (F)

[**LET**] <variable>=<expression>—assigns the value of a numeric or string expression to the variable to the left of the equal sign. Usually, the optional **LET** at the beginning of the command is left off. You can set variables to numeric constants and fixed strings, or assign keyed or calculated values to variables with the **LET** command.

```
10 A=10
20 B=A*2
30 INPUT X$
40 Y$=X$+STR$(A)
50 PRINT Y$
60 GOTO 30
```

Here line 10 assigns the value 10 to the numeric variable A, whereas B becomes 20 by the statement in line 20 (the value of 10 times 2). After you key a string in line 30, Y$ is assigned the string value of whatever you keyed (X$) joined to the string value of A. Thus, if you key "MONSTER," Y$ will have the value "MONSTER 10." (S)

LIST [[<first-line>] - [<last-line>]]—lists all or part of a program in memory on the screen and (optionally) to other devices, such as a printer, a disk file, or a cassette file. (See the **CMD** statement.) Be aware that a listing to disk or cassette cannot be reloaded back into memory with the **OLD** command. Instead, the file can be used as data only, to be read by a BASIC program. (C)

LIST	causes a listing of the entire program to the screen (stops when the **CLEAR** function is keyed)
LIST 10-100	lists from lines 10 to 100 only
LIST -200	lists from the beginning of the program to line 200
LIST 200-	lists from line 200 to the end of the program

LOAD ["<file name>"] [,<device>] [,<address>]—brings a program into memory from a device (such as disk or tape). When **LOAD**ing from tape, the file name parameter can be left out, causing the next program file on tape to be read. When **LOAD**ing from disk, the file name is normally given, but "*" will **LOAD** the first file on the directory. If the address parameter is left out (as it normally is), the program will **LOAD** starting at memory location 2048. (C)

LOAD	(loads next program from tape)
LOAD "PROG1",8	(loads PROG1 from disk)

LOG(<numeric>)—provides the natural logarithm function, or the inverse of the **EXP** function. **LOG** is generally used for mathematics and engineering applications. (F)

```
10 PRINT LOG(3)
```

M

MID$(<string>,<numeric-1> [,<numeric-2>])—allows you to get a substring of the string in parameter 1, starting from the position of numeric-1 for a length of numeric-2 characters. If the second numeric variable is omitted, the substring will be from the starting position to the end of the original string.

```
10 X$="THIS IS STRING 1"
20 Y$=MID$(X$,9,6)
30 PRINT Y$
RUN
STRING
```

Y$ in this program becomes the 9th character to the 14th character of X$. (F)

N

NEW—erases whatever program lines are in memory, in preparation for keying in a new program. (C)

```
NEW
```

NEXT [<counter>] [,<counter>] ...—must be paired with a **FOR** statement. (See **FOR**.) If you fail to end a **FOR** statement with a **NEXT** statement later on in the program, the program will not run because of a **FOR-NEXT** error condition. One **NEXT** statement can end several nested loops when the counters are separated by commas.

```
10 FOR I=1 TO 100
20 PRINT I
30 NEXT I
```

Notice that the **NEXT** statement in line 30 must possess the same control variable (I) as the **FOR** statement in line 10. (S)

NOT <expression>—can be used in two ways: (1) to produce the "twos-complement" of the operand that follows, or (2) to reverse the meaning of a relationship test. (O)

```
10 X=10:Y=30
20 IF NOT X=Y THEN 40
25 PRINT "LINE 25"
30 IF NOT (X=Y) THEN 50
40 PRINT "LINE 40"
50 STOP
```

Here "NOT X" produces the twos-complement of 10, which is -11. Therefore, line 40 prints.

O

ON <variable> **GOSUB** <line number> [,<line number>] ...—passes control to the line number in the line list for a subroutine. Determining which line number to use is based on whether the integer value of the numeric expression is 1, 2, 3, etc. If it is 1, control passes to the subroutine in the 1st line number of the list. If 2, control transfers to the line number of the second subroutine, and so on. After the subroutine encounters a **RETURN** statement, control returns to the next statement after the **ON-GOSUB** statement. (S)

```
10 PRINT CHR$(147):REM CLEAR SCREEN
20 PRINT "1=SELECTION 1"
30 PRINT "2=SELECTION 2"
```

```
 40 PRINT "3=SELECTION 3"
 50 INPUT S
 60 ON S GOSUB 80,100,120
 70 GOTO 10
 80 PRINT "THIS IS SELECTION 1"
 90 RETURN
100 PRINT "THIS IS SELECTION 2"
110 RETURN
120 PRINT "THIS IS SELECTION 3"
130 RETURN
```

ON <variable> **GOTO** <line number> [,<line number>] ...—passes control to the line number, based on the integer value of the numeric expression. When this branching occurs, an unconditional **GOTO** branch does not return to the next line after the **ON-GOTO**. As with **ON-GOSUB**, if the value of the numeric expression is 1, 2, 3, etc., control passes to line number 1, 2, 3, and so on.

```
 10 PRINT CHR$(147):REM CLEAR SCREEN
 20 PRINT "SELECTION 1"
 30 PRINT "SELECTION 2"
 40 PRINT "SELECTION 3"
 50 INPUT S
 60 ON S GOTO 80,100,120
 70 GOTO 10
 80 PRINT "SELECTION 1"
 90 STOP
100 PRINT "SELECTION 2"
110 STOP
120 PRINT "SELECTION 3"
130 END
```

Notice that in this example, after the branch to lines 80, 100, or 120, the program ends because of the **STOP** and **END** statements. If, however, the **ON-GOTO**s branched to quite different locations within a larger program, each of the program segments could be quite long and could then branch conditionally or unconditionally to other parts of the program. (S)

OPEN <file-num>,[<device>] [,<address>] [,"file name> [,<type>] [,<mode>]"]—prepares a file on an external storage device (such as a tape or disk) for use by a BASIC program. The program must first check to see whether there is such a file before the program can actually use the file. In the **OPEN** statement, then, you describe to the computer the file's characteristics in order for the computer to verify that everything is correct and to proceed with the rest of the program. If a problem exists, you are given a "file open" error message when you try to open the file.

The file number must be an integer between 1 and 255. Usually, you use the lower numbers because they are easier to keep track of when using the files.

Filename means the actual name that identifies, for the program, where the file resides. For example, "ANYNAME" refers to the disk file with the name ANYNAME.

```
10 OPEN 1,1,0,"FILE1"
20 OPEN 2,8,2,"DISK1,S,R"
30 OPEN 3,8,3,"DISK2,S,W"
40 OPEN 4,4
50 OPEN 128,2,0,CHR$(8)
```

In the above examples, line 10 opens a file called FILE1 on cassette for input. The file number (to which **INPUT#** and **PRINT#** statements refer) is the first 1; the second 1 refers to the device (tape). The 0 indicates input. (A third 1, in place of the 0, would have indicated output.) Line 20 opens a disk file called DISK1 for input. (The R indicates "read.") An 8 for device indicates the primary disk drive. In line 30, the W indicates "write," which means that the file DISK2 is opened for output. The S in lines 20 and 30 means that both files are sequential; that is, the records are read sequentially, one after another, starting at record number 1. Line 40 opens file #4 on device 4 (the 1525 Commodore printer). Line 50 opens file #128 on device 2 (the RS-232 user port). The file number 128 causes a line feed to be automatically generated after each carriage return (sent at the end of each line). File numbers of less than 128 do not generate the automatic line feed. Finally, **CHR$(8)** causes a baud rate of 1,200 bits per second. (S)

<operand> **OR** <operand>—can be used in two ways (like **NOT** and **AND**). When used for calculations, **OR** produces a bit value of 1 if, in bit position 1, either of the two operands (or both) has a 1. In a logical comparison, **OR** causes a statement to be true if either of the two expressions is true. (O)

```
10 IF X=Y OR X=Z THEN PRINT "YES"
```

P

PEEK(<numeric>)—allows you to read the value in the memory location specified by the numeric expression (must be from 0 to 65,535 to be a valid memory cell). The value read back will be in the range of 0 to 255.

```
10 X=PEEK(197):IF X=64 THEN 10
20 PRINT X
30 GOTO 10
```

These lines read the value of the key being depressed. X will be 64 if no key is pressed; and when you key something, its value will print in line 20. (F)

POKE <location>,<value>—puts or **POKE**s one character into a memory location. (The byte, or character, will have a value from 0 to 255.) With **POKE** or **PEEK**, you can cause certain system functions to be performed. For example, using the following statements, you can display a character on the screen at a specified row (R) and column (C):

```
 5 PRINT CHR$(147)
10 R=5:C=5:POKE 1024+C+40*R,ASC("1")
20 POKE 55296+C+40*R,1
30 INPUT X$
```

In this example a 1 is displayed at Row 5, column 5. (S)

POS(<dummy>)—gives the current cursor position on the screen. The result will be from a leftmost 0 to a rightmost 79. And on a 40-character display, 40-79 refer to the second screen line. (F)

```
 5 PRINT "XX";
10 PRINT POS (0)
```

PRINT [<variable>] [<,/;><variable>] ...—displays data on the screen. You can enclose literals or strings with quotation marks after the **PRINT** statement. Or you can **PRINT** variables, functions, or punctuation marks (which are used to format the data). Semicolons or blanks between items cause the next variable to be **PRINT**ed right after the previous value **PRINT**ed. Commas cause the next variable to be **PRINT**ed at the beginning of the next zone. (Each **PRINT** zone is composed of ten spaces.) (S)

```
10 PRINT "HELLO"
20 A=10
30 PRINT A,A*2
40 PRINT CHR$(147):REM CLEARS SCREEN
```

PRINT# <file number> [<variable>] [<,/;><variable>] ...—writes data to a file that has been **OPEN**ed for output. To put commas between variables, you can set a string to **CHR$(44)**, the ASCII value for a comma, and **PRINT** it between variables.

```
 5 OPEN 1,1,1, "TAPE1"
10 CO$=CHR$(44)
20 INPUT "A";A
30 INPUT "B";B
40 INPUT "C";C
50 PRINT# 1,A;CO$;B;CO$;C
```

```
60 IF A=-999 THEN 80
70 GOTO 20
80 CLOSE 1
```

R

READ <variable> [,<variable>] ...—"reads in" variables from **DATA** statements to the variables listed in the **READ** statement.

```
10 DATA "Bacon, Matt"
20 DATA "Sparkman, Mike"
30 DATA "LaDuke, Steve"
40 DATA "Suddeth, Pat"
50 DATA "Nealy, Carl"
60 DATA "Zangmaster, John"
70 DATA "Stewart, Bobby"
80 DATA "Stokes, David"
90 DATA "Howard, Todd"
100 DATA "Rush, Todd"
110 DATA "Brown, Art"
115 DATA "END"
120 READ NAME$
130 IF NAME$="END" THEN 160
140 PRINT NAME$
150 GOTO 120
160 END
```

In this illustration the **READ** statement reads in names from the **DATA** statements until a name that contains "END" is found. If it is not found, an "out of data" error occurs when line 120 tries to read another variable from the **DATA** statements and finds they have all been used. (S)

REM [<remark>]—allows you to put in your programs explanatory **REM**arks that have no effect on actual program execution. When the program is **RUN**, each **REM** statement is actually skipped over for the next statement. (S)

```
10 REM THIS IS A TYPICAL REMARK STATEMENT SERIES
20 REM IN THIS PROGRAM, YOU WILL INPUT A VALUE
30 REM TO WHICH THE PROGRAM WILL COUNT
40 INPUT "VALUE TO COUNT TO: ";V
50 FOR I=1 TO V
60 PRINT I
70 NEXT I
80 END
```

RESTORE—tells the program to start reading **DATA** from the first **DATA** statement within the program.

```
10 DATA 10,4,5,3,-999
20 READ A
25 PRINT A
30 RESTORE
40 READ B
45 PRINT B
```

In this program line 20 will **READ** the value 10 into A. Then line 30 **RESTORES** the data pointer back to the beginning so that line 40 also **READ**s 10 into B. (S)

RETURN—passes control from the subroutine being performed to the line after the **GOSUB** statement. (See also **GOSUB**.) (S)

RIGHT$(<string>,<numeric>)—returns a substring taken from the rightmost number of characters indicated by the numeric variable in the second parameter. (F)

```
10 A$="THIS IS IT"
20 PRINT RIGHT$(A$,2)
RUN
IT
```

RND(<numeric>)—generates random numbers. With **RND**, you can make choices that are arbitrary (by chance). Using a seed (the number in parentheses following **RND**) of 0, a truly random number is generated from the hardware "jiffy clock" of the Commodore 64. A positive seed will create the same "pseudorandom" sequence every time the program is **RUN** with that seed. (F)

```
20 INPUT "READY? (HIT ENTER): ":R$
30 V=INT(6*RND(0))+1
40 PRINT V
50 GOTO 20
```

These statements, for example, simulate a throw of a six-sided die.

When you select a random number between 1 and some ending number, the result is the integer value of (the maximum value times a random number generated greater than 0 and less than 1) + 1. (F)

RUN [<line number>]—starts program execution at the lowest line number when one is not given. If a line number is given, the program executes from the one specified.

```
RUN
RUN 50
```

The second command starts execution at line 50. (C)

S

SAVE ["<file name>"] [,<device number>] [,<address>]—saves a copy of the program in memory to the device specified in the file name. (C)

SAVE	saves to cassette
SAVE "NAME1",8	saves to disk the file named NAME1

To save the same file name to disk when that file already exists, you need to prefix the file name with "@0:":

```
SAVE "@0:NAME1"
```

SGN(<numeric>)—returns -1 if the numeric expression is less than 0. If the expression is 0, then 0 is returned. if the expression is positive, 1 is returned. (F)

```
10 A=10
20 PRINT SGN(A)
30 B=-20
40 PRINT SGN(B)

RUN
 1

-1
```

SIN(<numeric>)—returns the trigomometric sine of the angle in parentheses, where the angle is expressed as radians. To convert an angle in degrees to radians, you need to multiply by PI and divide by 180 (or just multiply the angle in degrees by .01745329251944). (F)

The sine, then, of any angle in degrees is determined in the following lines:

```
10 PRINT CHR$(147)
20 INPUT "ANGLE IN DEGREES: ";D
30 S=SIN(D*.01745329251944)
40 PRINT S
50 GOTO 20
```

SPC(<numeric>)—generates the indicated number of spaces either to the screen in a PRINT statement or to a file (disk, tape, or printer). (F)

```
10 PRINT "THIS HAS";SPC(10);"10 SPACES"
```

SQR(<numeric>)—gives the square root of the numeric expression.

```
10 FOR I=1 TO 100
20 PRINT I,SQR(I)
30 NEXT I
```

These lines give you a square root table for all integers between 1 and 100. (F)

STATUS or **ST**—gives the completion **STATUS** for the last input/output operation to a file. A **STATUS** of 0 indicates successful completion of the last I/O statement. (F)

```
10 OPEN 2,8,2,"FILE1,S,W"
20 INPUT X$
30 PRINT# 2,X$
40 IF ST>0 THEN 70
50 IF X$="END" THEN 70
60 GOTO 20
70 PRINT ST
80 CLOSE 2
```

STEP <expression>—is used in the **FOR-NEXT** statement. If the **STEP** increment is omitted, an increment of +1 is assumed for the loop. (S)

```
10 FOR I=1 TO 100 STEP 5
20 PRINT I
30 NEXT I
```

STOP—stops a program at various points. **STOP** is similar to the **END** statement, except that **END** is usually the last statement in a program. Ordinarily, there is only one **END**, but any number of **STOP** statements may appear in a program, although this recurrence is not necessarily the best programming procedure. (S)

```
200 INPUT "NUMBER BETWEEN 1 AND 10:";N
210 IF N<1 THEN 240
220 IF N>10 THEN 240
230 GOTO 250
240 STOP
250 PRINT "OK YOUR NUMBER WAS WITHIN LIMITS"
260 GOTO 200
```

STR$**(<numeric>)—changes a numeric value to a string value, allowing you to do string manipulations with it (such as determine its length or do a **MID$). (F)

```
10 A=10
20 A$=STR$(A)
30 PRINT LEN(A$)
40 PRINT MID$(A$,2,1)

RUN
 3
1
```

SYS <memory location>—accesses a machine-language program at the specified memory location. When the program has been terminated and an RTS (ReTurn from Subroutine) instruction is encountered, control returns to the next BASIC statement. (S)

SYS 64738 ("cold starts" the Commodore 64, removing any program from memory)

T

TAB(numeric expression)—causes the **PRINT** or **DISPLAY** statements to tab to a certain column before printing the next item. The line

```
10 PRINT "HELLO";TAB(10);"THERE"
```

results in

```
HELLO     THERE
```

TAB can be used for either output to the screen or formatting a printout to a printer. (F)
TAN(radian expression)—provides the trigonometric tangent function of the angle expressed in radians. **TAN** is similar to the **SIN** and **COS** functions. To evaluate an angle in degrees, use the same method to convert degrees to radians as was used with the **SIN** function. (F)

TIME or **TI**—reads the "jiffy clock" that is set to zero when the system is started. When reading or writing to tape, the 1/60th-second counter is turned off.

```
10 PRINT INT(TI/60)
```

This line prints how many seconds have elapsed since system startup. (F)

TIME$** or **TI$—gives a 6-digit hour, minute, and seconds value that is updated by the "jiffy clock." **TI$** can be set within a program to keep track of real time. (F)

```
10 INPUT "6 DIGIT HR/MIN/SEC";HM$
20 TI$=HM$
```

```
30 FOR I=1 TO 1000: NEXT I
40 PRINT TI$
50 GOTO 30
```

U

USR(<numeric>)—causes a BASIC program to jump to a machine-language subroutine that has been user-supplied at a memory location pointed to by the starting address in memory location 785-786. This address can be loaded with a **POKE** statement. The numeric argument is stored in the register at memory location 97. After the Assembler routine accesses that variable, the result is returned there. (F)

V

VAL(string expression)—converts a string expression to a numeric expression. **VAL** is the reverse of the **STR$** function, since **STR$** converts a numeric expression to a string expression.

```
10 A$="109"
20 A=VAL(A$)
30 PRINT A;A*2
```

Here the value 109 is put into the numeric variable A, and line 30 prints 109 and 218. (F)

VERIFY ["<file-name>"] [,<device>]—can be used to check the contents of a program file on tape or disk with the program in memory. If there are differences, the message "?VERIFY ERROR" will be displayed. (C)

SAVE "PROG1",8	(saves PROG1 to disk)
VERIFY "PROG1",8	(verifies that PROG1 has the same contents as the program in memory)

W

WAIT <location>,<mask-1>,<mask-2>—causes the program to wait in suspended execution until some external event has occurred. Use of this statement can cause an infinite pause (from which you can recover by keying **RUN/STOP** and **RESTORE** simultaneously). The **WAIT** command is rarely be used by most programmers. (S)

Appendix
Commodore 64 Products

Many products are available for the Commodore 64 computer. Spreadsheet programs are priced reasonably, a number of fine word-processing packages exist, and sophisticated game programs are also popular. Some of these software programs and several hardware products are briefly described in the following sections.

Software

Easy Script 64 is an excellent word-processing package that can interface to non-Commodore letter-quality printers that are attached to the RS-232 user interface port. Such features as underlining, search and replace, right justify, automatic scrolling through a document, centering, page numbering, and many other features make this word processor a beneficial writer's companion at a very reasonable price.

Easy Quiz 64 allows you to create lessons and multiple-choice quizzes.

Magic Desk is known as Commodore's answer to Lisa™, Apple®'s computer that can respond to commands given by a "mouse"—an apparatus much like a joystick. Magic Desk, which is quite reasonably priced, allows you to type letters and file information by selecting a function with a joystick. The screen presents a picture of an office with a desk, a typewriter, a wastebasket, a file cabinet, etc. You simply move a pointing hand (with a joystick) to the illustration representing the function you want performed.

Microsoft's Multiplan has been released in a CBM version. This spreadsheet package should be both powerful and advanced, as well as reasonably priced.

Public Domain Software is becoming available at Commodore dealers. A complete set of approximately 650 programs on over fifty disks can be purchased for about $250, but individual disks can be obtained practically for the cost of the disk and the time to reproduce the software. The Disk Bonus Pack, for instance, contains a number of programs, including a single-drive disk copying program.

Simon's BASIC has been hailed by many magazines as possibly providing a new standard for Commodore 64 BASIC. Simon's BASIC will provide 114 new commands. These include structured commands, such as REPEAT-UNTIL, which enables procedures to be performed by a procedure name instead of by a GOSUB to a line number. Using names that make sense for a procedure can make programming much easier. Another structured command, RENUMBER, allows you to resequence the line numbers in a program. (A limitation is that GOTOs are not changed, but the structured format of Simon's BASIC is supposed to help eliminate GOTOs.) TRACE allows you to follow the program logic through statement numbers to debug programs. PRINT AT and PRINT USING extend the capabilities of PRINT commands.

Some of the many games that are available include the following: Jupiter Lander, Kickman, Sea Wolf, Radar Rat Race, Avenger, Wizard of Wor, Star Post, and Gorf. All these and more are available on cartridges that plug into the cartridge port. Adventure games on disk include Zork I, II, and III; Suspended; Starcross; and Deadline (INFOCOM® games developed under a licensing agreement between Commodore and INFOCOM, Inc.).

Business software, such as General Ledger, Accounts Payable, Accounts Receivable, Payroll/Check Writing, and Inventory Management are available.

Other programming aids, such as Logo, Pilot, Screen Editor, Assember 64, and Nevada COBOL, are also available from Commodore dealers.

A new edition of the *Commodore Software Encyclopedia* is available from Commodore dealers at a list price of $19.95. The encyclopedia contains over 800 pages of nearly 2,000 entries of Commodore and non-Commodore software available worldwide.

A new publication, *INFO 64,* provides a lengthy list of Commodore software and hardware in the publication's fall, 1983, *Quarterly Review and Product Guide for the Commodore 64.* Subscriptions are not available, but look for this guide at computer stores.

COMMODORE and *POWERPLAY* are two magazines published by a division of Commodore that offer information about home computing. Other magazines, such as *Micro, Compute,* and *Commander* have much information about CBM products.

Hardware

The Commodore Executive 64, a new portable attache computer, has a built-in, six-inch color monitor; a single 170K diskette drive (with a second disk option); 64K of RAM; and a low-profile, full, upper- and lower-case, detachable keyboard. This computer is fully compatible with the 64 and includes a Commodore serial bus, a C-64-compatible external bus, and an IEEE-488 interface. The display has 25 lines of 40 columns, with 16 colors and graphics. The machine also includes music and sound capabilities with an external video port.

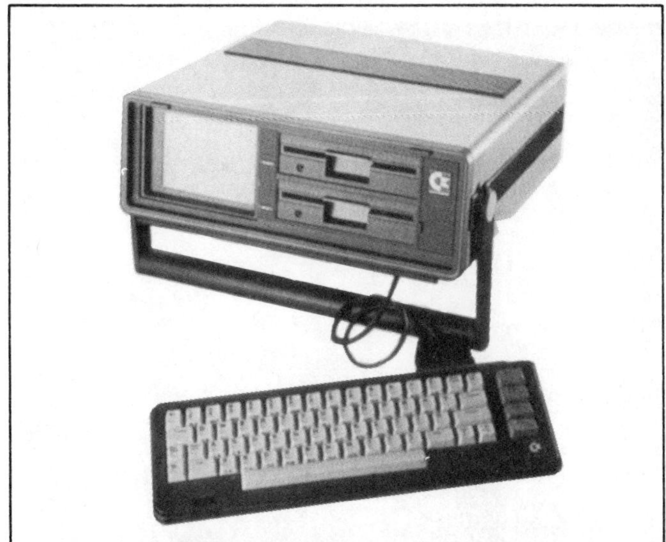

The portable Commodore Executive 64

The Commodore 64 processor is one of the lowest priced computers available, considering its many features and memory capacity. Features include 64K of RAM; a 40-character-by-25-line screen display on a user-supplied color monitor or a television; music and sound synthesis; 4 programmable function keys; 16 colors; 8 programmable "sprites" for 3-dimensional graphics; and a 6510 microprocessor.

The Commodore 64 Computer

The 1520 plotter printer is an 80-column graphics printer that can be used with the Commodore 64 or VIC-20. Charts and graphs can be drawn with 4 colors.

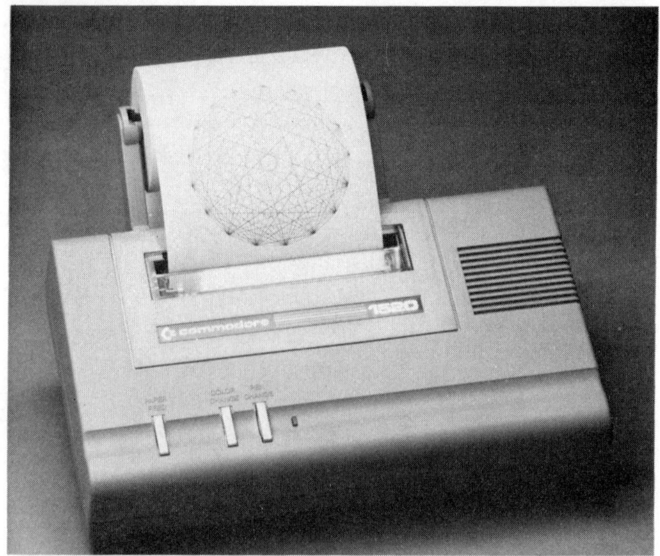

The 1520 Plotter Printer

A 1525 dot-matrix printer provides a 30-character-per-second, 80-column printout at 10-characters-per-inch spacing. This printer can accept variable-width paper, from 4.5 to 10 inches wide. The ribbon is single color, with an inked roller built in to the cassette. The 1525 can also produce Commodore graphics characters, special symbols, dot-addressable graphics, upper- and lower-case characters, and numbers.

The 1525 Dot-Matrix Printer

The 1541 disk drive provides a high-capacity (over 170,000 characters per diskette) storage and retrieval device for the Commodore 64. The device offers faster storage that is much higher than that of the 1530 Datassette tape recorder. Furthermore, the device can read and write disks of the Commodore 4040 and 2031 models (which can be used on the highly popular PET CBM computers). The 1525 printer and the 1541 disk drive are connected serially in daisy-chain fashion to the serial bus of the C-64.

The 1541 Disk Drive

The 1530 tape recorder provides a low-cost, yet reliable means of recording and retrieving programs and data. The recorder draws its power from the interface cable that connects it to the C-64.

The 1530 Datassette Recorder

A 13-inch color monitor (1701) provides an excellent quality video display with a built-in speaker and audio amplifier. The monitor can be connected through either a 2-pin, video-audio front input, or a 3-pin, audio-chroma-luma rear input. The screen resolution is quite good.

The 1701 Color Monitor

Two 300-baud (approximately 30 characters per second) modems (1600 and 1650) allow you to communicate with other computer systems and information systems, such as CompuServe™. The 1650 model provides auto-answer and auto-dial features, and full-/half-duplex modes. Both models include a cassette tape with sophisticated terminal software.

The 1650 Modem

The 1600 Modem

The 1011A RS-232-C interface cartridge allows you to interface to the Commodore 64 standard RS-232 modems, printers, and other devices. All the programs in this book that access a printer can print either to a 1525 printer or to an RS-232 printer at 1200 baud.